T0290173

GREATEST GAMES
ARSENAL

GREATEST GAMES
ARSENAL

THE GUNNERS' FIFTY FINEST MATCHES

PAUL DONNELLEY

First published by Pitch Publishing, 2018

Pitch Publishing
A2 Yeoman Gate
Yeoman Way
Worthing
Sussex
BN13 3QZ
www.pitchpublishing.co.uk
info@pitchpublishing.co.uk

A CIP catalogue record is available for this book
from the British Library.

ISBN 978-1-78531-207-6

Typesetting and origination by Pitch Publishing
Printed and bound in India by Replika Press Pvt Ltd

CONTENTS

Dedicated once again to the Serious Girl even though she doesn't like football.

Dial Square 6 Eastern Wanderers 0

Friendly. Saturday 11 December 1886, kick-off time unknown
Venue: Tiller Road, London E14
Dial Square: Various colours
Eastern Wanderers: Colours unknown
Referee: Unknown
Attendance: Unknown

Dial Square	Eastern Wanderers
Fred Beardsley	Unknown
David Danskin (captain)	
Porteous	
Gregory	
Bee	
Wolfe	
George Smith	
Moy	
Whitehead	
Morris	
Duggan	
Scorers: Unknown	

THE story is familiar to all Arsenal fans – on 1 December 1886 a group of workers from the Royal Arsenal armaments factory in Woolwich met at the Royal Oak[1] pub at 27 Woolwich New Road, Greenwich, London SE18, and a football team was formed. The moving force was an exiled Scotsman by the name of David Danskin. He was born on 9 January 1863 on Back Street, Burntisland, Fife, the second child of six of Janet Burton and David Danskin. He began working as an apprentice engine fitter at Kirkcaldy.

In 1885, he moved south and found a job at the Royal Arsenal as a mechanical engineer. A keen amateur footballer, he had already played for Kirkcaldy Wanderers alongside Peter Connolly and Jack McBean, two future Arsenal players. David Danskin moved south to Kent along with thousands of his fellow Scotsmen.

A couple of former Nottingham Forest players, Morris Bates and Fred Beardsley, also arrived at the factory looking for work and, along with Danskin, formed the impetus for a works football team. They named themselves Dial Square, after the gun-machining workshop where many of them worked.

---

1   The pub, near to Woolwich Arsenal station, changed its name to The Pullman. In June 2005, construction began on the Docklands Light Railway extension to Woolwich Arsenal, and the pub and several buildings nearby were demolished in 2007.

They arranged a match with Eastern Wanderers and caught the Woolwich Ferry to the Isle of Dogs. The game was played in less than salubrious conditions. Elijah Watkins, a friend and colleague of Danskin, became the club's first secretary.

Of the club's debut match on 11 December 1886, Watkins was to say, 'Talk about a football pitch! This one eclipsed any I ever heard of or saw. I could not venture to say what shape it was, but it was bounded by backyards as to about two-thirds of the area, and the other portion was – I was going to say a ditch, but I think an open sewer would be more appropriate. We could not decide who won the game because when the ball was not in the back gardens, it was in the ditch; and that was full of the loveliest material that could possibly be.

'Well, our fellows did not bring it all away with them, but they looked as though they had been clearing out a mud-shoot when they had done playing. I know, because the attendant at the pub asked me what I was going to give him to clear the muck away.'

In the event, Dial Square ran out 6–0 winners, although the score was disputed because the pitch had no markings and the goals no crossbars.

A fortnight later, on Christmas Day, 15 players gathered in the Royal Oak and officially adopted the title of Royal Arsenal, having decided that no one had heard of Dial Square and everyone was aware of Royal Arsenal.

They each paid a subscription of sixpence, and David Danskin contributed three shillings of his own money from his weekly wage of around 35 shillings. The first item the club bought was a handmade football, which the workers used at lunchtime for a kickabout.

Arsenal were on their way, and soon had a kit when Nottingham Forest kindly donated a set of redcurrant shirts (the same colour that they wore in their last season at Highbury).

Except … except … the story of Arsenal's origins raises many more questions than it answers. For a start, why did a team from south London (then Kent) travel to east London for their first match? Were there no suitable pitches in Kent? How did the Dial Square team get there? The official biography by Steve Stammers, among many other books, refers to the side getting 'the ferry from Woolwich but the ferry did not begin running until 23 March 1889. The Blackwall Tunnel? No, that did not open until 22 May 1897. The Greenwich foot tunnel, "the Pipe"? That opened on 4 August 1902.'

In fact, every detail that we have about the 'first' match rests on the testimony of one man – Elijah Watkins – in a letter he wrote to *Football Chat* in 1902. However, he does not mention the date or the final score.

The account is repeated in 1906 in *Association Football and the Men Who Made It*. The game is then mentioned in the *Woolwich Herald* in 1911, which stated that the club was 25 years old, having played its first game on 11 December 1886, beating Eastern Wanderers 6–0.

It is possible that the first match never actually occurred as it is recorded, or never occurred at all – or is it a mélange of different matches, teams and players?

At least that was the view of football historians until the facts emerged. Important research was carried out, and there is a mention in the sporting newspaper *The Referee* published on 12 December. It states: 'Dial Square v. Eastern Wanderers (A).–At Millwall: The first-named won by six goals to nil.' *The Referee* got its information from club secretaries.

In the edition of *The Referee* published on 2 January 1887, Watkins placed an advertisement for opponents: 'Dial Square F.C. (A.) have open for good medium clubs Jan. 22, Feb. 19, all dates in March. E. Watkins, 43 Park-rd., Plumstead.'

So how did they manage to play Eastern Wanderers? Were there no local teams? It would appear not. Erith, their opponents in the club's second game, were not formed at the time of the first match.

Eastern Wanderers had been playing in the previous season and had enough players to put out two teams. Based at Millwall, their secretary was David W. Galliford of 9 Marsh Street, Cahir Street, Millwall, London E14. It may have been that Watkins knew Galliford or knew someone who knew someone at Eastern Wanderers and thus the fixture was arranged.

It is now established beyond any doubt that the first game played by the club now known as Arsenal was on 11 December 1886, that it was against Eastern Wanderers and that they won by the convincing margin of six goals to nil.

Woolwich Arsenal 2 Newcastle United 2

Football League Division Two. Saturday 2 September 1893, kick-off 3pm
Venue: Manor Field, Plumstead Marshes, Kent
Woolwich Arsenal: Probably red shirts, blue shorts and black stockings
Newcastle United: Black and white striped shirts, white shorts, black stockings
Referee: J.C. Tillotson (Birmingham)
Attendance: 6,000[2]

Woolwich Arsenal	Newcastle United
Charlie Williams	Andrew Ramsay
Joe Powell (captain)	Harry Jeffery
Bill Jeffrey	James Miller
Daniel Devine	Robert Crielly
Bob Buist	Walter Graham
David Howat	Joseph McKane
Duncan Gemmell	J. Bowman
Jim Henderson	Tom Crate
Walter Shaw	Willie Thompson (captain)
Arthur Elliott	Jock Sorley
Charlie Booth	Joseph Wallace
Manager: None – a players' committee consisting of Fred Beardsley, Arthur Brown and Jack Humble selected the team	*Manager:* Boardroom committee
	Scorers: Crate 65 minutes; Sorley 80 minutes
Scorers: Shaw 6 minutes; Elliott 48 minutes	

I N 1888, Royal Arsenal moved to the Manor Ground, then known as Manor Field, where they stayed for two years. The club's first match there was a 3–3 draw against Millwall Rovers, on 11 February 1888. There were no stands, and the club borrowed wagons from the army for spectators to sit in. The club had changed its name to Royal Arsenal some time after its first match and before 7 January 1887. There is a theory that the name was changed to Woolwich Arsenal when the club voted to turn professional in May 1891, as they were not allowed to use the name Royal. This is not true. The name Royal Arsenal was used during the 1891/92 and 1892/93 seasons. In fact, the name change did not become official until 26 April 1893, when The Woolwich Arsenal Football and Athletic Company Limited (company number 38703C) was incorporated. On 28 April, the assets of Royal Arsenal Football Club were transferred to The Woolwich Arsenal Football and Athletic Company Limited.

After a financial disagreement with the owner of the Invicta Ground, Woolwich Arsenal returned to the Manor Ground, where they would stay for 20 years. In 1893, Arsenal became the first club to

---

2 Some sources list the attendance as 10,000.

issue shares to raise money; 860 people bought 4,000 shares, valued at £1 each.

The scheme was not met with universal praise. One letter writer to the *Kentish Independent*, the local newspaper, commented, 'The funding of a soccer club should be left to working men and those who know the game. Surely allowing clerks or accountants to control a football club by buying shares is a retrograde step.'

The 1893/94 season of the Football League began on the first Saturday in September. After a season playing friendlies against Football League opponents and non-league sides, Woolwich Arsenal had finally been elected to the league (along with Liverpool, Middlesbrough Ironopolis and their first opponents, Newcastle United) that summer.

The first Football League match in London saw the Novocastrians travel down from Tyneside to King's Cross on the morning of the game, as they could not afford to stay in hotels. The Newcastle side then took cabs straight to the Manor Ground.

A crowd of 6,000 (or possibly 10,000) people turned out to watch Woolwich Arsenal take on Newcastle United at the Manor Ground, Plumstead.

The weather was fine, and there was a light wind blowing in Kent. Woolwich Arsenal won the toss and elected to play with the wind behind them. Newcastle kicked off, and Willie Thompson took the first kick in the Football League in London.

With just six minutes (some sources say eight) of play gone, Walter Shaw scored Woolwich Arsenal's first league goal. The first half was not one of high skill, and Shaw's goal was described as very soft. Woolwich Arsenal kept the visitors penned into their own half, and it was not until just before half-time that Newcastle began putting some passes together; they were unlucky not to equalise.

In the second half, Woolwich Arsenal extended their lead in the 48th minute when Arthur Elliott scored. Rather than parking the bus, the Londoners allowed the Geordies to get back into the game.

In the last 15 minutes, the Novocastrians rallied, and Tom Crate scored after 65 minutes before Jock Sorley equalised to ensure the honours were shared. In the last ten minutes, however, the match could have gone either way.

Of the new boys, the season ended with Liverpool as Division Two champions with 50 points, Woolwich Arsenal in ninth place with 28 points, and Newcastle United eight points and five places above them.

Middlesbrough Ironopolis finished 11th in the division, but were in a perilous financial position and resigned from the league on 30 May 1894 and disbanded on 5 June that year, after five years of existence. Bootle (1892/93) and Middlesbrough Ironopolis – the Nops – are the only two clubs to have spent just a solitary season in the Football League.

Woolwich Arsenal goalie Charlie Williams lost his place in the side when the club signed Harry Storer in May 1894, and he left for Manchester City, beginning a long tradition that sadly continues to this day of players joining the Sky Blues. While at Hyde Road, he became the first keeper to score a goal from open play (against Sunderland at Roker Park on 14 April 1900). In 1902, he moved south and signed for Tottenham Hotspur. With his playing career over, he turned to management and managed the Denmark national side. In 1911, he began coaching teams in South America, where he stayed for the rest of his life, dying in 1952.

Joe Powell, Woolwich Arsenal's first captain, also became the first professional Gunner to die. He was serving in the Walsall 80th Staffordshire Regiment when Arsenal signed him in December 1892. He missed just three matches in the inaugural season. The next year, he again missed three games, and in 1895/96 he missed five games out of 30 and scored his only goal in a 5–0 victory against Loughborough Town on 4 January 1896.

He started in eight of the first ten matches of the 1896/97 season, but fell awkwardly while playing in a United League match against Kettering Town on 23 November and broke his arm. Powell came down with tetanus and blood poisoning. The arm was amputated, but he died six days later on 29 November. He was just 26. He had played 203 competitive matches for The Arsenal.

Glasgow-born Duncan Gemmell played in the first five matches of the opening season, lost his place to Gavin Crawford and never played for the first team again. Dumfries-born Jim Henderson scored 86 goals for Woolwich Arsenal in 137 competitive games – averaging a remarkable 0.6 goals per game. He lost form in the 1894/95 season and was released in the summer of 1895, when he returned to Scotland.

The club also released Walter Shaw at the end of the same season. Arthur Elliott is said to have moved to Tottenham in the summer of 1894, but there is no record of him playing for the Lilywhites.

On 26 January 1895, there was crowd trouble during a match against Burton Wanderers, and the Football League ordered that the Manor Ground be closed for five weeks.

Woolwich Arsenal played a game each at New Brompton's Priestfield Stadium (against Burton Swifts) and at Lyttelton cricket ground, Leyton (against Leicester Fosse). In 1904, the club built a second stand, which became the first to be nicknamed the Spion Kop. At first, attendances at the Manor Ground numbered around 20,000, but they began to drop, not least because of the venue's comparative isolation in an industrial area.

Plumstead was difficult to reach by public transport – northern fans had to get into central London and then take a 40-minute train journey from Cannon Street. On occasion, some opposing teams did not make the ground in time for kick-off.

The engineering works next door spewed out noxious fumes and occasionally raw sewage. The *Liverpool Tribune* said that Arsenal were the 'team who played at the end of the earth'.

The *Derby Post* reported on 15 January 1891, 'One of the Derby chaps was heard to mutter: "A journey to the molten interior of the earth's core would be rather more pleasant and comfortable an experience than our forthcoming visit to the Royal Arsenal."'

In 1910, with Woolwich Arsenal facing bankruptcy, two meetings were convened at Woolwich Town Hall on 22 January, to discuss the club's future. The first gathering was only for shareholders, and they were told about the club's financial crisis.

At the second meeting, open to all, the money problems were again a main topic, and a Voluntary Committee was created to raise £1,000 for the club. In the audience for the second meeting was the London property magnate and Fulham chairman Henry Norris.

On 19 February, Woolwich Arsenal played Fulham in a friendly. Only about 2,000 fans turned up to the match, and the club's league gates stayed low, adding to the financial woes. It looked as if Woolwich Arsenal would go the way of many other football clubs – out of business. Players still joined, though.

On 4 March, the amateur George Grant signed for Woolwich Arsenal from Invicta FC. Turning professional, he played for Woolwich Arsenal, The Arsenal and Arsenal.

On 18 March, again at Woolwich Town Hall, a meeting was held to discuss possible voluntary liquidation and the creation of a new company to keep a football team in the area. Norris was not there, but his right-hand man, William Hall, was.

Woolwich Arsenal were so short of money that they were unable to pay the players, and by that stage of the season they had only nine games to bring in enough cash to tide them over the close season (May to August).

Fortunately, the club's creditors were not demanding immediate payment and a local tailor, George Leavey, had stepped in on several occasions to pay the players' wages. By 1910, he was owed £3,600 (£410,000 at 2018 values).

At the meeting, someone (it is not known who) suggested that perhaps the solution was for Woolwich Arsenal to move to another ground. The club had debts of around £12,500 (£1.4 million at 2018 values).

On 20 March that year, Dr John Clarke, the head of the Voluntary Committee, began traipsing around Plumstead's pubs trying to sell shares in the new club for £1 each. Three days later, Spurs made an offer to buy all or part of Woolwich Arsenal. Glasgow Rangers did invest in Woolwich Arsenal and held the investment until forced to sell it in 2011, when they faced their own financial problems.

The following month, rumours began circulating that Henry Norris had established a firm interest in the club and was considering a merger with Fulham. It should be pointed out that Fulham would not be buying Woolwich Arsenal – the south-west London club had its own problems and lost £722 that financial year.

The Voluntary Committee did not manage to sell £2,000 worth of shares, managing only £1,200, so, on 25 April – two days after the end of the season – The Woolwich Arsenal Football and Athletic Company Limited was wound up. The following day, a new company with the same name was set up (which continues to this day after various name changes).

George Leavey, in a newspaper interview on 11 May, begged for help, as he was still personally responsible for the club's debts and faced financial ruin. With approaches to Chelsea and Spurs in the offing, Henry Norris was waiting on the sidelines, warming up.

A week later, a meeting was held at the Imperial Hotel in London to discuss the future of Woolwich Arsenal and a possible merger with Fulham. George Leavey was present for Woolwich Arsenal, and J.J. Bentley, Charles Sutcliffe and T. Harris were there on behalf of the

Football League Management Committee, but it is not known who attended for the Cottagers.

The Football League Management Committee immediately ruled out a merger between the two clubs. At Leavey's suggestion, three directors of Fulham joined the Woolwich Arsenal board, but only for a 12-month period. The Fulham directors would have a year to turn the club around, and guaranteed to keep the club in Plumstead for that duration. A new director on the Woolwich Arsenal board was Henry Norris. Not long after, Norris increased the time the club would guarantee to stay at Plumstead from one year to two.

On 8 June, he sat down with the club's secretary-manager, George Morrell, to assure him that his job was safe. One of the major problems for Woolwich Arsenal was diminishing attendances. A hard-core group of fans – known as the Torpedo Boys – stopped attending when the torpedo factory where they worked was closed and moved to Greenock in Scotland.

A week after Norris had assured Morrell his job was safe, there was more bad news when it was announced that more men would be made redundant as the need for materiel decreased after the end of hostilities in the Boer War.

On 9 July 1910, Woolwich Arsenal signed Willis Rippon, a promising centre-forward, who scored on his debut against Manchester United but then quickly faded and was sold in October 1911. That same week, Arsenal hired George Hardy as the first-team trainer – he stayed much longer than Rippon and was still with the club in 1927.

On 2 February 1927, Arsenal played Port Vale in an FA Cup fourth round replay. According to Tom Whittaker, 'Arsenal were pressing hard, but things were not going just right, and old George Hardy's eyes spotted something he felt could be corrected to help the attack. During the next lull in the game he hopped to the touchline, and cupping his hands, yelled out that one of the forwards was to play a little farther up field.'

Manager Herbert Chapman was furious at what he saw as the usurpation of his power and sent his trainer to the dressing room. After the match, which Arsenal won 1–0, Chapman sacked Hardy for gross insubordination, and he appointed Whittaker the following Monday, 7 February. The same month, Hardy became a first-team coach at Spurs.

Back to 1910, and on 13 July, The Woolwich Arsenal Football and Athletic Company Limited published its accounts, showing that it was £700 in debt, due to paying the players' wages in the close season.

Twelve days later, and two days after Norris's 45th birthday, he formally took over Arsenal in a meeting at the Mortar Hotel, Woolwich. It seems likely that only 20 or so people attended the meeting, at which George Leavey was appointed chairman and solicitor Arthur Gilbert became company secretary. Norris and his business partner William Hall loaned the new company £369 19s 4d (£42,500 at 2018 values), probably to pay the players' wages as they returned for training.

Norris also invited Jack Humble, an occasional early player, to return to the club. In 1891, he had come up with the idea of paying players, and in June 1893 he became the first chairman of Woolwich Arsenal. He retired from the board in 1907, but when Norris called, Humble answered.

Norris and Hall began to restructure the club and took out a loan – repayable over 15 years and at considerable personal risk – to pay off the second mortgage and bank overdraft. George Allison, in his autobiography, wrote that Henry Norris was 'one of the most far seeing men I have ever known. It was he alone who saw the possibility of taking the Woolwich Arsenal club, with all the attractions it could have, away from the obscurity and inaccessibility of Plumstead and putting it somewhere in the heart of London where it would have a chance of receiving better support.'

Norris was a man of foresight, not to mention deviousness, and he realised that Woolwich Arsenal could not flourish in Woolwich – they had just £19 in the bank. Sites in Battersea and Harringay were found and discarded before the club moved to north London and a new home at Highbury.

Woolwich Arsenal played their last match at the Manor Ground on Saturday 26 April 1913, a 1–1 draw against Middlesbrough watched by just 3,000 people. Once the venue was no longer home to football, the ground became derelict. It was later demolished and the land redeveloped. Today, it is an industrial estate once more. The Manor Ground was on the land that is now Nathan Way, Griffin Manor Way and Hadden Road.

Woolwich Arsenal 2 Leicester Fosse 1

Football League Division Two. Saturday 6 September 1913, kick-off 2.30pm
Venue: Highbury, Avenell Road, London N5 1BU
Woolwich Arsenal: Redcurrant shirts, white shorts, black stockings with two red and one blue hoop at top
Leicester Fosse: Blue shirts, white shorts, black stockings
Referee: J.H. Pearson
Attendance: 20,000

Woolwich Arsenal	Leicester Fosse
Joe Lievesley	Ron Brebner
Joe Shaw	Thomas Clay
Joe Fidler	Samuel Currie
George Grant	Douglas McWhirter
Percy Sands	James Harrold
Angus McKinnon	William Mills
David Greenaway	Horace Burton
Wally Hardinge	George Douglas
George Jobey	Henry Sparrow
Archibald Devine	Tommy Benfield
Thomas Winship	Thomas Waterall
Secretary-manager: George Morrell	*Secretary-manager:* Jack Bartlett
Scorers: Jobey 45 minutes; Devine 78 minutes (pen.)	*Scorer:* Benfield 20 minutes

AFTER being relegated at the end of the previous season – finishing bottom of Division One, five points adrift of the also relegated Notts County – Arsenal began life in Division Two with a new ground: Arsenal Stadium, Highbury and 'The Home of Football' – three names for the same place. A football ground next to a London Underground station in north London became an iconic sporting venue and an architectural one. Built in 1913 on the six-acre recreation fields belonging to St John's College of Divinity, they were leased on 20 February for 21 years at a cost of £20,000 (£2.1 million at 2018 values) from the Ecclesiastical Commissioners. The church signatory to the deal was Randall Davidson, the Archbishop of Canterbury, who just happened to be a personal friend of Woolwich Arsenal chairman Henry Norris.

The stadium was designed by Archibald Leitch and cost £125,000 (£13.1 million at 2018 values) to be built. (Leitch had previously worked on Hampden Park, Ibrox and Parkhead in Glasgow, and Goodison Park on Merseyside.) Local residents opposed the building of the stadium, as did representatives from Clapton Orient, Chelsea and Tottenham Hotspur, who feared a decrease in gate size and thus revenue. Tottenham demanded an extraordinary general meeting of the Football League to stop Woolwich Arsenal's move to the area. This motion was defeated at the annual general meeting on 26 May 1913. Woolwich Arsenal took possession of the site on 28 June, with ten weeks to build a stadium.

Many fans in south London also objected to the move. Paul Donaldson wrote to the *Kentish Gazette* complaining, 'Mr Norris has decided that financial gain is more important than protecting our local club. He is making a mistake – you cannot "franchise" a football club – Woolwich Arsenal must stay near Woolwich. Would Norris advocate moving Liverpool to Manchester? People like him have no place in Association Football.'

Another, Walter Bailey, wrote to the *Kentish Independent* thus, 'There is, and has been, sufficient support to run the team on a business basis ... Many clubs in different parts of the country would be glad of such support. Woolwich has been found guilty of apathy ... because it cannot furnish the huge gates that Tottenham and Chelsea get. The most distant part of London to which they intend moving will effectively prevent those who helped to make the club, and can morally claim it as their birthright, from having anything to do with it. Is this right?'

The financial argument won, and Norris overcame the residents' objections by saying that 30,000 supporters every Saturday was not all that many and, in any case, they would be good for business. The local newspapers did not carry much in the way of protest, because they had been silenced by Norris's contacts within the Fourth Estate. Norris promised that no matches would be played at the new ground on Sundays, Good Friday, Easter Monday and Christmas Day, and that alcohol would not be served there and gambling on-site was also banned.

That is not to say that the Gunners' fans did not enjoy a drink, however, in the ground. They bought drink in the local hostelries and took it into Highbury.

In 1925, the club bought the stadium outright at a cost of £64,000 (£3.6 million at 2018 values). The college became a tenant of Arsenal until the Second World War, when a fire destroyed the building.

Leicester Fosse, who had finished 15th in Division Two the previous season, were the first visitors to the new stadium. Arsenal had a number of debutants – George Jobey had moved from Newcastle United in May, and Joe Lievesley and Wally Hardinge had signed from Sheffield United the following month.

A crowd of 20,000 packed into the still unfinished stadium. Admission was sixpence, but the workmen had left open the exit doors, so, had they been of a mind, hundreds could have just walked in for free. As it was, they queued four or five deep in Avenell Road to get into the ground, where the pitch was also incomplete and had a distinctive slope. The southern end of the ground (later the Clock End) had to be lowered five feet, while the Gillespie Road End – the Laundry End and later, of course, the North Bank – had to be raised 11 feet. Before the 1913/14 season, 200 men worked on flattening the pitch and building what would become the terraces.

Leicester Fosse got off to the better start and had most of the possession in the first half. On the 20-minute mark, Leicester's Tommy Benfield scored the first goal at Highbury. George Douglas and William Mills combined to get the ball to Benfield, who beat Lievesley with a cracking shot that gave the Woolwich Arsenal keeper no chance.

On the stroke of half-time, Mr Pearson, the referee, awarded the home side a corner. Thomas Winship curled the ball in, and debutant Jobey scored the first Woolwich Arsenal goal at Highbury, heading the ball into the net.

In the second half, the home team came more into the game and pressurised the Fosse even when they went down to ten men.

Geordie Jobey was also the first player to go off injured at Highbury. He was kicked in the back, and the injury looked serious. There was no warm water in the dressing room, and he had to be taken there on a stretcher, to be looked after by ambulance men and a doctor. He was taken home on the back of milkman David Lewis's cart by trainer George Hardy and was out of action for the next four games.

The match looked to be heading for a probably deserved draw when a Fosse defender panicked and handled the ball. Scottish international Archibald Devine made no mistake from the penalty spot, and the ten-man Gunners ran out 2–1 winners.

The Leicester goalie, Ron Brebner, competed in the 1908 Olympics in London and 1912 Olympics in Stockholm, Sweden. On 14 November 1914, he died, aged 33, from injuries he had received guarding the Leicester Fosse goal.

The scorer of the first goal at Arsenal Stadium also died prematurely. Sergeant Tommy Benfield of the 6th Battalion of the Leicestershire Regiment was killed, aged 29, by a German sniper on 19 September 1918.

Woolwich Arsenal played well that season and very nearly went back up at the first attempt (as did Notts County, who ran out champions). The club finished a creditable third, four points behind County and with the same tally as runners-up Bradford Park Avenue.

The Arsenal 7 Nottingham Forest 0

Football League Division Two. Saturday 24 April 1915, kick-off 3pm
Venue: Highbury, Avenell Road, London N5 1BU
The Arsenal: Red shirts, white shorts, black stockings
Nottingham Forest: White shirts with a red stripe shoulder to shoulder across the chest, white shorts, red stockings
Referee: H.T. Yates (Bolton)
Attendance: 10,000

The Arsenal	Nottingham Forest
Joe Lievesley	Harry Iremonger
Percy Sands (captain)	Alfred Fisher
Joe Shaw	Tommy Gibson
John Graham	Jack Armstrong (captain)
Chris Buckley	Joe Mercer
Frank Bradshaw	George Needham
Jock Rutherford	John Derrick
Henry King	Tim Coleman
Bob Benson	Fred Harris
Billy Blyth	John Lockton
Charles Lewis	John Bell
Acting manager: James 'Punch' McEwen	*Manager:* Bob Masters

Scorers: King 15 minutes, 53 minutes, 56 minutes, 85 minutes; Benson 19 minutes, 58 minutes; Rutherford 90 minutes

THE previous August, the conflict that became known as the Great War and later the First World War broke out, but the football leagues carried on as normally as they could. The Football League began on 1 September 1914, and there was a rush for many footballers and fans to sign up – most expected the war to be over by Christmas and did not want to miss out on what they thought would be excitement.

When Arsenal moved to Highbury, their Manor Ground home was rented out to a new team, Woolwich FC. As Woolwich Arsenal were playing in the Football League in the 1913/14 season, their tenants were competing in the Kent League and FA Amateur Cup. However, in August 1914, the club's directors decided it was not possible to continue and Woolwich FC folded. The government eventually stepped in and bought the Manor Ground, which became a fuse factory in the Royal Arsenal.

The Football League continued with the fixtures as normal, although some clubs found their selections were hampered by players who had signed up for the army and thus were unavailable. The Arsenal began their season with a 3–0 victory over Glossop at Highbury. A return a week later saw them fare even better, beating Glossop[3] (who finished the season propping up the other teams) 4–0 away. By the time they had played their ninth game of the season, they were top of the table and looking forward to getting back into Division One.

In an echo of more recent seasons, however, The Arsenal were unable to maintain a winning consistency, and by the time January rolled around, the side was in fourth place. A 1–0 defeat at Hull on 2 April condemned the club to another season in Division Two.

Eleven days later and with two matches to play, The Arsenal parted company with secretary-manager George Morrell. The club realised that the conflict with Germany was unlikely to be over any time soon and told Morrell that he and all the staff would be released at the end of the season. He returned to his native Scotland, where he became manager of Third Lanark on 18 August 1917. He stayed with the club for four years, leaving on 30 April 1921. He died in 1931.

James 'Punch' McEwen was appointed caretaker manager for the final games – Preston North End away on 17 April, when the team went down by three goals to nil, and Nottingham Forest, languishing in 18th place.

Ten thousand fans travelled to Highbury for what they thought would be the final Division Two game of the season, little knowing that it would be the club's last fixture outside of the top league.

In what would be his second and last game in charge, McEwen made an experimental if not downright eccentric change: regular left-back Bob Benson, who had played 33 games that season in that position, was picked to play at centre-forward.

Playing for Forest was former Arsenal legend Tim Coleman, who was, until Jimmy Brain beat the record in 1927, the club's top goalscorer with 84 goals in 196 games.

After 15 minutes, Charlie Lewis crossed and Harry King opened The Arsenal's account. Not long after, Forest goalie Harry Iremonger stopped Benson from adding to the tally. In the 19th minute, he was powerless to stop the new centre-forward from scoring the second, playing a one-two with Jock Rutherford.

Iremonger's brilliance kept the score down to two by the time Mr Yates, the referee, signalled the end of the first half.

---

3   Until the First World War, Sir Samuel Hill-Wood, a future chairman of Arsenal, funded Glossop.

The second half was an entirely different match. King almost scored and then did get his second on 53 minutes. Three minutes later, he got his hat-trick from a Rutherford cross. That man Rutherford also made the fifth as he crossed to Benson, who drilled home his second. Benson relished his performance at number nine, and took a shot every time he saw the goal or the whites of Iremonger's eyes.

With just five minutes of the 90 to play, Lewis crossed for King to head past the unfortunate Forest goalie.

And, at the final knockings, Rutherford, who had made goals for others, got his own name on the scoresheet as The Arsenal ran out 7–0 victors. Rutherford scored the last goal of the game, the last goal of the season and also, as it turned out, The Arsenal's last goal outside the top league. It was also the last first-team match played under the name The Woolwich Arsenal Football and Athletic Company Limited. The name was officially and legally changed to The Arsenal Football Club Limited. The team showing so much promise and achieving their biggest win in 11 years never played together again.

It was Joe Lievesley's last game for the club – he retired at the end of the season and died in October 1941 – but most of the players reconvened after the war. Not striker Benson, though.

A miner by profession, Benson joined Woolwich Arsenal on 18 November 1913 from Sheffield United for a fee of £200. He made his debut against Bristol City 11 days later. Although he was a full-back, Arsenal on occasion used him as a centre-forward, and he was a killer penalty taker, with, it was claimed, an 80-yard run-up to kick the ball. He made 52 appearances for the first team.

During the First World War, Benson began work in the Royal Arsenal munitions factory. On 19 February 1916, with his wife and father-in-law, he made a rare visit to Highbury to watch his former club play Reading in the London Combination. When they got into the ground, Benson told his wife that he was 'going to see the boys'.

As the crowd waited for the match to begin, a murmur went up that The Arsenal were a man short – Benson's former full-back colleague Joe Shaw was apparently unable to get permission from the munitions factory to play. Benson persuaded club secretary John Peters, who was in charge that day, to let him play, and pulled on an Arsenal shirt for what would be the last time.

His father-in-law said that the stresses and long hours in the munitions factory meant he was nowhere near fit enough to play.

Benson shrugged off the warning. It was the first time he had played in more than a year, and his lack of match fitness showed. Fifteen minutes into the second half, he collapsed on the pitch with exhaustion. He staggered to the bench but was still unable to catch his breath. Trainer George Hardy helped him to the dressing room, but, despite his ministrations, Benson died in the trainer's arms, aged just 33. He was buried in his Arsenal shirt.

Three months later, on 6 May 1916, Arsenal played a Rest of London Combination team in a testimonial (the first of its kind) for Benson's widow before a crowd of more than 5,000. His death was later put down to a burst blood vessel in a lung.

When the 1914/15 season came to a conclusion, the Football Association and Football League shut for the duration of the war, and local competitions were arranged.

Arsenal finished fifth in the Division Two table, above Birmingham City on goal average – The Arsenal's was 1.68 and Birmingham's was 1.59.

There was no football, but that did not stop Henry Norris keeping himself busy. He began recruiting soldiers for the War Office and was appointed colonel for his efforts. On 13 June 1917, King George V knighted Norris in recognition of his recruitment drive.

The Great War ended with the Armistice, signed at 6am on 11 November 1918. When football returned to the country, wounded veterans of the Great War were given free admittance to Highbury – a generosity that cost the club around £100 (£5,400 at 2018 values) a match.

With the resumption of football, it appeared that the club would continue where they had left off, in Division Two. John McKenna of the Football League Management Committee suggested that the two divisions be expanded from 20 to 22 clubs. A meeting was convened at 2.30pm on 10 March 1919 at the Grand Hotel in Manchester to debate the issue, which would be decided by an election.

During the war, clubs had played in regional leagues, with Arsenal and Spurs in the London Combination.

At the end of the last full season, Chelsea and Spurs had finished in 19th and 20th places in Division One. Derby County and Preston North End had finished first and second in Division Two. On 2 April 1915, Manchester United had played Liverpool, but it became apparent that the match had been rigged in the Red Devils' favour.

This gave them the extra point that put them above Chelsea and thus avoided relegation.

Chelsea chairman Claude Kirby wrote to the Football League Management Committee demanding that Chelsea's relegation be voided because of the northern shenanigans.

Towards the end of January 1919, Spurs wrote to every league club explaining why they should not be consigned to Division Two. On 3 February, the Manchester-based weekly sports paper *Athletic News* published an article that rubbished Spurs' right to stay in the top division and put forward the case that The Arsenal should take their place in Division One. The Arsenal, the magazine wrote, had been born in a munitions factory, and their players and supporters had thus played an important role in winning the war. The club had also been instrumental in bringing football to the south, and had for many years been the only London side in the Football League.

After various propositions were put forward and discarded, it was agreed that Chelsea should stay in Division One and that the final place should be decided between Spurs, Barnsley, Wolverhampton Wanderers, The Arsenal, Birmingham City and Hull City. An outside suggestion was Nottingham Forest, but, since they had finished 18th in Division Two, no one really rated their chances.

After a debate, a vote was taken and The Arsenal came top with 18 votes. Spurs received eight, Barnsley five, Wolverhampton Wanderers four, Nottingham Forest three, Birmingham City two and Hull City only one. A Spurs spokesman said, 'We shall take our defeat like sportsmen.'

In spite of what has been written in many histories by both pro- and anti-Arsenal camps, there is absolutely no evidence to suggest that Sir Henry Norris had anything underhand to do with Arsenal's promotion – no backroom deals, no bribes, nothing.

The simple truth then was that The Arsenal were (as they still are) a bigger and more popular club than their north London rivals, and that is why they got the nod into Division One.

Leicester City 6 Arsenal 6

Football League Division Two. Easter Monday, 21 April 1930, kick-off 3pm
Venue: City Stadium, Filbert Street, Leicester, Leicestershire, LE2 7FL
Leicester City: Blue shirts, white shorts, black stockings with two white hoops at the top
Arsenal: Red shirts, white shorts, red stockings with white tops
Referee: A. Button (Wednesbury)
Attendance: 27,241

Leicester City	**Arsenal**
Joseph Wright	Dan Lewis
Adam Black	Tom Parker (captain)
Jack Brown	Horace Cope
Johnny Duncan	Alf Baker
Arthur Woolliscroft	Alf Haynes
Norman Watson	Bob John
Hugh Adcock	Joe Hulme
Ernest Hine	David Halliday
Arthur Chandler	David Jack
Arthur Lochhead	Alex James
Len Barry	Cliff Bastin
Manager: Willie Orr	*Manager:* Herbert Chapman
Scorers: Adcock 26 minutes, 42 minutes; Lochhead 28 minutes, 82 minutes; Hine 66 minutes; Barry 79 minutes	*Scorers:* Halliday 21 minutes, 58 minutes, 60 minutes, 62 minutes; Bastin 47 minutes, 77 minutes

I T was regarded as a normal end-of-season match. With only five days to go to Arsenal's second appearance in the FA Cup on the horizon (see page 30), it was expected that Herbert Chapman would, in the manner of Arsène Wenger in the League Cup of today, play an inexperienced team. What was also interesting in light of the modern fixtures was that in 1930 the FA Cup Final was not the last match of the domestic campaign. Arsenal had two more league games after the final – home matches to Sunderland and Aston Villa – and lost them both.

Arsenal and Leicester had met in the Highbury fixture just three days earlier, on Good Friday, and played out a 1–1 draw.

A number of fringe players were hoping to get picked so they could impress Chapman and perhaps get the chance for Wembley glory. Among those he chose was David Halliday, a reserve forward and another Scot who was so integral in the early days of the club. Halliday was born in Dumfries on 19 December 1901, and in October 1929 signed for the Gunners for £6,500 from Sunderland, where he had been the Division One top scorer in 1928/29 with 43 goals.

Halliday never really got a chance at Highbury, staying just over a year, although he managed an average of a goal a game, undoubtedly helped by four in this match.

The match turned out to be the highest scoring draw in English football history at that time. Dan Lewis – the 'villain' of the 1927 FA Cup Final disaster against Cardiff City – had been vying with Charlie Preedy for the goalie's jersey all season, but in the run-up seemed to have conceded the green shirt to the one-month-younger Preedy. Chapman brought Lewis back for this match.

After just two minutes, David Jack had the ball in the net, only for the referee to disallow his effort for offside. Halliday scored the first of his four in the opening 45 minutes, but when half-time came around, Leicester were up by three goals to one. Lewis had managed to get a hand to Hugh Adcock's shot, and Tom Parker appeared to clear it off the line, but the linesman signalled that the whole of the ball had crossed the line. Arthur Lochhead put in a second for the Blues before Adcock hit the third.

Chapman must have given an inspiring team talk in the dressing room, because in the second half Arsenal came out with all guns blazing. By the 63rd minute, they were in the lead by five goals to three. Cliff Bastin scored to make it 3–2, while Halliday hit a hat-trick in five minutes, Joe Hulme on the wing assisting in all three goals.

Ernie Hine pulled one back for the Blues before Bastin restored the two-goal advantage. However, Leicester City, runners-up in the previous season, had the same never-say-die attitude they showed when they won the Premier League, and Len Barry scored the Filbert Street side's sixth with 11 minutes left on the clock. Arsenal had two more chances in the final minutes but could not convert them. Alex James had a shot cleared off the line, and Halliday was denied a fifth.

As it turned out, scoring four goals on the eve of the cup final was not enough to guarantee a Wembley place, and it also turned out to be Halliday's last game in an Arsenal shirt. In November 1930, he was sold to Manchester City for £5,700, £800 less than Chapman had paid for him. Ironically, Halliday went on to manage Leicester City from June 1955 to November 1958, taking them to the Division Two title in 1957.

Arsenal 2 Huddersfield Town 0

FA Cup Final. Saturday 26 April 1930, kick-off 3pm
Venue: Wembley Stadium, Middlesex, HA9 0WS
Arsenal: Red shirts, white shorts, red stockings
Huddersfield Town: Blue and white striped shirts, white shorts, black stockings with sky blue tops
Referee: T. Crew (Leicester)
Attendance: 92,488

Arsenal	**Huddersfield Town**
Charlie Preedy	Hugh Turner
Tom Parker (captain)	Roy Goodall
Eddie Hapgood	Bon Spence
Alf Baker	Jimmy Naylor
Bill Seddon	Tom Wilson (captain)
Bob John	Austen Campbell
Joe Hulme	Alex Jackson
David Jack	Bob Kelly
Jack Lambert	Harry Davies
Alex James	Harry Raw
Cliff Bastin	Billy Smith
Manager: Herbert Chapman	*Manager:* Clem Stephenson

Scorers: James 16 minutes; Lambert 88 minutes

THREE years of hurt – and untold washed goalies' jerseys – never stopped them dreaming. Arsenal were determined to avenge the humiliation of losing their first FA Cup Final against underdogs Cardiff City, when Arsenal goalie Dan Lewis seemed to have a shot from the Bluebirds' Hughie Ferguson covered, only for it to slide into the goal off his shiny new jersey with just 16 minutes remaining. From that day forward, no Arsenal shot-stopper has ever taken to the field in an unwashed jersey.

The following season, 1927/28, Arsenal almost avenged their defeat, reaching the semi-finals; and in 1928/29 they reached the sixth round.

In 1929/30, their league position was disappointing, finishing a lowly 14th, but they made up for that by reaching the FA Cup Final for a second time.

It was the beginning of the greatness brought to the club by Herbert Chapman. In fact, Chapman, described by his biographer as 'a little ruddy and a little chubby', began his time in north London at the wrong end of the Seven Sisters Road. He signed for Spurs as a player in 1905 for £70 with a weekly pay packet of £4 (£465 at 2018 values). In his first season, he scored 11 goals, but in the second season he was unable to maintain his place in the team and netted just three times.

At the end of that season, Chapman left and became player-manager of Northampton Town and led them to a Southern League title. In 1912, he took over at Leeds City and took the Peacocks to their highest league position – fourth in Division Two. As Chapman was improving the side, the First World War began; and during the Great War the club found itself embroiled in a financial scandal, breaking a ban on paying players.

The club was thrown out of the Football League after eight matches of the 1919/20 season – the only club to be expelled from the league mid-season, and the only one to be expelled for financial irregularities.

Chapman found himself banned from football, but appealed, and the ban was lifted. On 31 March 1921, he became manager of Huddersfield Town, winning an FA Cup and two First Division titles in a period of four years. He left on 10 June 1925, just before the side completed a hat-trick of consecutive league titles.

Chapman had seen an advertisement in the Manchester-based weekly sports paper *Athletic News* published on 11 May 1925. The advertisement placed by Sir Henry Norris read:

> *Arsenal Football Club is open to receive applications for the position of TEAM MANAGER. He must be experienced and possess the highest qualifications for the post, both as to ability and personal character. Gentlemen whose sole ability to build up a good side depends on the payment of heavy and exhorbitant [sic] transfer fees need not apply.*

Five days after the advertisement appeared, Arsenal sacked manager Leslie Knighton after two disappointing seasons where the club just about avoided relegation.

In the 1924/25 season, Sir Henry had warned Knighton that winning the FA Cup was his last chance of glory. In the first round on 14 January 1925 at Upton Park, Arsenal met West Ham in a 0–0 tie. A friend of Sir Henry was a Harley Street doctor, and he gave the Arsenal team a box of 'courage pills' to take before the match. The silver capsules, probably amphetamines, gave the players 'a red-hot thirst' and heart rate of more than 160 beats per minute. Unfortunately, on the first two occasions they took them, the match was called off. A week later, on 21 January, the two teams met for the replay at Highbury. The Hammers, not on the drugs, kept pace with the Gunners and held them to 2–2. Five days later, the teams met for a second replay (at Stamford Bridge) and West

Ham won 1–0. Arsenal had played without the 'benefit' of the 'courage pills'.

In his autobiography, Knighton claimed that Sir Henry had kept a tight hold on the purse strings and had refused to let him spend money on quality players. A closer examination of the facts shows this to be untrue: the manager had generous funds at his disposal.

Chapman's salary was £2,000 a year (£107,500 at 2018 values and double what he was getting at Huddersfield). On joining the club, he had promised it would take five years to achieve success, and this cup final was played almost five years to the day since his arrival at Highbury.

When he took over, Chapman began dismantling Knighton's side, and indeed nine of the 11 players who took to the Wembley pitch for the 1930 FA Cup Final had been his signings. On 5 February 1926, Chapman signed pacey winger Joe Hulme from Blackburn Rovers for a fee of £3,500. Hulme went on to play 461 games for Arsenal in all competitions and scored 170 goals. To strengthen the defence, Chapman signed right-back Tom Parker from Southampton in March 1926 for £3,250. Parker was unfortunate to be playing at the same time as Roy Goodall and Tom Cooper, who restricted his England appearances to just one full cap and three trials. Parker would succeed Charles Buchan as captain.

With Buchan, the club became embroiled in a financial scandal. In 1925, Chapman arranged to buy Buchan, who was worth £4,000 or £5,000 despite being in his thirties. Norris arranged to pay Sheffield United £2,000 up front plus £100 for every goal Buchan scored in his first season. Buchan, who ran a sports shop, asked for extra money as compensation for his loss of shop income. This was agreed, but payments were made under the counter. Chapman would later deny any knowledge of this money, although, for a man so immersed in every aspect of the club, it seems highly unlikely that he was unaware of what was going on.

Hulme described Buchan as, 'The most tactically astute footballer I ever played alongside. Some players are that – fine players – but Buchan was much more than that in the way he thought about the way the game was played. His logical brain was totally the equal of Herbert Chapman.'

In June 1926, Chapman signed centre-forward Jack Lambert from Doncaster Rovers for £2,000. On 6 September, Lambert made his debut against Bolton Wanderers at Burnden Park, but it was not for four more years that he became a regular. In the 1929/30 season, he scored 18 times in 20 league matches and a goal in the 1930 FA Cup Final. The next season, he scored 38 goals in 34 league games, including seven hat-tricks. In October 1933, he was sold to Fulham, where he stayed for two years. In 1936, Lambert became coach of Margate, Arsenal's nursery club. Two years later, he returned to Arsenal as reserve team coach.

However, before he had the chance to see his protégés move into the first team, he was killed in a car accident on 7 December 1940 at Enfield, Middlesex. He was 38.

It would appear that in January 1927, Chapman learned that Sir Henry had forged his signature on a cheque for £170 for the sale of the Arsenal reserve team bus and that it was not banked in a club account.

In February, William Hall learned about the forgery and told Sir Henry that people at Fulham knew of what had happened and that John Dean, the Fulham chairman, was threatening to go to the FA to ask for an inquiry into the matter. Hall urged his friend to resign, but Sir Henry determined to bluff it out. Instead, it was Hall who resigned as a club director.

On St Valentine's Day, the Arsenal board held a meeting at which the cheque matter was discussed. As manager, Chapman attended and said that he handed the cheque to Sir Henry in July 1926 but had heard nothing more until January 1927. Sir Henry would later say that after the board meeting and until July of that year he was 'openly and continuously insulted' by Chapman.

On 29 March, Sir Henry's solicitor and Arsenal director, J.J. Edwards, went to court to obtain writs for defamation against Joe Bradshaw, John Dean, Edward Liddell and James MacDermott for their comments on Norris and the cheque for the sale of the Arsenal reserve team bus.

The Football League began an investigation into Arsenal's finances, and Charles Sutcliffe and Fred Rinder, the chairman of Aston Villa, began looking into the club's accounts during the first weekend in April. The two men learned that the £170 for the sale of the bus had not yet been paid into the club's bank account. Sir Henry showed Sutcliffe a promissory note that he had presented to Harry John Peters in early July 1926, Edith Norris's bank paying-in book and the envelope Peters had used to take the promissory note to the bank. The two Football League men were convinced that a court case would follow.

On 5 April, Sir Henry wrote to Chapman confirming that the £170 cheque for the bus had not yet reached the company's account, and enclosed with the letter a cheque for £250 to be paid into its account.

On 26 May, Edwards wrote to Sutcliffe confirming that Sir Henry would resign from Arsenal Football and Athletic Company Limited at the next AGM. Sutcliffe replied the next day saying that the Football League's investigations into Arsenal would end. On 3 June, Sir Henry sold 25 shares in Arsenal Football and Athletic Company Limited to George Allison, who in due time became a director. On 27 June, the Football Association Emergency Committee announced that an inquiry would be made into Arsenal's financial affairs. Four days later, Sir Henry wrote to his fellow board members announcing that he would be standing down as chairman and as a director. The FA committee to investigate Arsenal consisted of Sir Charles Clegg of Sheffield Wednesday; the chairman, John McKenna of Liverpool; Arthur Kingscott of Derby County; Harry Keys of West Bromwich Albion; Arthur Hines, a referee and linesman; and A.J. Dickinson, also of Sheffield Wednesday.

On 9 July, Chapman wrote a letter setting out what he knew about the £170 cheque for the Arsenal reserve team bus. Five days later, Fred Wall interviewed Peters on the FA's behalf about the cheque. On 18 July, Sir Charles stood down as chairman through ill health and was replaced by Charles Sutcliffe. At 2pm on 20 July, the FA Commission of Inquiry hearing against Arsenal opened at the Royal Victoria Station Hotel, Sheffield. Present was every director of Arsenal plus Sir Henry and Peters. The meeting was adjourned and a second session fixed for 8 August. The board attended again, as did Sir Henry and William Hall. The committee heard from Chapman, Peters, Knighton and Clement Voysey, a former player. Two days later, Sir Henry wrote to the FA in a bid to explain that the payments to players that he had made (against FA rules) were made with his own money from his own bank account; they were not financed by Arsenal. Over the next weekend (13–14 August), Sir Henry was told what was going to be in the FA report. Sir Henry's lawyers went to court on 23 August for an injunction preventing the publication of the report of the FA Commission of Inquiry into Arsenal. The request was refused.

The following day, the *Daily Mail* ran an article – untrue as it turned out – that the FA Commission's report would not be published. On 26 August, all the club directors were sent the report and ordered along with Sir Henry to attend the FA Council meeting on 29 August to hear the findings. Sir Henry refused to attend. The next day was the opening of the 1927/28 season, and Arsenal played away to Bury and lost 6–1. That day, solicitors Rogers, Gilbert and Rodgers sent a letter to all Fleet Street newspapers telling them not to publish the FA report. On the Sunday, the sports editor of the *Daily Mail* told Sir Henry that his newspaper intended to publish the report despite the legal warning. They offered the former Arsenal chairman the chance to offer his side of events. Sir Henry refused on the grounds that the matter was *sub judice*.

Representatives of Arsenal gathered at the FA's offices in Russell Square, Bloomsbury, London at 3pm on 29 August to hear the report. Three directors – William Hall, George Peachey and Jack Humble – were present, but Sir Henry Norris was not. The damning report found Sir Henry and Hall guilty of taking excessive expenses from the club's accounts; it declared Peachey and Humble guilty of not doing anything to prevent them.

Norris, Hall, Humble and Peachey were all banned from taking any further part in the management of a football club. A furious Sir Henry said the report more than implied that he had taken money from Arsenal for his own personal benefit. The FA denied their report made any such inferences.

The report stated:

- Sir Henry paid C.R. Voysey a signing-on fee of £200, which was against Football League rules.
- It restated the findings of the 1923 investigation into Sir Henry's deal with centre-forward H.A. White but did not comment further.
- The accounts of Arsenal Football and Athletic Company Limited showed payments totalling £539 had been made to D. Ryder, Sir Henry's chauffeur over the period 4 June 1921 to 5 May 1923; and payments of £539 over the same period to H. Denham, William Hall's chauffeur. Hall denied the payments to Denham.
- Arsenal's accounts showed a payment of £143 9s 8d towards the costs for a legal case brought by its player Jock Rutherford. The FA Commission believed the payment was against Football League rules.

- Sir Henry had at first refused to give any details concerning a cheque for £125 cashed during May 1926 and payable to Queensborough Motor Company. Other directors of the club, including William Hall, knew nothing about the cheque; Chapman and Peters did not know of the company or its address. When the FA demanded further details, firstly J.J. Edwards, acting for Sir Henry, said that all evidence about the cheque had been lost; and then Sir Henry revealed the money was for one season's use of his car on club business.

- A cheque for £170 originally payable to Arsenal Football Club Limited had been endorsed as follows: 'Arsenal Football Club Ltd, H Chapman, Secretary. Pay to the order of Lady Norris.' The endorsement had been signed with the names of Herbert Chapman and Edith Norris. Sir Henry admitted that the endorsement was in his handwriting.

- The expense claim Sir Henry put in to cover January 1926 to 7 May 1927 included items of furniture not authorised by Arsenal's directors; and travel expenses, which the FA did not allow directors to claim from their club.

On 30 August, the *Daily Mail*, and only that newspaper, published the FA Commission of Inquiry's report. Sir Henry issued a writ against the Football Association for libel. On 2 September, Jack Humble resigned as a director of Arsenal, but George Peachey went to the club's ground and attempted to attend a board meeting. He was 'forcibly excluded', and the meeting went ahead with the three directors present: Samuel Hill-Wood, the new chairman, J.J. Edwards and newcomer George Allison. Five days later, Peachey began proceedings against Arsenal for his exclusion, saying it had no legal basis because the FA had exceeded their power. When it became apparent that Peachey was likely to win his case, the FA wrote to Arsenal threatening to expel them unless Peachey's removal as a director stood.

On 10 September, the *Daily Mail* ran a story about what had occurred at the delayed AGM, a meeting that Sir Henry had considered private. It mentioned the £664 that Sir Henry had been ordered to repay the club. He issued a writ against the newspaper claiming their report suggested that he had acted dishonestly. On 16 November, Sir Henry's lawyers claimed that he did not owe the club any money because he had not personally received any of it. There is no evidence that he did repay any of the money. That same day, Peachey won his court case and, having been vindicated, immediately resigned as a director of the club.

In February 1929, the Lord Chief Justice found for the FA, and they banned Sir Henry from football for life. It was alleged that in 1928, Sir Henry had told Arsenal to take it easy against Manchester United and Portsmouth so that struggling Spurs would be relegated. Nothing was proved, but such was Sir Henry's reputation at the time that it was generally believed. As Arsenal began to gain honours in the 1930s, the man who had done so much for the club was forced to watch from the stands. He died from a massive heart attack at his home, Sirron Lodge, Vine Road, Barnes Common, London SW13 on 30 July 1934, six months after Herbert Chapman. He left £72,051 4s 1d (£4.8 million at 2018 values). Sir Henry bequeathed £100 to Leslie Knighton, the manager he sacked to be replaced by Herbert Chapman. Norris was buried in the family plot in East Sheen cemetery on 1 August.

On 13 October 1928, Chapman bought David Jack – the first player sold for a five-figure transfer fee. His club, Bolton Wanderers, had fallen into financial trouble, and the wily Yorkshireman arranged for the negotiations to be held in the bar of the Euston Hotel in London. Bolton wanted £13,000 for the forward. Bob Wall, Chapman's assistant and later general manager and a club director, recalled: 'We arrived at the hotel half-an-hour early. Chapman immediately went into the lounge bar. He called the waiter, placed two pound notes in his hand and said, "George, this is Mr Wall, my assistant. He will drink whisky and dry ginger. I will drink gin and tonic. We shall be joined by guests. They will drink whatever they like. See that our guests are given double of everything, but Mr Wall's whisky and dry ginger will contain no whisky, and my gin and tonic will contain no gin."'

The cunning Chapman persuaded the Bolton contingent to accept £10,890 (the previous record stood at £6,750). Sir Charles Clegg, the president of the Football Association, immediately issued a statement claiming that no player in the world was worth that amount of money.

David Jack – the first player to score in an FA Cup Final at Wembley and the first to play for two different clubs in Wembley finals – did not turn up for training on 18 October, which worried trainer Tom Whittaker, who feared that the club had bought a crocked player. He went round to Jack's house to find him relaxing, his feet on the mantelpiece and a cigarette in his mouth (one of 25 he smoked a day).

Jack calmly explained that he was well and fit but always had Thursdays off at Bolton. Whittaker soon put an end to that nonsense, and Jack, who always arrived at the ground in spats, made his debut for Arsenal on 20 October against Newcastle United at St James' Park, when the Gunners won by three goals to nil. In his first season, he was the club's top scorer with 25 goals in 31 matches. David Jack retired on 5 May 1934 after scoring 139 goals for Arsenal in 234 matches at all levels.

Chapman continued to strengthen his squad and bought Herbie Roberts (December 1926 for £200), Eddie Hapgood (October 1927 for £1,000), Cliff Bastin (May 1929 for £2,000) and Alex James (June 1929 for £8,750).

The second road to Wembley began on 11 January 1930 at home to Chelsea, when the Gunners won by two goals to nil. It took them two attempts to bypass Birmingham City, drawing 2–2 in London before winning by a solitary goal at St Andrew's. Their next two ties saw them travel to Ayresome Park, where they dispatched Middlesbrough 2–0 with Lambert and Bastin scoring, and to the Boleyn Ground in east London, where they comfortably saw off West Ham United 3–0, Lambert getting a brace.

They were drawn against Hull City in the semi-final and played out a 2–2 draw at Elland Road – Arsenal were two goals down with ten minutes left before Jack and Bastin pulled them level – before winning the replay 1–0 at Villa Park thanks to a Jack goal. Huddersfield, on the other hand, sailed through each of their ties, dispatching their opponents with relative ease.

Dan Lewis had hoped to be selected to make up for his error three years earlier, but a knee problem reoccurred during the 6–6 match with Leicester City (see page 28), and Charlie Preedy was chosen instead. Lewis dropped from first to fourth choice, never played for Arsenal again, and was transferred to Gillingham in May 1931. He died in July 1965.

On the team bus to the game, Preedy told his team-mates, 'I know you think I'm the worst goalkeeper in the world. I probably am, but today I'm going to play like I'm the best.'

The 1930 final began a tradition that continues to this day. For the first time, both teams entered the pitch side-by-side in tribute to Herbert Chapman. The sun shone on Wembley.

HM King George V watched the match, making his first public appearance in 18 months after an illness. Arsenal director George Allison provided the BBC radio commentary.

Arsenal were missing centre-half Herbie Roberts, and reserve Bill Seddon was selected. Huddersfield were favourites to win, but on five minutes Arsenal won a free kick. Alex James went to take it and then feinted, allowing Tom Parker to smash the ball into the stomach of his opposite number, Tom Wilson.

James crossed the ball for Lambert to head goalwards but Huddersfield goalie Hugh Turner pushed it away. Bastin was next, with a header that went just wide, before Lambert headed over.

With a quarter of an hour gone, Roy Goodall fouled James. Before Mr Crew could get his whistle to his lips to allow play to continue, James passed the ball to Bastin, who took it to the corner flag and crossed, whereupon James opened the scoring, putting the ball into the bottom corner of Turner's net.

James later said, 'Turner had positioned himself so well that I saw that I could only hope to beat him by some deception. So I sliced the ball with the outside of my right foot and sent it swerving beyond the reach of the goalkeeper's right hand.'

Throughout the season, James had been taking free kicks as the first notes of the referee's whistle sounded, with the result that he was usually made to retake them, which annoyed Chapman because it destroyed the flow.

Tom Whittaker said, 'It is strange that he helped to win the cup by virtually disobeying an order from his chief.'

The second half was disrupted by, for some, an unwelcome visitor. With Arsenal one up, the LZ127 Graf Zeppelin flew over the stadium accompanied by 12 aircraft. The engine noise made the fans look up and distracted them from the game. Hulme remembered 'a droning sound which got louder and louder. I realised what it was, but I was so focused I played on.' Parker said, 'I glanced up, saw what it was, and didn't give another second's thought. I'd seen a Zeppelin over London before anyway.'

Bernard Joy wrote in *Forward Arsenal!*: 'It cast a shadow of events to come, which were to be nearly disastrous for both the country and Arsenal.'

It was only when the aircraft dipped its nose, perhaps in salute to the king, who raised his hat to it, that the crowd broke into a round of applause and cheers, although reportedly some booed.

The second half was rather scrappier than the first, and Huddersfield pounded Arsenal's goal for most of the half. With no substitutes, both sides felt fatigued in the hot sun. David Jack was unable to run, and Parker 'had terrible cramps in both legs'. Huddersfield's Alex Jackson was hobbling after an enthusiastic tackle from Bob John.

Then, with two minutes to go, James 'held the ball long enough to make the halves and backs uncertain of his intentions. Then he pushed the ball straight down the middle where Lambert, between the two backs, could not be challenged promptly by either.'

Lambert scored Arsenal's second to guarantee their name on the trophy. So tired were the players that when Lambert looked up to be congratulated, there were no other Arsenal players near him.

'None of us had the legs to chase after Jackie,' said Parker. Fifty years after he collected the trophy from the king, he recalled, 'I'm old now and no one recognises me in the street, which suits me. I'm not a vain man, modest in fact. But inside I'll always have the honour of being the first Arsenal captain to lift not just silverware but the FA Cup. It's marvellous.'

Arsenal's Bill Seddon, who died in January 1993 at the age of 91, was the last surviving player to appear in the game.

Arsenal 3 Liverpool 1

Football League Division One. Saturday 18 April 1931, kick-off 3.30pm
Venue: Arsenal Stadium, Avenell Road, London N5 1BU
Arsenal: Red shirts, white shorts, red stockings with white tops
Liverpool: White shirts with red collar and cuffs, black shorts, red stockings
Referee: Unknown
Attendance: 39,143

Arsenal	**Liverpool**
Bill Harper	Elisha Scott
Tom Parker (captain)	James Jackson (captain)
Eddie Hapgood	Tommy Lucas
Charlie Jones	Tom Morrison
Herbie Roberts	Norman James
Bob John	Jimmy McDougall
Joe Hulme	Harold Barton
David Jack	Gordon Hodgson
Jack Lambert	Dave Wright
Alex James	Archie McPherson
Cliff Bastin	Gordon Gunson
Manager: Herbert Chapman	*Manager:* George Patterson
Scorers: Jack 25 minutes; Bastin 65 minutes; Lambert 70 minutes	*Scorer:* Roberts (o.g.) 3 minutes

HAVING enjoyed the sweet taste of victory the year before, Arsenal were determined to carry on dining at the silver service restaurant of success. The FA Cup was one thing, but Herbert Chapman wanted more – he wanted the league title.

Chapman had the team he wanted and was determined that they would exploit their talent for maximum success. They scored 14 goals in their first four games, and did not lose a match until their tenth, when they went down 4–2 at Derby County.

On 8 November 1930, they beat Aston Villa 5–2. Apart from after their first game, Arsenal were never out of the top two all season, and after going top on 5 February 1931, they never let go of first place.

The title was achieved at Arsenal Stadium in a match against Liverpool in mid-April – two weeks before the end of the season. Arsenal's title rivals, Aston Villa, fell too far to catch up. Despite the three-one score line at Highbury it was not a walkover. A wind-assisted Herbie Roberts own goal from a Harold Barton cross gave the visitors an unexpected advantage, and the wind kept Arsenal pinned in their own half for much of the first period. In the days before the technical area, Herbert Chapman looked nervous in the dugout.

When the wind dropped, Arsenal began to put together some moves. Alex James passed to Cliff Bastin, who smacked a belter against the underside of Liverpool's crossbar before goalie Elisha Scott managed to claw it away.

On 25 minutes, Liverpool did not clear their lines from a corner and David Jack put the ball away for the equaliser.

The players went in for their half-time refreshments at one goal apiece. In the second half, the wind got up again and Arsenal played into it. Just past the hour mark, James found Jack Lambert in space; he passed to Bastin, who put the ball beyond Scott's reach to give Arsenal the lead.

Five minutes later, Lambert put the game beyond doubt with Arsenal's third, and the league trophy was on its way south to Highbury for the first time.

It was a remarkable season. Cliff Bastin played in all 42 games, Tom Parker in 41, Herbie Roberts and Alex James in 40 and Eddie Hapgood in 38. The one position where Arsenal found difficulty was between the sticks. Chapman started the season with Dutchman Gerrit Keizer (also spelled Keyser). The first foreign player to play for Arsenal, he joined the club in 1930, aged 19, even though he was still technically on the books of Ajax. He said that he came to England to improve his English. He made his debut in the 4–1 victory over Blackpool at Bloomfield Road on 30 August 1930, and kept goal for the first dozen games that season.

On Saturdays, he would play for Arsenal and then fly back to Holland that night to play for Ajax the next day, earning him the nickname 'The Flying Dutchman'. As with many keepers, Gerrit Keizer's performances ranged from the erratic to the brilliant.

Herbert Chapman eventually tired of Keizer; he dropped him in October and never picked him for the first team again. In July 1931, Keizer moved to Charlton Athletic. He continued to shuttle between London and Amsterdam, ostensibly bringing football kits with him. In 1947, Dutch customs officers discovered that he was also importing British bank notes, then an offence. He was fined 30,000 guilders and given a six-month prison sentence. Out of jail, he started a successful greengrocery business and in 1955 became a director of Ajax. He died on 5 December 1980.

Herbert Chapman picked Scotsman Bill Harper for one game, then Charlie 'Spider' Preedy for one before reverting to Harper.

In November 1925, Arsenal had paid what was then the record fee of £4,500 for a goalkeeper when Harper joined from Hibernian.

He made his Arsenal debut against Bury on 14 November 1925, in a game that Arsenal won 6–1. He stayed at the club for 19 months before joining Fall River Marksmen in Massachusetts in the US. Three years later, after playing for various American teams, he returned to Arsenal. He made more than 70 appearances between the posts for the Gunners – his last was away to Blackburn Rovers on 31 August 1931 – before moving to what was to become his second home, Plymouth Argyle, where he stayed for 54 years in various roles.

Harper played 13 league and cup games before Charlie Preedy took over. Preedy had ten games in goal before Harper resumed for the rest of the season.

Arsenal finished seven points clear of second-placed Aston Villa and achieved 60 points, a record (in the days of two points for a win) that stood until 1969 when Leeds United attained 67. Arsenal scored 127 goals – 67 at home and 60 away – but even that was not the most. Aston Villa scored one more. Arsenal failed to score in just one match – at home to Huddersfield Town – and scored four or more on 17 occasions. Manchester United finished bottom.

This began a run of success unheralded until Sir Alex Ferguson's reign at Old Trafford:

> 1930: FA Cup winners
> 1931: League champions
> 1932: League runners-up; FA Cup runners-up
> 1933: League champions
> 1934: League champions
> 1935: League champions
> 1936: FA Cup winners
> 1938: League champions

The *Daily Express* joked that Arsenal would probably win the Boat Race and the Grand National if they bothered to enter those competitions.

Chapman, the architect of the modern Arsenal, was not around to see the second half of the triumph. He spent 31 December 1933 with his family at their home, 6 Haslemere Avenue, Hendon, Middlesex, and then travelled up north to watch Bury play Notts County. Arsenal's next opponents at Highbury were Sheffield Wednesday, so Chapman went to see them beat Birmingham City 2–1. Then after spending the night at his brother's home, Chapman returned to London and consulted Arsenal's doctor, Guy Pepper.

Despite catching a cold, Chapman ignored Dr Pepper's advice to rest and decided to watch Arsenal's third team at Guildford. Arsenal beat Guildford City 4–0, and among the players was 15-year-old Denis Compton, a future brilliant English Test batsman.

Finally, Chapman went home to bed – but the cold had turned to pneumonia, and Chapman died at 3am at his home on Saturday 6 January 1934. He was 59.

The match against Sheffield Wednesday went ahead before a 45,156 crowd, but Arsenal only managed a 1–1 draw. They also lost their next three games.

Herbert Chapman was buried four days later at St Mary's, Hendon. The pallbearers were Cliff Bastin, Eddie Hapgood, Joe Hulme, Alex James and Jack Lambert.

Aston Villa 1 Arsenal 7

Football League Division One. Saturday 14 December 1935, kick-off 3pm
Venue: Villa Park, Trinity Road, Birmingham, B6 6HE
Aston Villa: Claret shirts with light blue sleeves, white shorts, black stockings with claret and blue stripe at top
Arsenal: White shirts, black shorts, blue and white stockings
Referee: J.M. Wiltshire (Sherborne)
Attendance: 60,891

Aston Villa	**Arsenal**
Harry Morton	Alex Wilson
Danny Blair	George Male
George Cummings	Eddie Hapgood (captain)
Alex Massie	Jack Crayston
Tommy Wood	Herbie Roberts
Tommy Griffiths	Wilf Copping
Eric Houghton (captain)	Pat Beasley
James Williams	Cliff Bastin
Dai Astley	Ted Drake
Jack Palethorpe	Tim Rogers
Ronnie Dix	Ray Bowden
Manager: Jimmy McMullan	*Manager:* George Allison
Scorer: Palethorpe 61 minutes	*Scorers:* Drake 15 minutes, 28 minutes, 34 minutes, 46 minutes, 50 minutes, 58 minutes, 76 minutes

HAT-TRICKS are comparatively rare in football matches, four goals are rarer still – but seven goals by one player in a match is virtually unheard of. But that's how many Arsenal forward Ted Drake scored against Aston Villa at Villa Park in the mid-1930s.

The 1935/36 season got off to a mixed start for Arsenal, as they won four of their first ten matches, including a 6–1 thrashing of Grimsby Town and a 5–1 walloping of Blackburn Rovers. Arsenal won their eighth game of the season in early December against Middlesbrough and prepared to travel to the Midlands to play Aston Villa, who were floundering at the bottom of the table, on 14 December. Villa had just spent £24,000 on five new players and were expected/hoping to improve.

Arsenal forward Ted Drake had been suffering with a cartilage problem that would mean he missed most of the second half of the season, but he had warmed up for his visit to the area by hitting two against Wolverhampton Wanderers three weeks earlier.

There was a standing joke at Arsenal that if the groundsman did not cut the grass properly, Drake could trip over one of the blades and injure himself.

Ted Drake was a gas fitter from Southampton when, in March 1934, George Allison signed him for £6,500, the first addition after Herbert Chapman's death. He said, 'I was just a lad from Southampton. I scored a few goals for the Saints, but to supplement my wages I still did shifts as a gas fitter. Then, when I got a call saying that Arsenal were interested in me, I immediately jumped into a different world. It was pure fantasy.

'To be honest I didn't stop being bowled over by Highbury from the minute I arrived.'

Drake scored on his debut, and in his first season at Highbury scored 42 goals in 41 games – still the club record for most goals in one season. He hit four goals four times and three hat-tricks.

Against Villa, Drake's left knee was strapped and his arm was bandaged as he took to the pitch before nearly 60,000 fans. Arsenal were also without Alex James and Joe Hulme, and manager George Allison was at home in bed at Hendon with the flu.

Aston Villa had more possession than Arsenal in the first half, but, thanks to Drake, the Gunners still went in for their half-time refreshments three goals to the good.

The first came off a Pat Beasley pass that Drake put in at the near post. Never one to do the same thing twice, his second goal came from a Cliff Bastin pass that he put into the net at the far corner. In the 34th minute, Beasley took a chance himself, but the ball was parried by Harry Morton and Drake was there to mop up and make it three.

The players had only been on the pitch 60 seconds for the second half when Drake made it four. After a mistake by Villa centre-half Tommy Griffiths, Drake took the ball to the byline and hit it goalwards at an acute angle. Harry Morton was unable to stop it.

Four minutes later and Drake made it five; and eight minutes after that, six. In his only game for Villa, Jack Palethorpe scored what could probably not even be termed a consolation goal to make it 6–1, before Drake hit his seventh with nearly 15 minutes left on the clock.

He claimed he should have had an eighth as the ball hit Morton's bar and bounced over the line, but J.M. Wiltshire, the referee, waved away his claim. Morton later admitted that Drake had been unfairly penalised.

'I was very lucky that day. It's the kind of day that any striker dreams of,' he said, 'where your team-mates put chance after chance on a plate for you. And although what happened was – I suppose – noteworthy, I look back with only casual interest because we didn't win the league that season.'

It was claimed at the time that Drake's haul equalled that of Jimmy Ross, who hit seven for Preston North End against Stoke City in 1888. However, years later it was revealed that the Preston forward had only scored four. Drake's record did not stand for long – only 12 days, before Bunny Bell of Tranmere Rovers hit nine in a 13–4 defeat of Oldham Athletic in Division Three North. He might have hit ten, but missed a penalty.

Arsenal finished a lowly sixth at the end of the 1935/36 season, although they did have the consolation of an FA Cup triumph, with Drake scoring the only goal of the game (see page 48). Aston Villa were relegated for the first time in their history. Indeed it was the reverse fixture at Highbury that helped to seal their doom. Drake scored the winning goal for Arsenal and said, 'I'm sorry' as he put the ball over the line. Later he said, 'I was tempted to miss. I thought I'd better not.'

At Arsenal, Ted Drake scored 139 goals in 184 competitive games, plus 94 goals in other matches, including 91 in wartime football. After he was forced to retire, he became manager of Hendon (August 1946), Reading (1 June 1947 to 1 June 1952) and Chelsea (1 June 1952 to 30 September 1961), where he led 'Drake's Ducklings' to the Division One title in 1955 – the first man to play in and manage a championship-winning team – before becoming assistant manager of Barcelona for six months in early 1970. That ended because of language difficulties and Drake being unable to cope with the heat.

Arsenal 1 Sheffield United 0

FA Cup Final. Saturday 25 April 1936, kick-off 3pm
Venue: Wembley Stadium, Middlesex, HA9 0WS
Arsenal: Red shirts with white sleeves, white shorts, blue and white hooped stockings
Sheffield United: Red and white striped shirts, black shorts, black stockings with thin red and white hoops at the top
Referee: Harry Nattrass (County Durham)
Attendance: 93,384

Arsenal	Sheffield United
Alex Wilson	Jack Smith
George Male	Harry Hooper (captain)
Eddie Hapgood	Charlie Wilkinson
Jack Crayston	Ernest Jackson
Herbie Roberts	Tom Johnson
Wilf Copping	Archie McPherson
Joe Hulme	Harold Barton
Ray Bowden	Bobby Barclay
Ted Drake	Jock Dodds
Alex James (captain)	Jack Pickering
Cliff Bastin	Bertie Williams
Manager: George Allison	*Manager:* Teddy Davison
Scorer: Drake 74 minutes	

BACK to Wembley for the third time in the 1930s, this time Arsenal's opponents were Sheffield United from Division Two, on Saturday 25 April 1936. It was the only FA Cup Final attended by HM King Edward VIII during his short reign, which ended in December of the same year with his abdication so he could marry the American double divorcée Wallis Simpson.

A crowd of 93,384 saw Ted Drake score the only goal of the game 15 minutes from time, as Arsenal won their second FA Cup, six years after their first triumph.

As Arsenal had finished sixth in the league, the FA Cup was their only chance of glory. In a reverse of Arsène Wenger's League Cup policy, manager George Allison rested his best players in the league and kept his strongest team for the cup. It resulted in a fine of £250 for the club by the Football League. Remarkably, there were no newsreel cameras to capture the events, because Wembley officials had banned them after a dispute over match fees. Gaumont British Film Company offered £900, but the Wembley bosses wanted £1,500. The stadium chiefs gave in, but by this time Gaumont had reduced their offer to £500. No compromise could be reached, so Wembley's official cameraman took the only film. Enterprising reporters hired autogyros to fly above the stadium to watch the match. The BBC broadcast the match live on the wireless from 2.30pm and, for the first time, used commentators. The debuting pairing were Ivan Sharpe and Norman Creek.

Arsenal's road to Wembley began with a series of journeys up and down the country. In the third round they went to the south-west to play Division Three South's Bristol Rovers at Eastville Stadium. Arsenal missed a penalty, and Rovers went a goal up in the first half. It seemed as if a giant-killing act could be on the cards to match the disaster against Walsall on 14 January 1933. Arsenal eventually began to assert themselves, and equalised in the 65th minute before scoring four times in 14 minutes – including Ted Drake and Cliff Bastin both bagging a brace – to run out 5–1 winners.

It was up north for the next two rounds, where they saw off Liverpool 2–0 at Anfield on 25 January 1936, five days after the death of King George V. Both sides wore black armbands. The crowd of 60,000 sang 'Abide with Me' and 'God Save the King' before the match, which was described by programme editor W.M. Johnston as going 'down in Arsenal history as one of the most glorious performances ... the triumph was complete and outstanding ... in spite of [Liverpool's] excellence they were well and truly beaten, and eclipsed in every department. The form of our team ... was superb'. In the fifth round, they were drawn against Newcastle United and were held 3–3 by the Magpies, who had triumphed 2–1 in the 1932 final.

The ground was packed, with 64,484 fans inside and thousands more locked out. Arsenal took the lead each time but the Magpies equalised on all three occasions.

The replay on home turf four days later – the first FA Cup tie played at Arsenal Stadium for two years – was an easier task, and Arsenal won 3–0, including two penalties. Nearly 130,000 people saw the two matches. They stayed at home for the quarter-final, while their opponents travelled south from Yorkshire. Arsenal easily beat Barnsley from Division Two, 4–1.

In the semi-final, Arsenal played Grimsby Town at Leeds Road, the home of Huddersfield Town, and won thanks to a goal from Bastin in a match whose one-sidedness was not reflected in the scoreline.

Arsenal's most recent appearance in the final had come four years earlier, while the Blades had not graced the FA Cup Final since 1925, when they beat Cardiff City – the team who were to beat Arsenal two years later for the only time the cup has been won by a team from outside England.

Sheffield United had an additional incentive to win – their city rivals Sheffield Wednesday had won the cup in 1935.

Both teams were made up of nine Englishmen and two Scotsmen, and, despite the apparent clash, both sides sported red and white shirts. Drake returned to the side after injuries had blighted his season. On the morning of the final, manager George Allison gave the captaincy to Alex James, a decision that earned him the continuing enmity of Eddie Hapgood. The boss moved Ray Bowden to inside-right and Bastin to outside-left, meaning there was no place for Pat Beasley, who had played four matches and scored three goals in the run-up to the final. In those days there was none of this modern-day nonsense about every Tom, Dick and Harry getting a medal, or players who did not even make the final eleven changing from their civvies into their kit so they can get a medal they are not entitled to. Beasley signed for Arsenal in May 1931 for £550, and was left out of the 1932 final because Joe Hulme recovered from injury. Beasley won two league championship medals with the Gunners, but was sold in October 1936 to Huddersfield Town for £750. He played in the 1938 FA Cup Final, but was on the losing side.

The wind caused problems for both sides, on occasion blowing the ball away. With just three minutes gone, Alex Wilson dropped the ball and could not pick it up again sufficiently quickly. There was little protection for the keeper in those days, and Jock Dodds and Bobby Barclay hassled Wilson before an Arsenal defender kicked the ball away. In fact, Wilson looked unsteady for much of the first half as the Blades overwhelmed their superior opponents. Right-back George Male had the 'game of his life'.

Cliff Bastin and Ray Bowden were ineffectual up front for Arsenal, while Jack Smith played well between the sticks for the Blades, and the score was 0–0 at half-time.

In the second half, Arsenal began to show their superiority, and Smith did exceptionally well to protect his goal.

With 16 minutes to go, James passed to Bastin, who went past United captain Harry Hooper and crossed the ball into the middle for Drake, who hit it with his left foot into the roof of the net.

Not long after, the Blades attacked. Harold Barton raced down the right wing and crossed to Dodds, who headed against the bar. He later said, 'I was just about to direct the ball down into the net when a wee fellow called Wilf Copping went up behind me and, in striving to get to the ball, punched me in the back. This had the unfortunate effect of knocking my head backwards so the ball thudded against the crossbar instead of nestling itself in the back of the net. But for that, who knows, things might have turned out different.'

It was Drake's solitary effort that sent the cup to north London and not South Yorkshire, although he was penalised by referee Harry Nattrass five times for unsporting use of elbows.

Arsenal gave a silver watch to each player's wife.

The shirt worn by James in the match is displayed in the Arsenal Museum. Dodds, who died on 23 February 2007, was the last surviving player from the game.

On 27 April 1936, Allison received a letter from David Danskin, the man without whom Arsenal would not exist. He was in the Municipal Hospital in Coventry and had listened to the game on the wireless. He congratulated the team on their success.

REG'S DOUBLE SEALS ANOTHER CUP VICTORY

Arsenal 2 Liverpool 0

FA Cup Final. Saturday 29 April 1950, kick-off 3pm
Venue: Wembley Stadium, Middlesex, HA9 0WS
Arsenal: Gold shirts, white shorts, gold stockings
Liverpool: White shirts, black shorts, red and white hooped stockings
Referee: A. Pearce (Bedfordshire)
Attendance: 100,000

Arsenal	Liverpool
1 George Swindin	1 Cyril Sidlow
2 Laurie Scott	2 Ray Lambert
3 Wally Barnes	3 Eddie Spicer
4 Alex Forbes	4 Phil Taylor (captain)
5 Leslie Compton	5 Bill Jones
6 Joe Mercer (captain)	6 Laurie Hughes
7 Freddie Cox	7 Jimmy Payne
8 Jimmy Logie	8 Kevin Baron
9 Peter Goring	9 Albert Stubbins
10 Reg Lewis	10 Willie Fagan
11 Denis Compton	11 Billy Liddell
Manager: Tom Whittaker	*Manager:* George Kay
Scorer: Lewis 17 minutes, 62 minutes	

ARSENAL had not been to Wembley for 14 years when they reached the final of the 1950 FA Cup; opponents Liverpool had never been there.

The road to Wembley began on a cold January afternoon in north London when Sheffield Wednesday came to visit. A single goal from Reg Lewis was enough to send the Gunners through to the fourth round, where they were drawn at home to Swansea Town on 28 January.

The Londoners beat the visitors from Wales by two goals to one, with a penalty from Wally Barnes and Jimmy Logie's goal seeing off the Swans.

Arsenal stayed in London for the fifth round when they met Burnley on 11 February. Two goals saw off the Lancastrians, with Lewis and Denis Compton bagging the spoils.

On Saturday 4 March, Arsenal played their fourth consecutive cup tie at home when they beat Leeds United by a solitary goal from that man Lewis again.

Remarkably, they stayed in London for the semi-final. Arsenal drew Chelsea from west London, and the tie was played at White Hart Lane. The match ended with the teams sharing four goals. Arsenal's pair came from Freddie Cox (in the dying seconds of the first half) and

Leslie Compton. A replay was held four days later, and Arsenal won by a solitary goal in the 14th minute of extra time scored by Cox.

Three days later, on 25 March, the second semi-final was played and it, too, was a local derby. Liverpool beat Everton 2–0 in a tie played at Maine Road, the home of Manchester City, with the vital goal scored by future Liverpool manager Bob Paisley. To everyone's surprise, manager George Kay, who had captained West Ham United in the first Wembley final in 1923, dropped him from the final. Liverpool centre-forward Albert Stubbins rallied behind his disheartened team-mate: 'Bob was shattered to be left out. He was very low and contemplating leaving the club, but I told him not to make any hasty decisions.'

The Arsenal team ran out at Wembley having reached the final without leaving London. The weather was wet, very wet. Liverpudlians had applied for almost ten times their allocation of 11,500 tickets for the final (7,000 standing and the remainder seated).

Liverpool were made slight favourites for the cup by the bookies, and head-to-head form favoured the Scousers, as they had beaten Arsenal twice already that season.

Despite playing for Arsenal, captain Joe Mercer still lived on Merseyside and owned a grocer's shop in Wallasey. He usually trained with Liverpool, but in the week running up to the final he was asked not to, lest he inadvertently give away the final game plan. He trained on his own in the afternoons, while Arsenal went to Brighton to prepare. Mercer was also named the Football Writers' Association Footballer of the Year.

King George VI was introduced to the teams – Arsenal captain Joe Mercer did the honours first. Queen Elizabeth stayed in the stand.

Liverpool captain Phil Taylor won the toss and Arsenal kicked off. The Gunners attacked from the kick-off, but the Liverpool defence was strong enough to see them off.

Jimmy Payne made a run down the right wing but was unable to get the ball near the Arsenal goal. The Liverpool defence of Taylor, Laurie Hughes and Bill Jones kept Arsenal at bay.

Payne crossed, and George Swindin grabbed it at the second attempt to defy the Scousers from scoring.

Mercer passed to Denis Compton on the left wing, who shot away with the ball. He passed to Peter Goring, who sent it on to Logie, who in turn played it to Cox out on the right, but he was unable to stop it running out of play.

After 17 minutes, Arsenal won a corner, which Denis Compton took. The ball came in to Logie, who passed to Lewis, who put it past Wales international Cyril Sidlow in the Liverpool goal.

That was the only goal of the first half, and Liverpool attempted to regroup at half-time. They kicked off the second half but almost immediately came under pressure from the Gunners. Sidlow was one of the first keepers to launch an attack by throwing the ball out rather than kicking it.

Seventeen minutes into the half, a centre from Cox was put away by Lewis for his second goal, putting the match beyond Liverpool's grasp.

Mercer led his players up to collect the medals, but there was an error and he was given a loser's one until the king spotted the mistake and rectified it. As Denis Compton walked up the steps to accept his prize from the king, he became the only Test cricketer with an FA Cup winner's medal.

Denis Compton, the first sportsman to advertise Brylcreem, spent the whole of his football career at Arsenal and the whole of his cricket career with Middlesex. He joined the MCC ground staff at Lord's in 1934. Four years later, he scored his first Test century against Don Bradman's touring Australia. He played 78 Tests, scoring 5,807 runs with an average of 50.06, and hitting 17 centuries with a highest score of 278. A winger, he made his debut for the Gunners against Derby County on 26 September 1936, and won the league in 1948 and FA Cup two years later. By the 1950 final, he was already into his 30s, inclined to run out of puff, and troubled by a notorious knee injury. In the first half, in his own words, he 'played a stinker'; in the second, fuelled by a mammoth slug of whisky administered by Alex James, he put in a dazzling performance.

Magnanimous in victory, Joe Mercer said to a post-match interviewer, 'This is the greatest moment of my life to be holding the cup here at Wembley. And while we are very, very pleased to have won it, I would like to say how wonderful the Liverpool boys have been in their defeat.'

Liverpool centre-forward Albert Stubbins also holds an unusual record. He was the only footballer to appear on the cover of The Beatles' *Sgt. Pepper's Lonely Hearts Club Band* LP. It was said that he was included because John Lennon liked his name. Paul McCartney sent him a copy of the record with the message, 'Well done, Albert, for all those glorious years of football. Long may you bob and weave.'

Arsenal 3 Burnley 2

Football League Division One. Friday 1 May 1953, kick-off 6.30pm
Venue: Arsenal Stadium, Avenell Road, London N5 1BU
Arsenal: Red shirts with white sleeves, white shorts, blue and white hooped stockings
Burnley: White shirts, black shorts and stockings
Referee: R.F. Leafe (Nottingham)
Attendance: 51,586

Arsenal	Burnley
1 George Swindin	1 Des Thompson
2 Joe Wade	2 Jock Aird
3 Lionel Smith	3 Doug Winton
4 Alex Forbes	4 Jimmy Adamson
5 Ray Daniel	5 Tommy Cummings
6 Joe Mercer (captain)	6 Joseph Brown
7 Don Roper	7 Roy Stephenson
8 Jimmy Logie	8 Jimmy McIlroy
9 Peter Goring	9 Bill Holden
10 Doug Lishman	10 Les Shannon
11 Ben Marden	11 Billy Elliott
Manager: Tom Whittaker	*Manager:* Frank Hill
Scorers: Forbes 10 minutes; Lishman 15 minutes; Logie 21 minutes	*Scorers:* Stephenson 8 minutes; Elliott 74 minutes

ARSENAL had not won the league for five seasons when they set out on 23 August 1952 against Aston Villa in a bid for glory. Arsenal won 2–1 but were without Wally Barnes (who was to miss the entire season through injury), Jimmy Logie, Freddie Cox and Reg Lewis, who would never play for the club again.

Five days later, Manchester United came to Arsenal Stadium and were beaten by the same margin. Defeats in September against Derby County and Charlton Athletic saw the side drop to seventh, and they were booed off the pitch by discontented fans.

Peter Goring defended his team-mates: 'Perhaps the Arsenal fans, used to success down the years, have become a little spoilt. There have been a great deal of changes in the first team due to injuries, and [the fans] need to stick with us.'

Results improved, and on Christmas Day Arsenal beat Bolton Wanderers 6–4 at Burnden Park.

The Highbury crowd, though, continued to be unhappy with the way the side played, and the press were also critical. One player hit back, saying he was 'ashamed of the crowd and considered them the most unsporting collection in the country'.

Arsenal got better and mounted a real challenge for the title. Preston North End beat Derby County 1–0 in their last match of the season, played on 30 April. Tom Finney scored the winner from the penalty spot, which meant that they led Arsenal by two points at the top of the table. The Gunners' final game was played on the eve of the FA Cup Final – Blackpool had dispatched them 2–1 in the sixth round.

Arsenal had beaten Bolton 4–1 at home on 15 April to take them to the top of the league. Three days later, they beat Stoke 3–1 at home before facing two away games – they played a goalless draw at Cardiff City and then lost 2–0 to Preston at Deepdale. Preston then left for a European tour, leaving the fate of the title entirely in the hands of the Gunners. Arsenal had a slightly better goal difference than the Lancastrians, so went into their last game knowing a victory over Burnley would be enough to take the title.

Burnley were managed by Scotsman Frank Hill, who had been signed for Arsenal by Herbert Chapman in May 1932 for £3,000 from Aberdeen. Hill made his debut for the Gunners on 15 October 1932 against Blackburn Rovers, a match Arsenal won 3–2. He won three league championship medals at Highbury, although he was never a first-team regular. He played 76 league games for Arsenal before joining Blackpool in the summer of 1936, and later went on to manage the Iraqi military side.

It was a rainy Friday night at Highbury, with a kick-off time of 6.30pm. The muddy pitch did not make for skilful football, and Burnley started the better. Not all the Burnley players were full-time professionals. Tommy Cummings worked as a colliery engineer, and Roy Stephenson was a National Coal Board draughtsman.

After eight minutes, George Swindin initially thwarted a Burnley attack but then dropped Billy Elliott's cross, allowing Stephenson to get in and give the visitors a lead.

Within two minutes, Arsenal had pulled level when Alex Forbes's speculative shot from 25 yards was deflected past Des Thompson in the Burnley goal – it was his only goal of the season.

Five minutes later, Thompson saved from a Don Roper shot, conceding a corner. Roper took the kick, and Jimmy Logie dummied, allowing Doug Lishman to volley past Thompson into the roof of the net for his 22nd goal of the season.

On 21 minutes, Roper passed to Ben Marden, whose overhead kick let Jimmy Logie put the ball past Thompson from close range.

The rain kept falling and made the pitch something of a quagmire in the second half, and the players struggled to get the ball moving. On

70 minutes, Bill Holden pressurised Swindin but the Arsenal keeper was too strong. Four minutes later, the referee awarded Burnley a controversial corner kick. Stephenson took it and the ball landed with Jimmy McIlroy; he passed to Elliott, who hit the ball on the volley to make it 3–2.

The last 15 minutes were a battle, but Arsenal managed to hold on to win their seventh league championship, overtaking Aston Villa and Sunderland, who each had six titles.

Both Arsenal and Preston North End had 54 points; both teams had 21 wins, a dozen draws and nine losses, but Arsenal's goal average was 1.516 while Preston's was 1.417, which meant Arsenal had won the league by 0.099 of a goal per game.

After the match, the crowd gathered outside the Marble Halls shouting for Joe Mercer. Finally, the 38-year-old Arsenal captain acquiesced and appeared on the stadium steps.

Waving to the crowd, he said, 'This has been the most wonderful day of my life, and now I am sorry to tell you that you have seen me playing for the last time. I am retiring from football.'

His wife, Norah, added, 'Joe has been promising to retire for years. He has been playing since he was 15. I can hardly believe this. In fact I will not believe it has happened until next season has started and Joe is still out of football.'

In fact, Mrs Mercer's scepticism was well founded. Her husband had said he was retiring each year since the 1950 FA Cup Final victory.

Sure enough, in the next season, 1953/54, Mercer was back in an Arsenal shirt and played in 19 league games and the Charity Shield. However, his career really did come to an end on 10 April 1954 against his hometown club, Liverpool, when he broke his leg. He was registered with the Football League for the 1954/55 season but did not appear.

It was also a fitting way for Ray Daniel to end his career at Arsenal – he moved to Sunderland in June for £27,500.

Burnley's Les Shannon would go on to become Arsenal's first-team coach under Billy Wright from 1962 until 1966.

This was Arsenal's last trophy under Tom Whittaker and, indeed, they were not to win anything for the next 17 years.

Arsenal 4 Manchester United 5

Football League Division One. Saturday 1 February 1958, kick-off 3pm (part floodlight)
Venue: Arsenal Stadium, Avenell Road, London N5 1BU
Arsenal: Red shirts with white sleeves, white shorts, blue and white hooped stockings
Manchester United: White shirts and shorts with red trim, white stockings with red tops
Referee: G.W. Pullin (Bristol)
Attendance: 63,578

Arsenal	Manchester United
1 Jack Kelsey	1 Harry Gregg
2 Stan Charlton	2 Bill Foulkes
3 Dennis Evans	3 Roger Byrne (captain)
4 Gerry Ward	4 Eddie Colman
5 Jim Fotheringham	5 Mark Jones
6 Dave Bowen (captain)	6 Duncan Edwards
7 Vic Groves	7 Kenny Morgans
8 Derek Tapscott	8 Bobby Charlton
9 David Herd	9 Tommy Taylor
10 Jimmy Bloomfield	10 Dennis Viollet
11 Gordon Nutt	11 Albert Scanlon
Manager: Jack Crayston	*Manager:* Matt Busby
Scorers: Herd 58 minutes; Bloomfield 61 minutes, 63 minutes; Tapscott 77 minutes	*Scorers:* Edwards 10 minutes; Charlton 34 minutes; Taylor 44 minutes, 71 minutes; Viollet 64 minutes

F only the watching fans could have known that the match they were about to watch would be the last played on English soil by the Busby Babes. The youthful team assembled by Matt Busby at Old Trafford were expected to sweep all comers before them for many years, but fate was to intervene. They were already reigning champions. When the Red Devils arrived at Arsenal Stadium, the mid-table Gunners were on a modest 27 points from 28 games, while United were lying third with 36 points, also from 28 games.

As always, the Metropolitan Police Central Band entertained the fans before kick-off with a selection of tunes including 'The Teddy Bears' Picnic' and Florrie Forde's Favourites.

What a cracker the match turned out to be – thrilling end-to-end stuff that kept fans on the edges of their seats. After ten minutes, Duncan Edwards – regarded by many as the greatest footballer who ever strapped on boots – put United one in front, Arsenal goalie Jack Kelsey not having a chance to block the powerful shot as the ball rolled under his body and into the goal. 'Tubby' Bobby Charlton threw away his shin pads and, with his socks around his ankles, put the northerners two up after half an hour. Tommy Taylor made it 3–0 after Kelsey parried the ball, and that was the way the score stayed until the second half.

Arsenal refused to lie down and die, and David Herd pulled one back before Jimmy Bloomfield scored twice to pull the score back to 3–3. The recovery came to an end in the 64th minute, when Scanlon ran down the wing, with Stan Charlton again left struggling, before delivering an outswinging cross from which Viollet scored with a rare header – 4–3 to United.

Eight minutes later, Taylor burst between two Arsenal defenders on the right-hand byline and, from an apparently impossible angle, smashed the ball between an ill-prepared Kelsey and the near post for his 131st and last goal for the club – Arsenal 3, Manchester United 5.

Derek Tapscott scored what would be his last goal for Arsenal to take the score to 5–4 – he moved to Division Two Cardiff City in September 1958 for £10,000. It ended that way, although Vic Groves almost equalised.

David Herd, who would go on to a seven-year career at Old Trafford, described the first half: 'Stunning. I had never seen an English side do the things they did. We were all attacking teams in those days, raiding wingers, two potential strikers and a midfield that tended to pour forward. But United did it all at a different pace. In a way, I was almost enjoying it.'

The *Daily Telegraph*'s Special Correspondent said of the first 45 minutes, 'The Babes played like infants in paradise. The ball, it seemed, had been placed in the arena for their own amusement. With the utmost abandon and cherubic cheerfulness, the Manchester United marvels kicked, headed and dribbled among themselves. When, on rare occasions, an Arsenal player knocked them sliding in the mud, or momentarily took their ball away, it was all part of the fun.'

'The players came off arm in arm. They knew they had fashioned something of which to be proud,' wrote the gentleman from *The Times*.

Dennis Evans said, 'Everyone was cheering, not because of Arsenal, not because of United but because of the game itself. No one left until five minutes after the game. They just stood cheering.'

'They just kept coming at us, and the score could easily have been 10–7,' said Jack Kelsey. 'It was the kind of game, even one which was played in ankle-deep mud, which could pack grounds all over the country. It was the finest match I ever played in, and in Duncan Edwards, Manchester United had a player with all the promise in the world. Even in the conditions that day, his strength stood out. He was a colossus.'

Derek Tapscott later commented, 'I were the last fella to score against the Busby Babes in England. But I wish to God I wasn't.'

Postscript: On 14 January 1958, United had beaten Red Star Belgrade 2–1 at Old Trafford in the European Cup. United chartered a plane to take them to Yugoslavia for the second leg, which they drew 3–3 (Bobby Charlton getting two and Dennis Viollet the other), although they led 3–0 at one stage. Twice in the space of a few days, United had thrown away three-goal leads.

After a night on the town celebrating, the United players travelled to the airport for the journey home. The British European Airways Flight 609 was delayed leaving Zemun Airport, Belgrade, for an hour because United outside-right Johnny Berry had packed his visa into his suitcase. The plane did not have a sufficient range to travel directly to Manchester and so made a stop at Munich in West Germany to refuel, landing at 1.15pm.

After the plane received new supplies and the players attempted to warm themselves with hot tea, an attempt to take off was made and abandoned because Captain James Thain, the pilot, noted a fluctuation of boost power to get off the ground.

A second attempt was also abandoned because Captain Thain thought the engine sounded odd, and the players were told to disembark. It was 2.35pm. With a light snow now falling much more heavily, it looked as if the passengers would have to spend the night in Munich. Indeed, Duncan Edwards sent a telegram to his landlady saying that he would not be home until the next day: 'Flights cancelled. Flying tomorrow. Duncan'.

However, after 15 minutes the passengers were recalled to the plane. By this time the runway at Munich-Riem Airport was covered in slush. At 3.03pm, Captain Thain and first officer Captain Kenneth Rayment attempted a third take-off. Some of the United players had been part of a card school, and before the third attempt they all moved to the back of the plane apart from Albert Scanlon. (He was the only one of the school to survive, albeit with terrible injuries. He left United in 1960, disappointed by the way that he believed the club had treated him, and died on 22 December 2009.)

As the plane built up momentum, the atmosphere inside was tense. Someone laughed nervously and Johnny Berry snapped, 'I don't know what you're laughing at, we're all going to die.' Devout Catholic Liam Whelan said, 'Well, if it happens, I'm ready.'

The plane did not achieve sufficient speed to take off and skidded off the runway, crashing through a fence and into an empty house, a tree and a wooden hut.

Twenty-three of the 44 people on board perished as a result of the crash, including eight of the United squad. Among them was left-back Geoff Bent, a 25-year-old grammar school boy, who had not properly recovered from a second broken leg and had only travelled as back-up to left-back and club captain Roger Byrne, who died two days before his 29th birthday and prior to learning the news that he was to become a father for the first time. Wing-half Eddie Colman, 21, was the youngest to die – he still lived with his parents on Archie Street, later to be used in the opening credits of *Coronation Street*. His fellow wing-half Duncan Edwards passed away in Munich's Rechts der Isar Hospital at 2.15am on 21 February 1958, aged 21.

The fatalities also included centre-half Mark Jones, 24, who liked nothing better than his pipe, his birds (some say pigeons, others budgies) and taking his dog Rick for a walk; outside-left David Pegg, 23; centre-forward Tommy Taylor, 26, who had scored 131 goals in 191 games; and inside-forward Billy Whelan, 22. Nine players survived, but two of them, Johnny Berry (d. 16 September 1994) and half-back Jackie Blanchflower (d. 2 September 1998) – the brother of Tottenham Hotspur's Danny – never played again.

United secretary Walter Crickmer, 57, also died, along with the 63-year-old first-team trainer, Tom Curry, and former United centre-half turned coach Bert Whalley, 45, who was also a Methodist lay preacher. Matt Busby suffered extensive injuries and was the only club official to survive the crash. Eight of the nine journalists on board also died: Alf Clarke (*Manchester Evening Chronicle*); Donny Davies (*Manchester Guardian*), 65, who had also been a first-class cricketer for Lancashire; George Follows (*Daily Herald*); Tom Jackson (*Manchester Evening News*); Archie Ledbrooke (*Daily Mirror*); Henry Rose (*Daily Express*); 47-year-old Eric Thompson (*Daily Mail*) and, on the way to hospital, Frank Swift (*News of the World*), aged 44.

The programme for United's next home match (against Sheffield Wednesday on 19 February 1958 in the fifth round of the FA Cup) contained no players' names, just 11 blank spaces. The cause of the crash was the build-up of slush on the runway, although the West German authorities blamed Captain Thain (Captain Rayment died of brain damage three weeks after the crash), and he was not absolved until 1969. He died on 6 August 1975 aged 54 of a heart attack, a broken man.

Documents declassified in 2007 showed that, while the English authorities privately took Captain Thain's side all along, they did not exert more public pressure to avoid embarrassing the West Germans in the fraught post-war atmosphere. Harry Gregg, the United goalkeeper and one of the survivors, later said of the pilot, 'Jim Thain was a good man and was crucified.'

Arsenal 3 Anderlecht 0

Inter-Cities Fairs Cup Final, second leg. Tuesday 28 April 1970, kick-off 7.30pm
Venue: Arsenal Stadium, Avenell Road, London N5 1BU
Arsenal: Red shirts with white sleeves, white shorts, red stockings with white stripe
Anderlecht: All white
Attendance: 51,612
Referee: Gerhard Kunze (East Germany)

Arsenal	Anderlecht
1 Bob Wilson	1 Jean-Marie Trappeniers
2 Peter Storey	2 Georges Heylens
3 Bob McNab	3 Maurice Martens
4 Eddie Kelly	4 Tomas Nordahl
5 Frank McLintock (captain)	5 Roland Velkeneers
6 Peter Simpson	6 Julien Kialunda
7 George Armstrong	7 Gerard Desanghere
8 Jon Sammels	8 Johan Devrindt
9 John Radford	9 Jan Mulder
10 Charlie George	10 Paul van Himst (captain)
11 George Graham	11 Wilfried Puis
Substitutes	*Substitutes*
12 Geoff Barnett	12 Pierre Hanon
13 Sammy Nelson	13 Werner Deraeve
14 Ray Kennedy	14 Jean Cornelis
15 Peter Marinello	15 Gerard Bergholtz
16 John Roberts	16 Alfons Peeters
Manager: Bertie Mee	*Manager:* Pierre Sinibaldi

Scorers: Kelly 25 minutes; Radford 75 minutes; Sammels 76 minutes

IT had been a long time since any major silverware had adorned the Highbury boardroom. After Billy Wright left the club in 1966, Arsenal turned to physio Bertie Mee. He hired Dave Sexton as coach, because Mee's forte was not on the training pitch. Don Howe became reserve team coach. Sexton invigorated the team, and the Arsenal players began to believe in themselves. Then, on 23 October 1967, the team was due to play away at Wolverhampton Wanderers and the players climbed on the coach to Molineux. They were shocked to find out the reason that Sexton was not on board was because he had resigned to take over as manager of Chelsea. The players were so dispirited they lost 3–2.

On the Monday, captain Frank McLintock went to see Bertie Mee to ask him why he had allowed Sexton to leave. 'Dave wants to paddle his own canoe,' was the reply.

McLintock was furious. 'Fuck his canoe. This is bollocks. At last we're getting a team together and you're letting him go.'

Mee promoted Don Howe to first-team coach, but the players were still in mourning for Sexton. Finally, Howe lost his patience with them.

'Right, I have fucking had my fill of you lot. Dave Sexton's gone. I'm the coach now and if you don't do what I tell you, you can get out of here.'

Arsenal finished ninth in the league but reached the final of the League Cup – the bastard child of Alan Hardaker as Frank McLintock called it. The Gunners lost by a solitary goal to Leeds United.

However, defeat in the League Cup Final to Third Division Swindon Town at Wembley on 15 March 1969 did not stop Arsenal's journey into Europe. Rules in place at the time prevented the Robins from entering the Inter-Cities Fairs Cup, as only teams from the First Division were eligible.

Swindon's misfortune was Arsenal's opportunity, and they grabbed it with both hands. It was 17 years since they had won the league and 20 since they had lifted the FA Cup.[4] Arsenal's road to cup glory began on a cold night at Highbury when the visitors were Glentoran from Northern Ireland. The Irishmen did not prove much of a difficulty for the Gunners, who ran out easy 3–0 winners with two goals from George Graham and a third provided by Bobby Gould.

Bob Wilson was injured (a broken arm) for the second leg and Malcolm Webster, a promising young keeper, took his place between the sticks. Arsenal lost the match 1–0 but ran out 3–1 winners on aggregate.

Doncaster-born Webster had come up through the ranks at Arsenal, but his time had come too soon and he was not ready for first-team football following Wilson's injury. Bertie Mee gave him a three-game run in the league, but the 18-year-old was just too inexperienced.

Webster[5] moved on to Fulham, Southend United and finally Cambridge United, where he won a Division Four championship medal.

Mee looked northwards for a reserve goalie and settled on Everton's curly headed shot-stopper Geoff Barnett. Barnett had joined the

4   Oddly, in the 1969/70 season, Arsenal beat Southampton 2–0 in the second round of the League Cup after drawing at The Dell. They played out a goalless draw at Highbury against Everton before going down 1–0 at Goodison Park. (Everton went on to win the League, with Arsenal a disappointing 12th, achieving 42 points from 42 games.) In the FA Cup, they drew 1–1 with Blackpool (who ended the season as Division Two runners-up) before losing 3–2 at Bloomfield Road. Thus every cup tie Arsenal participated in that season was played over two games.

5   When Arsène Wenger bought Richard Wright on 5 July 2001 as a long-term replacement for David Seaman, Wright wanted to take Webster, by then goalkeeping coach at Ipswich Town, with him, but Arsenal already had their own goalkeeping coach and the move fell through. Wright's Arsenal career was less than spectacular, and he moved around before settling at Manchester City, where he stayed for four years but never made a first-team appearance.

Toffees in 1962 and showed much promise, winning schoolboy and under-21 honours for England.

Yet thanks to the continued excellence of Gordon West and Andy Rankin, Barnett could not break through into the first team. In seven years at Goodison Park, he made just ten appearances.

He signed for Arsenal for £35,000 in October 1969 and made his debut against Coventry City that month. He was between the sticks for both second round ties against Sporting Lisbon and kept a clean sheet over the two legs – saving a penalty in the goalless first leg in Portugal. Arsenal beat the Portuguese side 3–0 at Highbury, with another brace from George Graham and a goal from John Radford.

Round three saw Arsenal travel to France and Rouen, where they played out another first-leg goalless draw. Back at Highbury, Arsenal won from a solitary goal scored by Jon Sammels.

A trip behind the Iron Curtain beckoned in round four – or the quarter-finals – and Arsenal met Dinamo Bacău in Romania on 11 March 1970, winning 2–0 with Radford and Sammels providing the goals.

Fearful of what food might be provided, Arsenal took their own food with them to Romania, and as they settled down in the hotel restaurant, locals gathered at the windows to watch them eat. A week later back in London, the return leg was a rout, with Arsenal running out 7–1 winners. Charlie George, John Radford and Jon Sammels all got two, with George Graham getting one goal. In 2014, after 64 years, Bacău went out of business.

To the semis, and Arsenal had victory in their nostrils. To reach the final, they had to overcome the mighty Ajax of Amsterdam in Holland. In the end the result was rarely in doubt. Arsenal beat the Dutch side 3–0 at Highbury, and although they lost the away leg by a solitary goal, they sailed through to the final.

They faced Anderlecht in the final, and the first leg was played in Belgium. The Belgians were too good for the Gunners and cruised to a 3–0 lead. Their football was brilliant, with goals from strikers Johan Devrindt and the exceptional Jan Mulder.

Frank McLintock said, 'The continental sides didn't bombard you like British teams. Their build-up was much more patient, yet before you knew where you were, you could be two or three down.'

Right-back Peter Storey agreed, 'We were entrenched in the blood and thunder of the English league system, yet here was this bunch of crafty Belgians beating us with brainpower and the accuracy of their passing. They were unbelievably patient and we just let them weave their pretty patterns in front of us, then bang, they scored and we were 3–0 down after 70 minutes.'

No side had ever fought back and won from a three-goal deficit in a European final, so things looked bleak for the Londoners.

Charlie George had been on the end of some rough-housing from the Belgians, and in the 77th minute of the match Mee pulled him off, sending on Ray Kennedy, 18 and making only his fifth appearance in the first team.

Five minutes later, Kennedy rose to head the ball and, with his first touch of the game, hit the back of the net.

Bertie Mee said, 'Kennedy's goal was vital to us as it means we can face the second leg with confidence.'

In the Arsenal dressing room after the match, there was an air of general despondency. The side had reached their third final in three years and looked to have blown a great chance.

Captain Frank McLintock was especially upset. He was facing his fifth cup final defeat, and it looked like he was destined never to have a winner's medal in his cabinet. Originally a midfielder, he had been changed to centre-half by Don Howe, Arsenal's coach.

He was down but not out, and he gave a motivational speech that has entered Arsenal folklore. Coming out of the shower, McLintock said, 'You know they're rubbish really. If we get at 'em next week at Highbury, they'll cave in. We'll murder them.'

For the second leg at Highbury six days later, Bertie Mee picked an unchanged side. Arsenal's lifeline seemed to be the 82nd-minute goal scored in the away leg by Ray Kennedy.

In the home dressing room before kick-off, Mee addressed his players, telling them what they could do, what they were expected to do. Don Howe took over: 'Their two best forwards can be bullied. Well, bully them. Hit them hard and do it quick ... Don't let Jan Mulder start running at you. He can take four on and go straight past the lot of you.'

The Gunners kicked off at a high pace, and Anderlecht – with five of the Belgian World Cup squad in their ranks – were forced to defend. The Highbury pitch was muddy to begin with, and the 22 players churned it up further.

Apart from two players (Tomas Nordahl and Jan Mulder), the Anderlecht side was made up of Belgians. Although Belgian by nationality, the willowy 6ft 2in Julien Kialunda was eligible to play for the Republic of the Congo, and on this cold, wet and windy night in north London he looked as if 'he wished he was somewhere else miles away, preferably with a wide stretch of ocean between himself, Radford and the rest of Arsenal's hungry pounding forwards'.

Frank McLintock noted Kialunda 'couldn't head the ball for a free haggis supper'. Two years later, while playing for Anderlecht, Kialunda represented Zaire (as the country was by then known) at the 1972 African Cup of Nations. He gradually fell out of favour at Anderlecht as younger players like Hugo Broos, Gilbert van Binst and Jos Volders emerged and asked for a transfer, but the club asked 18 million Belgian francs for him, and most sides could not afford that kind of outlay. Finally, Anderlecht agreed to release him on a free transfer and he moved to Leopold Club Brussels, where he finished his career. After retiring, he briefly became Zaire's coach but did not bring success to the side. On 14 July 1987, aged 47, he died of Aids.

On 25 minutes, Arsenal won a corner that George Armstrong took. The ball reached Frank McLintock's head, but he could only knock it down as an Anderlecht defender approached. Just about maintaining control, the Arsenal captain passed out to Eddie Kelly a yard or two outside the semicircle on the edge of the box. He jigged forward and let go with a blasting shot that gave no chance to Jean-Marie Trappeniers, and the right-hand side of the net bulged as Arsenal took the lead.

Charlie George almost got the aggregate equaliser, but Trappeniers managed to bundle the ball away for another corner. Arsenal put the Belgian defence under huge pressure but were unable to make their touches count. The corner came in from Armstrong and McLintock got his head to the ball, but so did an Anderlecht player. The ball went to Kelly, who crossed it; Radford went for it, but Trappeniers was there – and both missed. The ball fell to McLintock on the goal line, and he put it back into the heart of the Anderlecht defence, where George got his head to the ball but could only put it out for a goal kick.

In the second half, Devrindt had a great chance to score but hit the ball straight into Bob Wilson's midriff. On the hour mark, Jan Mulder and Wilfried Puis combined to put Nordahl through, but he could only hit it against the post with Wilson nowhere in sight. Had that gone in, Arsenal would have been 4–2 down with each side having scored one away goal apiece. The Belgians might have won the game and the trophy in that moment.

Mulder and Paul van Himst both showed flashes of skill, but were overwhelmed by Arsenal's physicality. Mulder, in particular, was a true artisan, an expressionist and above all a player of bravery who took on everything thrown at him.

However brave and skilful they were, though, Mulder, van Himst and Devrindt were let down by their insipid defence.

With a quarter of an hour to go, Nordahl lost the ball to Graham, who sent Bob McNab up the left wing. He crossed, and John Radford's header found the back of the net in the 75th minute. The scores were level on aggregate, with Arsenal ahead on away goals counting double.

The Belgian side hit back, but Mulder's shot rebounded off the post. Arsenal were not done yet and wanted to win the game properly. A minute later, George got the ball and made an excellent cross that was met by Sammels, who smashed it into the back of Trappeniers's net.

It was the third year on the bounce that the Fairs Cup had been won by an English side, Arsenal following in the footsteps of Leeds United and then Newcastle United.

Frank McLintock led the team round Highbury on a lap of honour, and the crowd came on to the pitch from the North Bank and Clock End terraces to join in.

The captain said, 'On the night, as a team, we couldn't have played any better. Everyone was on fire and the crowd was really behind us. Winning that cup was so important to me and the club. The first trophy in 17 years. We were becoming a good team and now we had the confidence to go with it.'

Unlike the European Cup and European Cup Winners' Cup, the winners of the Inter-Cities Fairs Cup did not get automatic qualification for the next season – that was dependent on final league positions.

Arsenal 2 Stoke City 2

FA Cup semi-final. Saturday 27 March 1971, kick-off 3pm
Venue: Hillsborough Stadium, Owlerton, Sheffield, South Yorkshire, S6 1SW
Arsenal: Yellow shirts, blue shorts, yellow stockings with blue stripe
Stoke City: White shirts and shorts, white stockings with two red stripes at top
Referee: Pat Partridge (Middlesbrough)
Attendance: 53,456[6]

Arsenal	Stoke City
1 Bob Wilson	1 Gordon Banks[7] (captain)
2 Pat Rice	2 Eric Skeels
3 Bob McNab	3 Mike Pejic
4 Peter Storey	4 Jimmy Greenhoff
5 Frank McLintock (captain)	5 Denis Smith
6 Peter Simpson	6 Alan Bloor
7 George Armstrong	7 John Mahoney
8 George Graham	8 Mike Bernard
9 John Radford	9 John Ritchie
10 Ray Kennedy	10 Terry Conroy
11 Charlie George (Sammels, 75 mins)	11 Harry Burrows
Substitute	*Substitute*
12 Jon Sammels	12 Jackie Marsh
Manager: Bertie Mee	*Manager:* Tony Waddington
Scorers: Storey 60 minutes, 90+1 minutes (pen.)	*Scorers:* Smith 21 minutes, Ritchie 30 minutes

THE 55,000-strong crowd paid £80,000 in gate receipts to watch this FA Cup semi-final. It was a match that Arsenal were expected to win comfortably, but the genies who work their magic in the FA Cup had other ideas.

It was Arsenal's first FA Cup semi-final for 19 years. Four days before, they had been knocked out of the Fairs Cup by Cologne on the away goals rule. George Armstrong said, 'The media portrayed it as a David v Goliath encounter. We certainly weren't thinking like that. We were really annoyed at how we'd lost to Cologne and we just couldn't afford to lose this one.'

'Nothing would give me greater pleasure than to stick [a penalty] past Gordon Banks in the semi-final,' Peter Storey said in a press interview. 'That would really be something, wouldn't it?'

Gordon Banks had nine months earlier made what was regarded as the best save ever during England's World Cup match against Brazil in Mexico. He was now 33 and had been appointed Stoke's captain.

---

6   The attendance was given as 55,000 on *The Big Match*.

7   Banks's blue goalkeeping shirt bore no number.

Striker John Ritchie said, 'I'm never convinced that goalkeepers make the best captains. They're too far removed from the action for long intervals, and Gordon, possibly feeling that he had to intervene and fight his team's corner with officials, began to get a bit tetchy and irritable. He started to make a few mistakes.'

Arsenal's fans occupied the Kop End, while Stoke's were in Leppings Lane. The match was closely fought for the first 20 minutes. On 21 minutes, a corner came in from Burrows to the Arsenal box. The ball bobbled around before Peter Storey attempted to clear but only succeeded in hitting Denis Smith, and the ball rebounded past Bob Wilson to give the Potters a shock lead. 'A freak goal,' said commentator Brian Moore, 'that could have gone in off any one of five players.'

An Arsenal attack by Ray Kennedy was thwarted by the blue-shirted Gordon Banks, but then disaster almost struck when the goalie dropped the ball inside his six-yard box and could not retrieve it despite going to ground and attempting to grab it. The whistle blew, the referee deciding the ball had been kicked from the keeper by foul means. Watching video footage of the match today, though, it seems that there was no foul by George Graham – merely Banks attempting to take a kick and miscuing.

'It was a bit unusual to see a top goalkeeper behave like that,' said Ray Kennedy. 'It was a high pressure situation, but this was a guy who'd won the World Cup and had made that save from Pelé less than a year earlier in Mexico, so it was a bit unusual to see him shouting at pretty much everyone.'

John Ritchie concurred. 'It's true that of all the Stoke players, he was the least calm. I think Gordon was desperate to win the FA Cup and, as captain, he felt he had to fight our corner if things got tight in the game. It just got to him a bit, but he wasn't fully in control that day.'

Referee Pat Partridge awarded a free kick, but Banks then hit the ball straight at John Radford and had to recover quickly as the Arsenal number nine attempted to capitalise on Banks of England's error.

The ball fell to Graham, who passed to Charlie George, who feinted the ball to Radford. Ray Kennedy and George Armstrong were unable to do anything with the ball, and Peter Storey came in with a blistering shot that was saved by Banks, before Kennedy hit an effort that was turned around the post by the Stoke shot-stopper.

Stoke's second goal was due to a disastrous error by George. On the half-hour mark, Mike Pejic took the ball down the left wing before a neat flick by Harry Burrows was cleared by Peter Simpson, landing at the feet of George. He lazily kicked the ball back to Wilson, but Ritchie[8] was quicker off the mark and got the ball from the Arsenal keeper before going round him and putting the Potters 2–0 up. The moment is memorialised in stone outside Stoke's current home, the Britannia Stadium.

In the second half, Armstrong took a throw-in for the Gunners. The ball went over the head of Eric Skeels[9] to Kennedy, who lobbed the ball towards the penalty spot, where John Radford and George Graham leapt for the ball but were beaten by the Stoke defence. The ball dropped on the edge of the box, and it was Peter Storey who made amends for his first-half kick that had led to Stoke's opening goal. He smashed the ball towards the goal, giving Gordon Banks no chance and putting Arsenal back in the game.

Frank McLintock took a free kick, slipping over as he hit the ball. Charlie George went for the ball, but his header landed at the feet of Alan Bloor, who punted the ball up the field, where Jimmy Greenhoff picked it up.

In what seemed like acres of space, he began his assault on the Arsenal goal, chased by a frantic McLintock. The Arsenal captain had no chance as Greenhoff prepared to shoot. Bob Wilson came off his line and Greenhoff let fly – about three feet over the bar, much to McLintock's and the travelling Arsenal contingent's relief.

It would take something special or bizarre to get Arsenal back into the game as the seconds of Pat Partridge's added two minutes ticked away.

With very little on the clock, Armstrong took a free kick. He floated the ball into the Stoke penalty area, and Graham went for it as Banks came for the ball. In the mêlée, Jon Sammels went for a shot that was blocked before Kennedy hit the ball but it went off Banks for a corner. The normally unflappable Stoke and England goalkeeper remonstrated with Mr Partridge, as he had done for much of the afternoon, claiming that Graham had fouled him and in any case he had not managed to get a hand to the ball – but the referee was unmoved.

---

8   Ritchie is Stoke's all-time leading goalscorer, with 176 league and cup goals in 347 matches, covering two spells at the Victoria Ground. His career ended in 1974 with a double fracture of his leg. He died on 23 February 2007, aged 65.

9   Stoke's record appearance holder, having played in 592 matches in all competitions.

Stoke defender Denis Smith had managed to get a hand, his left, to the ball, but no one noticed.

John Ritchie said, 'In that era I'm not entirely sure George Graham's challenge should have been treated as a foul. I scored plenty of goals by being a damn sight more physical than that. I know that's almost a form of heresy from a Stoke player but Smithy's handball is more clear-cut than George Graham's shoulder barge.'

Corner to the Arsenal.

Banks, gloveless, licked his hands to give him some traction on the ball as he waited for the Arsenal corner to come in.

Forty-five seconds into stoppage time, Armstrong took the last-gasp corner. Several Arsenal players went for the ball, and it was headed towards Banks's goal, but John Mahoney flung himself at the ball to clear it. Initially, it appeared the clearance was made with the head, but Mr Partridge, closer to the action, signalled for a penalty.

Jon Sammels recalled, 'We knew that it was a penalty straight away but just in case Pat Partridge had forgotten, we all screamed in his face at top volume, pointing to our hands.'

Storey, the man feared by many players including some on his own side, stepped up to take the kick against probably the best goalkeeper in the world at that time.

Many a lesser man might have crumbled under the pressure.

Not Peter Edwin Storey.

None of the modern jiggling.

None of the modern feinting.

No Panenka.

Banks stood up and still; Storey hit the ball to his left, giving the goalie no chance: 2–2.

Two goals for Storey.

Lifeline for the Arsenal.

'It was one of those defining moments which I sensed would live with me forever. Miss and Arsenal would be out of the FA Cup and I'd never hear the end of it,' he said.

Storey was asked what he was thinking about as he prepared to take the kick. 'I was praying, really,' he said. 'It's got to go in. I can't miss it now. I should think it must be the most important kick I've ever taken in my life.

'I felt a bit down when we were 2–0 down at half-time. We came out and decided to have a go in the second half. It worked out in the end.

We gave them two goals, two bad goals but I thought we played quite well really.'

Speaking about his first goal – the thunderbolt that beat Banks – Storey said, 'I hit the ball on the volley. I didn't actually see it go in. It went through a crowd of players and I think it hit someone's shoulder.'

McLintock said, 'Despite his reputation as a hatchet man, he was an excellent footballer and would have been equally at home in any position in midfield or defence. He's been underrated because of his fearsome qualities in the tackle. On the pitch he was not very nice at all and could be quite frightening.

'Cold and focused, Peter was great at sensing danger and was unflappable when we were under pressure. His gift for the simplest, but most vital tasks – winning the ball then giving it – gave a framework for the way we operated.' Goalie Bob Wilson said of him, 'Off the field, he was shy and polite; on it, he was anything but, and could scare his own team-mates to death.'

Storey himself commented, 'I liked to get in and hit them hard early – you could still tackle from behind in those days and you knew if you flattened someone early on you would only get a warning from the ref. Sometimes it would be a hard, legitimate tackle, sometimes not legitimate but it was important to let the opponent know from the start that he was in for a long afternoon.'

The match had to go to a replay – no extra time and penalties in those days.

The venue chosen was Villa Park in the Midlands, the home of Aston Villa, and this time Arsenal gave no quarter before a crowd of 62,356.

Goals from Graham and Kennedy saw off the Potters and ended their FA Cup dream of a final against Liverpool.

Storey was injured at Highbury in the penultimate league game, also against Stoke City. Eddie Kelly came on for Storey and scored the winner. As a result, he missed the crucial game at White Hart Lane (see page xxx), which Arsenal had to triumph in to win the league.

From 1970, the losing semi-finalists played each other to decide who finished third and fourth in the competition. On 7 May, the day before the final, Stoke City met the other losing semi-finalists, Everton, at Selhurst Park, the home of Crystal Palace, and won 3–2 before a crowd of just 5,031 fans. The third/fourth place match was abandoned in 1974.

Tottenham Hotspur 0 Arsenal 1

Football League Division One. Monday 3 May 1971, kick-off 7.30pm
Venue: White Hart Lane, 748 High Road, Tottenham, London N17 0AP
Tottenham Hotspur: White shirts, blue shorts, white stockings
Arsenal: Red shirts with white sleeves, white shorts, red stockings
Referee: Kevin Howley (Teesside)
Attendance: 51,992

Tottenham Hotspur	Arsenal
1 Pat Jennings	1 Bob Wilson
2 Joe Kinnear	2 Pat Rice
3 Cyril Knowles	3 Bob McNab
4 Alan Mullery (captain)	4 Peter Storey
5 Peter Collins	5 Frank McLintock (captain)
6 Phil Beal	6 Peter Simpson
7 Alan Gilzean	7 George Armstrong
8 Steve Perryman	8 George Graham
9 Martin Chivers	9 John Radford
10 Martin Peters	10 Ray Kennedy
11 Jimmy Neighbour	11 Charlie George
Substitute	*Substitute*
12 Jimmy Pearce	12 Jon Sammels
Manager: Bill Nicholson	*Manager:* Bertie Mee
	Scorer: Kennedy 88 minutes

NORTH London derbies are always tense events. Even when one team (usually Spurs) is at or near the foot of the table, form does not matter. It is what happens on the pitch that counts.

Spurs were sixth in the First Division, but their reserves and youth teams topped the Football Combination and South-East Counties leagues respectively, in both cases from Arsenal in second position.

Arsenal met at South Herts Golf Club in Totteridge, their usual pre-match venue. None of the players exhibited nerves as they boarded the coach for White Hart Lane.

The journey usually took around half an hour, but the throng of fans meant it took much longer. About 100 yards from the entrance, Frank McLintock spotted his wife, Barbara, and George Armstrong's wife, Marje. He flung open the coach doors and got them aboard, much to Bertie Mee's fury. 'Women aren't allowed on the team bus,' he moaned.

It took the coach 20 minutes to travel the last 80 yards, and at one stage the driver switched off the engine to stop it overheating. In the end, the players dashed the last few yards into the ground.

Having already qualified for the FA Cup Final (see page 77), Arsenal needed to beat Spurs or come away with a goalless draw to take the league title. Any other result would hand the title to Don Revie's Leeds

United, who were top with 64 points. As well as the glory of beating Arsenal and thus getting north London bragging rights, Spurs would stop the Gunners from emulating their own Double feat of ten years earlier.

Around 52,000 piled into the ground, with police estimating that another 50,000 were locked out. The police insisted Spurs close the gates early. The Spurs board had not thought to make the match all-ticket, so fans began queuing early that morning in the hope of getting in. Some devotees who had been locked out had a lucky break. Steve Perryman turned up in a green MGB GT, and stadium staff had to open the gates to let him into the car park. As they did so, about a thousand supporters rushed through and, to their amazement, were admitted to the ground.

The match was tense, and neither side gave any quarter. In the opening minute, Pat Rice made a run for Arsenal and crossed for Charlie George. Pat Jennings anticipated and managed to push George's shot over the bar.

Then Tottenham's World Cup winner Martin Peters threatened Bob Wilson's goal and left the Chesterfield-born Scot stranded, but fortunately the shot clipped the bar.

Captain McLintock encouraged and cajoled his team-mates, while George Armstrong made the wing his own. In the 15 minutes leading up to half-time, Arsenal overwhelmed Spurs but could not force that goal.

As the second half got underway, Spurs attacked, and Wilson was injured in a tussle with Joe Kinnear as the Spurs man tried to score in a packed penalty area. George Wright needed all the magic in his sponge to get Wilson in a position to continue, while the Arsenal team surrounded Kinnear, remonstrating with him.

In the 75th minute, Armstrong played the ball to McLintock in space. The captain geared up to shoot, when the referee accidentally ran into him and Cyril Knowles cleared the ball.

Kevin Howley said, 'Christ, Frank, you've loosened my front teeth.'

'I ought to knock your teeth out, you daft bastard! I was just about to score the goal that would have won the league,' responded the Scot.

Knowles went up the touchline and found an unmarked Alan Gilzean, but, with seemingly acres of space and aeons of time, he fluffed it. 'That should have been it but I was so busy looking for a place to put it that I took my eye off the ball,' he remembered.

With just minutes on the referee's watch, Charlie George raced up the left wing and Jennings moved to cover his post for the shot. Instead he crossed to John Radford, who forced Jennings to make a brilliant save to prevent an Arsenal goal, but George retrieved the ball and chipped it back across the goal. Arsenal's young Fairs Cup hero Ray Kennedy climbed to head past Jennings via the underside of the bar.

Spurs attempted to equalise and thus deprive Arsenal of the title, but were unable. When Mr Howley blew the final whistle, the Arsenal fans went mad. The players nearest the dressing room made a dash for safety, but it took McLintock 15 minutes to get off the pitch as fans slapped his back in celebration. Kennedy was to say, 'That was the longest three minutes I have ever known. As Tottenham came back I remember thinking that perhaps it might have been better had my header not gone in.'

The players went to the White Hart in Southgate, arriving just before midnight, and were still drinking five hours later.

Arsenal 2 Liverpool 1 (aet)

FA Cup Final. Saturday 8 May 1971, kick-off 3pm
Venue: Wembley Stadium, Middlesex, HA9 0WS
Arsenal: Yellow shirts, blue shorts, yellow stockings
Liverpool: All red
Referee: Norman Burtenshaw (Great Yarmouth)
Attendance: 100,000

Arsenal	Liverpool
1 Bob Wilson	1 Ray Clemence[10]
2 Pat Rice	2 Chris Lawler
3 Bob McNab	3 Alec Lindsay
4 Peter Storey (Kelly, 64 minutes)	4 Tommy Smith (captain)
5 Frank McLintock (captain)	5 Larry Lloyd
6 Peter Simpson	6 Emlyn Hughes
7 George Armstrong	7 Ian Callaghan
8 George Graham	8 Alun Evans (Thompson, 68 minutes)
9 John Radford	9 Steve Heighway
10 Ray Kennedy	10 John Toshack
11 Charlie George	11 Brian Hall
Substitute	*Substitute*
12 Eddie Kelly	12 Peter Thompson
Manager: Bertie Mee	*Manager:* Bill Shankly
Scorers: Kelly 101 minutes; George 111 minutes	*Scorer:* Heighway 92 minutes

ARSENAL'S road to Wembley began at Yeovil at the start of January, and they ran out easy 3–0 winners. Then they stumbled. The Gunners made hard work of what most commentators assumed would be an easy tie at Fratton Park in the FA Cup fourth round on 23 January, only managing a 1–1 draw with Portsmouth. They did not make it easy for themselves in the 1 February replay at Highbury either, just winning 3–2. Charlie George recovered from the broken leg he had suffered on the opening day of the season at Goodison Park, when goalie Gordon West had fallen on his ankle, and replaced George Graham in the side. George scored from 20 yards out.

The fifth round match was away to Manchester City at Maine Road, and Arsenal won 2–1. Another replay was needed to see off Leicester City in the quarter-finals before the semi-final tie against Stoke City (see page 69). Before they could concentrate on the final, Bertie Mee's men had the tough task of going to White Hart Lane (see page 74).

With that job completed, Arsenal had to overcome Bill Shankly's Liverpool side that had finished fifth, 14 points behind the champions. Mee and coach Don Howe gave the players the Tuesday off and only

---

10 Clemence's shirt bore no number.

played gentle practice matches in the run-up to the big day. Mee arranged for the ground staff at London Colney to prepare a pitch that was similar to the one that the players would play on at Wembley.

Arsenal stayed the night before the match at the Grosvenor House Hotel. Bertie Mee was unable to name his side until the day before the big match, when Peter Storey passed a late fitness test. An ankle injury had left the Arsenal hard man with only a fifty-fifty chance of playing.

It was a blazing hot day in Middlesex, and the entertainment began, as it did in those days, at 11.45am with *Cup Final Grandstand* on BBC1, hosted by David Coleman. At 12.55pm, viewers were treated to *It's a Cup Final Knockout*, presented by David Vine and Eddie Waring, with teams representing both clubs, urged on by celebrity supporters DJ Pete Murray (Arsenal) and *Till Death Us Do Part* actor Anthony Booth (Liverpool) and players from the 1950 cup final between Arsenal and Liverpool: Joe Mercer, Reg Lewis and Wally Barnes of Arsenal plus Phil Taylor, Billy Liddell and Albert Stubbins of Liverpool.

Before the kick-off, Joe Mercer, Don Revie and Bobby Charlton provided expert analysis for the BBC. The corporation's commentary was by Kenneth Wolstenholme, while Brian Moore did the honours for ITV with analysis from Jimmy Hill.

At 2.25pm, the Community Singing was conducted by Frank Rea and the Band of the Coldstream Guards. Five minutes before the match was due to start, both teams were introduced to HRH the Duke of Kent.

The captains, Footballer of the Year Frank McLintock and Tommy Smith, the man he beat to the title, shook hands with 45-year-old referee Norman Burtenshaw, and Smith tossed the coin – McLintock called correctly and chose to defend the northern side of Wembley.

Bob Wilson remembered, 'Bertie had told us to be prepared for a cacophony of sound on the day. He was right. The noise was deafening, the atmosphere incredible.'

Liverpool had much the better of the first period of play, but Arsenal's defence held firm. Then the Gunners began to assert themselves and show why they were champions. Charlie George hit a long-range shot than almost beat Liverpool's 22-year-old keeper, Ray Clemence, who had cost £18,000 when signed from Scunthorpe United. Around the 22nd minute mark, John Radford broke free, which necessitated Clemence rushing off his line to clear. The resulting throw-in went nowhere and George Graham headed it out. Later, as Clemence tried to clear, Radford raised his leg to stop the keeper and gave away a free kick.

Mr Burtenshaw had words with the Arsenal centre-forward as Larry Lloyd wandered over to put his fourpennyworth into the mix. A Liverpool counter-attack was stopped, and Arsenal pushed forward; Kennedy met a cross poorly, before Arsenal's resident hard man, Storey, flattened Clemence, who needed a rub of the magic sponge from trainer Bob Paisley.[11] Not long after, the midfielder also barged Steve Heighway[12] off the ball to stop a Liverpool attack. He managed to escape referee Burtenshaw taking his name. In the 41st minute, the Reds goalie was called on to make a superb reflex save to stop George Armstrong's head opening Arsenal's account. Three minutes later, it was Bob Wilson's turn to stop Alec Lindsay scoring for Liverpool from a free kick after a foul by Peter Simpson. Wilson, his vision blocked by the wall, went down quickly to his left to stop the shot and then made it a double save when he prevented Chris Lawler from scoring. The teams went in at half-time without either having managed to break the deadlock. The second half started with both sides seemingly keen not to concede a goal.

Then, in the 51st minute, Ray Kennedy should have scored. From a free kick after a foul on McLintock, the ball went to Radford, who crossed – but, with just Clemence to beat, Kennedy miscued his shot and the ball bobbled wide. Not long after, George needed treatment from Arsenal trainer George Wright, and Storey showed signs of having not shaken off his injury. In the 56th minute, George blasted a shot from long distance but it went four or five yards wide. Eight minutes later and Storey could no longer continue; he was replaced by Eddie Kelly.

In the 67th minute, an Arsenal attack was blunted when it appeared a cross from Radford hit Smith's hand but the referee waved play on and the ball went out for a Liverpool throw-in. Radford argued with the linesman, but the officials refused to budge. Peter Thompson came on for Alun Evans as Arsenal piled on the pressure. Paisley was called

---

11 Later, as manager at Liverpool, Paisley became one of five managers to have won the English championship as both player and manager at the same club. The others are Bill Nicholson (Tottenham Hotspur), Howard Kendall (Everton), George Graham (Arsenal) and Kenny Dalglish (Liverpool).

12 Heighway was one of one of two graduates in the Liverpool side, Brian Hall being the other.

on again, this time to deal with Emlyn Hughes, who had taken a blow to the face.

The Gunners spent much of the last 20 minutes of normal time menacing the Liverpool goal. Graham had two chances to score, with only the hand of Clemence, tipping the ball on to the bar, and the left foot of Lindsay stopping the Arsenal taking the lead. It was a long throw from Radford that Graham headed goalwards before Clemence's left hand saved it and the ball was hustled away by Smith. From the resulting corner, Graham shot and Lindsay saved for the Reds.

Even before Mr Burtenshaw blew the final whistle, the players began to suffer in the heat, with Hughes collapsing with cramp. Kennedy got through with three minutes to go but shot wide. Liverpool had a couple of chances in the dying minutes of normal time, but Wilson kept the Arsenal in the game. With two minutes of stoppage time played, Toshack also collapsed with cramp. Wilson again saved his side with three minutes played. After 93 minutes, the scores were still level and referee Burtenshaw blew the whistle to signal the end of the game. The backroom boys came on to the pitch and Howe, the Arsenal coach, went round to the players doling out encouragement.

For the second year in a row, the FA Cup Final went to extra time. McLintock tossed the coin and Smith, winning, decided to change ends. Arsenal kicked off the first period of 15 minutes. Two minutes in and Liverpool played down the left-hand side and the ball found its way to left-winger Steve Heighway, who moved in on the Arsenal goal.

Wilson came out, expecting a cross, and left his right-hand post unguarded. Heighway looked up and shot past the Arsenal goalie, giving the Reds the lead. Showing that education standards have not necessarily risen since 1971, the man who wrote the on-screen ITV credits listed the Liverpool scorer as HEIGWAY.

Bob Wilson said later, 'My orders had been to help out the two central defenders, Peter Simpson and Frank, against the threat of John Toshack, and to go for everything. I was edging forward all the time when Steve Heighway caught me out.'

Buoyed by their advantage, Liverpool attacked and won a corner after Pat Rice cleared the ball. Thompson took the corner and Brian Hall hit it on the volley, causing Wilson to bring off a fine save at close distance. A few minutes later, McNab took Heighway's legs from under him; he lay on the turf shaking his leg as two players tried to help before Paisley came on to administer much-needed treatment. Mr

Burtenshaw had words with the Arsenal left-back but did no more than that.

The sun continued to beat down on Wembley, and although neither goalie wore gloves, Clemence sported what Brian Moore called 'a jockey cap'. In the second period of extra time with the sun in his eyes, Wilson donned a red 'jockey cap'.

Liverpool continued to press, but Arsenal were not beaten yet, and Radford performed an overhead kick, which led to a scramble in Clemence's area and – yes! George Graham put the ball past Clemence, except despite his celebrations he did not: replays showed that Eddie Kelly had become the first substitute to score in an FA Cup Final to put the Gunners level.

A few minutes later, Radford thumped the ball goalwards but straight into the arms of Clemence. With seconds to go until the end of the first period, Toshack had a chance but hit it yards over Wilson's goal, and then Mr Burtenshaw blew his whistle to signal the end of the first 15 minutes of extra time.

Arsenal trainer George Wright walked on to the pitch holding a white metal pail of cold water and a bag of sponges. The first player to get a cold sponge on his head was Charlie George. The Liverpool players also received the white bucket treatment from their trainer and future manager Paisley.

Captain Smith wrung out his soaked shirt as play started again. The heat began to take even more of a toll on the players – the number 11, Hall, went down with cramp. Most of the players had their socks around their ankles.

After an attack by Liverpool, the Gunners broke away and Smith foiled Kennedy in the Liverpool goalmouth to prevent the Arsenal man – who had been let go by Port Vale, his first club, supposedly with the words, 'You will never make a pro as long as you have got a hole in your arse' – from giving Arsenal the lead.

The subsequent throw-in by Radford fell to Peter Simpson – nicknamed Stan because of his supposed resemblance to Stan Laurel, the comedian – who hit the ball with an overhead kick, but Clemence saved. Armstrong gathered the ball and, much to the fury of George and Radford, tried to shoot but hit the side netting.

Seconds later, a ball from Radford found George just outside the Liverpool penalty area. He smashed the ball, giving Clemence no chance. The long-haired idol of the North Bank lay arms outstretched on the Wembley turf until his team-mates dragged him up to celebrate, McNab being the first on the scene.

It was a contrived move as George remembered, 'I used to think ahead of other people and I knew it would take quite a while to lift me off the floor. But I'm amazed people don't remember that I scored two goals against Man City in the fifth round and done exactly the same thing. I laid on the ground just their side of the halfway line. It wasn't something I just did in the final.'

Radford obviously did not remember, as he ran up to his team-mate and shouted, 'Get up, you lazy fucker. There are nine minutes left.' Exhausted, Liverpool pressed on but were unable to force the equaliser.

The Arsenal fans sang with gusto 'Good Old Arsenal', which had been written by ITV analyst Jimmy Hill. Arsenal had put out a request for a cup final song, and Hill asked Bertie Mee if he would mind if he contributed some words. John Radford tested Ray Clemence with a couple of minutes to go, but the Liverpool goalie gathered safely. In what was almost the last minute, Liverpool won a corner, which Hall took, but Bob Wilson was more than equal to the challenge and easily caught the ball. He dribbled the ball around his area before picking it up and kicking it upfield as Mr Burtenshaw blew to signal the end of the game.

Ten years after bitter rivals Spurs had achieved the same feat, Arsenal, in their 64th match of the season, had achieved their first Double. Charlie George said: 'I remember going to look round Wembley on the Friday. The younger players like Ray [Kennedy], Eddie [Kelly], Peter Marinello and myself hadn't played there before and for us it was an absolutely awesome place. Then we stayed that night at the Grosvenor House, Park Lane. Very nice. The match itself we should probably have won four- or five-one. Liverpool were a very good side with good youngsters like Steve Heighway and lots of experience in the likes of Tommy Smith and Chris Lawler, but we played much better than them. I wish I had a penny for every time the goal's been on the telly or spoken about. As soon as I hit it, I knew it was in. If Clemence had got to it, it would have broken his hand.'

Bob Wilson remembers: 'I still worry that my reputation would have been ruined forever if we had not equalised and gone to win the match. FA Cup headlines are littered with goalkeeping blunders. We got the craziest of goals to equalise through Eddie, though I still think George Graham got a touch.'

Arsenal, led by captain McLintock, went up to receive the trophy from the Duke of Kent. After the players from both teams had received their medals and were back on the pitch, the national anthem was played again.

Bob Wilson said, 'After the final whistle I dragged Frank back around the pitch, telling him to take it all in, to savour it. It is hard to explain the elation. After the match, we attended the banquet in the evening, interviews on *Match of the Day* with David Coleman, and front-row seats at Danny La Rue's nightclub in London where he put on a special show for us. The next morning, we toured Islington, where Frank fell asleep on the steps of the Town Hall. On the following Wednesday, we had to sing "Good Old Arsenal" live on *Top of the Pops*, lyrics courtesy of Jimmy Hill. The gold disc still hangs on the wall of my downstairs toilet at home.

'Years later, I spoke to Bill Shankly about the 1971 cup final, and, in his mind, having pipped Leeds, he believed we were very much in our prime, while his team were in transition with a young Emlyn Hughes, Steve Heighway and Ray Clemence in their first seasons. Shanks later admitted that he believed if we had met ten times, Arsenal would have won eight of those matches. His psychology was his great tactic and he certainly managed to wind me up before the game, saying it was a nightmare pitch for goalkeepers. The pitch had been soaking wet on the Friday but on the day it was ninety degrees with almost every player suffering from cramp in extra time.'

Frank McLintock would later say: 'The words used to describe us during the 1970/71 season – dull, sterile, unimaginative – reflect the generally dismissive tone levelled at us. Even the compliments we got – well organised, highly efficient, powerful – had the whiff of back-handed tributes.'

Years later, Peter Thompson of Liverpool recalled his manager Bill Shankly's pre-match team talk. 'He really didn't give Arsenal any credit. He said, "They're nothing to beat, these Cockneys from London."'

The Arsenal captain had been to Wembley four times before, twice for FA Cup finals with Leicester City and for two League Cup finals with the Gunners, and had been on the losing side on each occasion. On the fifth attempt, he tasted victory. If he thought it was to be the start of long glory days ahead for himself and the club, he was soon to be disillusioned.

Within 18 months, the manager told him that he was surplus to requirements. A criticism of Mee is that he broke up the Double-winning side too soon. However, not everyone wanted to stay. Charlie George fell out with the manager, leading him to leave for Derby County in July 1975 for a fee of £100,000.

'I thought he was a pompous little man,' George recalled. 'I was Billy Wright's last signing. Just after he signed me, we only had 3,900[13] people here for the last game of the season against Leeds, and we got beat 3–0. So the board decided on a change. To be fair, we won three trophies in three years. But a lot of that was down to the coaches, Don Howe and Dave Sexton, before him.'

Arsenal suffered mixed fortunes after the heights of the Double. They reached just one cup final – losing the FA Cup to Leeds United on 8 May 1972. In the league, they finished fifth, second (to Liverpool), tenth, 16th and 17th before Mee left the club[14], and on 9 July 1976 the former club captain Terry Neill was appointed manager. At 34, the man who at 20 had been the youngest club captain became the club's youngest manager.

Mee, who had been Manager of the Year in the Double year, moved to Watford as an assistant to Graham Taylor and later became a director of the Hornets. In 1984, he was appointed OBE for services to football.

He died aged 82 on 22 October 2001, and seven years later he was inducted into the National Football Museum's Hall of Fame.

---

13 In fact, the attendance at Highbury on 5 May 1966 was 4,554. On the same night, the European Cup Winners' Cup Final between Borussia Dortmund and Liverpool was screened live on television.

14 Bertie Mee was Arsenal's most successful manager in terms of wins, with 241 victories under his belt. His record stood until 2006, when Arsène Wenger beat it.

Arsenal 6 West Ham United 1

Football League Division One. Saturday 20 March 1976, kick-off 3pm
Venue: Arsenal Stadium, Avenell Road, London N5 1BU
Arsenal: Red shirts with white sleeves, white shorts, red stockings with white tops
West Ham United: White shirts, pale blue shorts and stockings
Referee: Kevin McNally (Hooton, Cheshire)
Attendance: 34,011

Arsenal	**West Ham United**
1 Jimmy Rimmer	1 Mervyn Day
2 Pat Rice (Stapleton)	2 Keith Coleman (McGiven)
3 Sammy Nelson	3 Frank Lampard
4 Trevor Ross	4 Billy Bonds (captain)
5 Terry Mancini	5 Tommy Taylor
6 Ritchie Powling	6 Kevin Lock
7 George Armstrong	7 Alan Taylor
8 Alan Ball (captain)	8 Alan Curbishley
9 John Radford	9 Billy Jennings
10 Brian Kidd	10 Trevor Brooking
11 Liam Brady	11 Keith Robson
Substitute	*Substitute*
12 Frank Stapleton	12 Mick McGiven
Manager: Bertie Mee	*Acting manager:* Ron Greenwood
Scorers: Ball 2 minutes, 30 minutes (pen.); Armstrong 33 minutes; Kidd 45 minutes, 52 minutes, 80 minutes	*Scorer:* Jennings 23 minutes

█ N 57-year-old Bertie Mee's last season in charge, Arsenal went into the derby game on an unbeaten five-match run, having staved off the spectre of relegation. John Radford returned to the team having been sidelined for some time.

Alan Ball woke up on the morning of the match feeling under the weather, and so he took what he thought were a couple of aspirins. It was only when he had swallowed them that he realised that they were actually sleeping pills. He spent some time in a cold bath in the dressing room, trying to wake up.

With just two minutes gone, Arsenal were awarded a free kick in their own half. Sammy Nelson played the ball up to Radford, and the centre-forward crossed the ball. George Armstrong left it for captain Ball to blast past Mervyn Day in the Hammers goal, with the West Ham defence in total disarray.

A few minutes later and Arsenal continued to put pressure on the West Ham goal as Ball took a throw-in to Brian Kidd, who passed back to his captain. Kidd, meanwhile, moved into a striking position as the ball came in. Pat Rice and Liam Brady went for the ball, and, as Trevor Brooking went to clear, Tommy Taylor brought down Kidd.

Referee Kevin McNally immediately pointed to the spot. Ball took the kick, but Day was equal to it and, going to his left, made a relatively easy save, stopping Arsenal going two ahead. Armstrong tried to follow up, but the ball was hustled away, West Ham winning a free kick.

With 23 minutes gone, West Ham attacked through Alan Taylor, who passed to Brooking on his left before Billy Jennings lost his markers in the Arsenal defence and headed past Jimmy Rimmer to equal the scores.

Arsenal counter-attacked, and a free kick from Brady floated into the West Ham area. Centre-half Terry Mancini was in the thick of it before Frank Lampard felled Kidd on 30 minutes and again Mr McNally pointed to the spot.

Ball versus Day part two, and this time Ball put his shot out of the West Ham keeper's reach into the bottom right-hand corner.

Three minutes later, number three came from a West Ham error. From the kick-off after Ball's goal, their players became confused as to what they wanted to do with the ball. Frank Lampard passed to Billy Bonds, who sent the ball forward to Kevin Lock, who in turn sent it to Tommy Taylor. He kicked the ball in error to Armstrong, who surged forward and gave Day no chance.

From a free kick, Brady hit the ball towards the West Ham goal, and Radford got his head to the ball but was thwarted when it hit the crossbar, only for Kidd to head the rebound in. There was some confusion until the referee signalled that the ball had indeed crossed the line before Day swiped it clear. Television cameras at the match were not sufficiently technologically advanced to see if the goal was good, but press photographs clearly show Day scooping the ball out of his goal from over the line.

In the second half, Arsenal carried on putting relentless pressure on the West Ham goal. Ball passed to Armstrong, who ran down the right touchline before crossing to Kidd, who took a shot, and, although Day got to it, there was too much momentum on the ball to stop it going in for number five.

West Ham were awarded a free kick, which Brooking took. Pat Rice got his head to the ball to head away, but only as far as Lampard, who belted the ball, bringing out a tremendous save by Rimmer that had his Arsenal team-mates applauding.

From the corner, Jennings got his head to the ball only to see it kicked away.

Arsenal thought they had a sixth when Ball passed through to Brady, who played it back to Ball, who slid it to Kidd to put the ball away only for the linesman to signal offside. A few minutes later, Kidd was again through on goal and hit a blistering shot straight against the crossbar.

A poor clearance from Day went to Ball, who saw Kidd making a run and passed to him. Kidd took the ball to the left side of the goal, and, just when fans thought he had gone too far, hit the ball past Day for Arsenal's sixth and – finally – his hat-trick: a header and one with each foot. This was the first time Arsenal had scored six goals in a game since September 1970.

'It was the happiest day of the season for us,' said Brian Kidd. 'In recent weeks we have been fighting against relegation so everything came right at the right time.

'The lads were making that many chances for me I was confident [the hat-trick] was going to come.'

Frank Lampard said: 'How can I analyse that? I was part of it. Maybe it had something to do with reaction to last Wednesday's [European] game. But there can be no excuses for it. They might have scored eight.'

Neither side finished the season well. Arsenal were 17th – their worst league position since 1925 – and West Ham a place below, both on 36 points but Arsenal ahead on goal average – 0.889 compared with West Ham's 0.676. This was the last season that goal average was used to determine the position of teams finishing level on league points. Goal difference was adopted for the 1976/77 season, a system originally suggested by Arsenal seven years earlier.

Arsenal also failed to progress past the first hurdle of both domestic trophies for the only time in their history, losing to Everton in the League Cup and Wolves in the FA Cup.

West Ham had been at the top of the table after 15 games, but then had a spectacular fall, gaining just 14 points from the remaining 27 games.

It was not long after the game that Bertie Mee announced his resignation, effective at the end of the season. It had been a terrible season, but the Highbury faithful gave him a great send-off after the final home game against Ipswich Town.

Arsenal 5 Newcastle United 3

Football League Division One. Saturday 4 December 1976, kick-off 3pm
Venue: Arsenal Stadium, Avenell Road, London N5 1BU
Arsenal: Red shirts with white sleeves, white shorts, red stockings with white tops
Newcastle United: Black and white striped shirts, black shorts, white stockings with two black stripes at top
Referee: Eric Read (Bristol)
Attendance: 34,053

Arsenal	Newcastle United
1 Jimmy Rimmer	1 Mick Mahoney
2 Pat Rice (Matthews, 70 minutes)	2 Irving Nattrass
3 Sammy Nelson	3 Alan Kennedy
4 Trevor Ross	4 Tommy Cassidy
5 David O'Leary	5 Aidan McCaffery
6 Pat Howard	6 Geoff Nulty (captain)
7 Alan Ball (captain)	7 Stewart Barrowclough
8 Liam Brady	8 Paul Cannell
9 Malcolm Macdonald	9 Micky Burns
10 Frank Stapleton	10 Alan Gowling
11 George Armstrong	11 Tommy Craig
Substitute	*Substitute*
12 John Matthews	12 Ray Hudson
Manager: Terry Neill	*Manager:* Gordon Lee
Scorers: Ross 23 minutes; Macdonald 28 minutes, 62 minutes, 89 minutes; Stapleton 45+2 minutes	*Scorers:* Burns 13 minutes, 76 minutes; Gowling 69 minutes

'THERE'S no way I'm not going to be on the scoresheet on Saturday,' was the boast by Malcolm Macdonald after he became Arsenal's most expensive buy.

The bandy-legged goal machine had cost £333,333.33 when new Arsenal manager Terry Neill poached him from Newcastle United on 28 July 1976. Supermac had been a star at Gallowgate under manager Joe Harvey, but when he resigned in 1975 and was replaced by Gordon Lee, Macdonald's time on Tyneside began to come to an end. The two men did not see eye to eye, as Macdonald had something of an ego and Lee operated a strict 'no stars' policy.

With Bertie Mee's departure and Neill's appointment from Spurs, Macdonald was his first big signing. Five months later, he picked up Alan Hudson from Chelsea for £200,000.

Macdonald signed a four-year contract and received five per cent of the transfer cost as a signing-on fee spread over the length of the contract.

When Macdonald agreed terms with Neill, it was a weekend and there were no office staff on hand to type out the contracts – so, because the manager was keen for his new signing to go on a pre-season tour of

Switzerland and Yugoslavia, Macdonald signed blank forms with the details to be filled in later.

The first tour match was on 10 August against Grasshoppers of Zurich, and en route the airline had managed to lose Macdonald's luggage, so he was not in the best of moods. Still, he scored twice – once with a header from the edge of the box and then with a shot from 35 yards out – as Arsenal ran out 3–0 winners (Liam Brady providing the third).

Back at home there was disquiet at the club as several senior players – Alan Ball especially but also Peter Simpson, Peter Storey and George Armstrong – did not rate Wilf Dixon, Neill's assistant who had replaced Bobby Campbell as coach. It should be remembered that in those days the backroom staff did not, unlike today, consist of dozens of specialist coaches, nutritionists, analysts and the like – there was, usually, the manager, the first-team coach and a trainer/physio.

Ball was openly insubordinate to Dixon, with whom he had worked, unsuccessfully, at Everton. 'You cannot teach me anything! Tell me what I can do to become a better player. You had ample opportunity at Everton and you failed miserably to improve any player there. What makes you so confident you can come to the Arsenal, the mighty Arsenal, and second time around, make me a better player? I want to hear it.'

To make things worse for Macdonald, he found he was being paid only £200 a week. Macdonald had a showdown with club secretary Ken Friar, who told him Arsenal's wage structure meant that the most any player could earn was £200 a week. The blank forms had been filled in to enable Macdonald to go on tour, and Neill, rather than Macdonald's accountant, who was present at the meeting, had supplied the figures. Again, things were different in those days when a player had to negotiate his contract personally – no agents allowed.

Then things got worse on the pitch. On tour Macdonald had begun to form a partnership with Frank Stapleton, so when Neill pinned up the team sheet, Macdonald was disappointed to see that he would be playing up front with John Radford. The Yorkshireman was not pleased either, knowing his and Macdonald's styles would not gel, and he wanted away with a big-money move to help with his future after retiring.

Neill refused to change the team, saying that he wanted to go 'for a bit of experience'. Radford was right. Arsenal lost 1–0 to newly promoted

Bristol City. Radford was dropped for the next game (away to Norwich City), with Stapleton returning to the side; he and Macdonald both found the back of the net in a 3–1 win.

Eventually, Neill bowed to 'experience' and sold Radford to West Ham United in December 1976 for £80,000, bringing to an end an Arsenal career that saw the blunt Yorkshireman play 746 games in all competitions for the club and score 328 goals.

By this time, Macdonald's wage complaints had been sorted thanks to chairman Denis Hill-Wood and Friar. He was paid a basic £500 each week, with various bonuses on top. It meant he earned two and a half times as much as club captain Ball. However, the Labour government's tax schedule meant that top earners paid 85.5 per cent tax, so only £90 went into Macdonald's bank account each week.

Arsenal played Newcastle three weeks before Christmas 1976, and it was a chance for Macdonald to show Lee what Magpies fans were missing. Some had argued that Newcastle had done better since jettisoning their folk hero than Macdonald had done since moving from the North East to north London.

Neill's other signing from Newcastle, Pat Howard, played, replacing the injured Peter Simpson – the only change from the side's midweek League Cup fourth round 2–1 defeat by Queens Park Rangers.

Going into the game – one of only three played that day because the country was blanketed in snow – Macdonald had hit seven competitive goals for the Gunners plus another seven in friendlies.

Arsenal kicked off, and Macdonald tapped the ball to Frank Stapleton, who almost slipped – but, thanks to the undersoil heating, the pitch was playable. It was hard down the centre but softer on the flanks, especially where the sun had shone.

Macdonald led Arsenal's first attack, which led to a throw taken by Armstrong that was put out by Tommy Craig for the first corner of the game. The kick was taken by Trevor Ross but came to nothing, and the ball was punted into the Arsenal half.

Sammy Nelson, gingerly, gathered the ball and passed it to David O'Leary, who passed it to Stapleton, but he was tackled for another Arsenal throw. A pass to Armstrong resulted in a neat cross, but O'Leary, who had pushed forward, could not reach the ball, and it was cleared by Newcastle captain Geoff Nulty.

Alan Gowling made a run down the left-hand side and crossed, only to see Ross whack the ball behind for a corner – to be applauded by goalie Jimmy Rimmer, wearing blue tracksuit bottoms to keep out the cold. His opposite number, Mick Mahoney, used to the inclement Geordie weather, needed no such comforts.

With less than 15 minutes on the clock, Newcastle attacked; Gowling headed on to Micky Burns, who caught Pat Rice flat-footed and went round the right-back, hampered by the icy conditions. Rimmer came out, but could do nothing to stop Burns putting the ball in the back of the Arsenal net.

The Gunners tried to counter, but Newcastle's ability to get men behind the ball quickly made the Arsenal attack seem leaden.

Then Arsenal began to gather their wits. Brady got the ball just outside the centre circle; he found Nelson, who crossed, but the Newcastle defence managed to get to the ball before Macdonald. The ball dropped to Stapleton, but it bobbled to Ross, who struck it goalwards. Mahoney got a hand to the ball, but not enough to stop it hitting his right upright and going in to bring the scores level.

The goal gave Arsenal the impetus, and captain Alan Ball, in his last appearance for the club, pushed the Gunners forward. A corner from Armstrong was met by Stapleton, who beat McCaffery but headed the ball over.

In another Arsenal attack a few moments later, Stapleton tussled with Irving Nattrass in the penalty area, and the Magpies right-back obstructed Arsenal's Irishman. Referee Eric Read awarded Arsenal an indirect free kick in the box.

Brady took the free kick to Ball, who floated the ball across the goal area. Macdonald rose above his former team-mates and headed firmly into Mahoney's goal: 2–1 to Arsenal. Unlike today's matches, when the managerial team often go as wild as the players on the pitch, the response on the Arsenal bench was muted. Physio Fred Street smiled, coach Wilf Dixon gave no reaction, kit manager Tony Donnelly sucked on his cigar and Neill tipped the ash off his cigarette.

Newcastle attacked and had two appeals for handball in the Arsenal penalty area turned down. The second, against Nelson, led to the left-back beginning another attack, but Macdonald was unable to get his second.

As half-time approached, Howard hoicked the ball towards the Newcastle goal. Macdonald got his head to it, and Stapleton picked up. He ran towards Mahoney's left, and just when it seemed he had gone too far, he shot and put it past Mahoney from an angle. Nulty kicked the ball away, but the linesman signalled to show that it had crossed the line. The Gunners went in 3–1 up.

As Newcastle began the second half, Supermac lost his feet and fell face down. The players were still reluctant to give it everything on the partly frozen pitch, and a back pass from Nelson put Howard under pressure; as he cleared it, the ball went out for a Newcastle throw.

Then an error put Burns through, and Rimmer had to be at his best to stop the Magpies pulling one back. A few minutes later and Mahoney had to perform a similar manoeuvre to prevent Arsenal extending their lead.

Ball then passed to Brady, who went on the kind of run that showed why he was so popular with the North Bank, and it was a great save from Mahoney that saved Newcastle.

The players tried to avoid the skid patch in the middle of the field, and the ball fell to Stewart Barrowclough, who took on Howard, and although he got the better of the Arsenal defender, the danger was cleared.

It was a pass by Brady resulting from the clearance that led to Arsenal's fourth. He found Ross, who then found Armstrong on the left. He crossed it to Stapleton in the centre, who either made a hash of his kick or gave an ever-so-subtle touch to Macdonald behind him, who slammed the ball home for his second. The Newcastle players were convinced that the Arsenal striker was offside, and Burns remonstrated with the linesman at some length.

The goal was the first time Macdonald had scored twice in a competitive match since arriving at Highbury, but better was to come.

Ball passed to Macdonald, who made a penetrating run into the Newcastle half but was unable to get his third; in desperation, McCaffery kicked it out for a throw-in. The pressure remained, and Brady forced Newcastle into conceding a corner.

Armstrong slipped as he took the kick, but it was still good enough for Stapleton to head to that man Macdonald, who hit the bar with a blistering shot. A few minutes later, Armstrong passed to Stapleton, who laid it off for Ball, who made a great cross that brought out a fine header from Macdonald and an even better save from Mahoney.

The Newcastle keeper had to continue his fine form as the corner came in and he punched clear.

Despite their clumsy defending, Newcastle managed to counter-attack. They had four black and white striped shirts in the Arsenal box against four defenders.

Alan Kennedy passed to Cassidy, who went down the right wing. The cross came in and Barrowclough dummied, letting it go through his legs before Gowling put it past an unsighted Rimmer.

The goal put the fire in the Geordies, and they pulled another back through Burns. The Arsenal defence was split on the through ball, and, despite Ball's best efforts, Burns beat the Arsenal goalie.

With ten minutes to go, Ball played Macdonald through and it looked finally as if the Londoner would get his hat-trick, but no – Mahoney foiled him again. The ball fell to Armstrong, whose shot was pushed by Mahoney on to the bar.

Burns made a break and got through for a one-on-one with Rimmer, but again the Arsenal keeper was equal to the task, although Burns almost managed to sink the rebound before Ross cleared it.

Armstrong made another blistering run, with John Matthews calling for the ball, but the winger believed that if he passed the substitute might be offside. He held on until Ross made a run up the right wing, then crossed for Macdonald to get his head to the ball and put it past Mahoney for his hat-trick.

Newcastle did not give up, and in the second minute of stoppage time Gowling went on a run down the right-hand flank. O'Leary made the tackle badly, and the Newcastle man was insistent the foul had occurred within the Arsenal box. Mr Read saw things differently and awarded a free kick outside the penalty area. Burns almost got Newcastle's fourth, but Rimmer was equal to it and pushed it away for a corner. The Magpies took the kick quickly, and the ball went out for another corner.

Barrowclough took the kick, and Paul Cannell's header was cleared off the line by Armstrong with his head before Nulty blasted one in that brought a brilliant reaction save from Rimmer.

The keeper took the resulting corner easily, and Mr Read blew his whistle for full time. It was two very welcome points for Arsenal, and the Gunners remained unbeaten over the Christmas and New Year period.

In the return fixture on 30 April 1977, Arsenal again won by a two-goal margin, with the goals from Macdonald and Matthews. The season finished with Newcastle in fifth, three places and six points above Arsenal, who had 43 points. Tottenham Hotspur's 27-year run in the First Division ended in relegation when they propped up the table with just 33 points and a goal difference of minus 24.

Things did not work out as well for his two star signings as Neill might have hoped. In the summer of 1977, the club went on a tour of the Far East and Australia. The team arrived in Singapore, and the players asked for £800 spending money and were upset when the club offered just £6 a day.

The players were told to attend a function with officials from Singapore and the British Embassy. After half an hour of chit-chat, Macdonald and Hudson walked out. The next day, Neill laid into them, telling them that they had embarrassed the club.

Two days later, on 12 July, Arsenal played Red Star Belgrade and lost 3–1 (Macdonald got the goal). The players lost around eight pints of fluid during the match, and a local Australian doctor suggested that they replaced the liquid by drinking water or beer.

Offering beer as a solution to dehydration was probably not what the club would have liked to hear, but the players took the medic at his word. Macdonald said he drank 22 pints and Hudson added a few gin and tonics to his diet.

Arsenal beat Singapore 5–1 on 16 July, with Macdonald hitting a hat-trick. The team flew to Sydney and stayed at the Rushcutters Hotel. Macdonald claimed that he was given a child's bed in his room – Hudson said it would have suited diminutive comedian Ronnie Corbett.

They played an Australian National XI on 20 July, losing 3–1, and then went down 3–2 to Celtic on 24 July at the Sydney Cricket Ground.

Neill banned the players from drinking, but they ignored him. Armstrong joined Hudson and Macdonald on a drinking spree. On their return to the hotel, Arsenal chairman Denis Hill-Wood bought Macdonald a gin and tonic in the hotel bar. Then Macdonald and Hudson both took sleeping pills and went to bed.

Unfortunately and unbeknown to the two players, Terry Neill had arranged a training session and sent the club captain Rice to their rooms to rouse the two sleeping players. It was too much for Neill, and he sent Hudson and Macdonald home and put both players on the transfer list.

Although George Armstrong asked to be sent home, Terry Neill refused. Liam Brady later admitted that at least ten other players should also have been sent home, for they had committed the same 'offence'.

Back home in England, Hudson never played for Arsenal again, although Macdonald and Neill made their peace. In October 1978,

Hudson was sold to Seattle Sounders for £100,000, half the money Neill had paid for him in December 1976.

Alan Hudson later admitted leaving Arsenal 'was the worst day's work I ever did. I just couldn't get on with the manager and I was fed up with the way things had gone for me on and off the pitch.'

Tottenham Hotspur 0 Arsenal 5

Football League Division One. Saturday 23 December 1978, kick-off 3pm
Venue: White Hart Lane, 748 High Road, Tottenham, London N17 0AP
Tottenham Hotspur: White shirts, dark blue shorts, white stockings
Arsenal: Red shirts with white sleeves, white shorts, red stockings
Referee: Trevor Spencer (Salisbury)
Attendance: 42,273

Tottenham Hotspur	Arsenal
1 Mark Kendall	1 Pat Jennings
2 Terry Naylor	2 Pat Rice (captain)
3 John Gorman	3 Steve Walford
4 Jimmy Holmes	4 David Price
5 John Lacy	5 David O'Leary
6 Steve Perryman (captain)	6 Willie Young
7 John Pratt (Jones, 66 minutes)	7 Liam Brady
8 Ossie Ardiles	8 Alan Sunderland
9 Colin Lee	9 Frank Stapleton
10 Glenn Hoddle	10 Steve Gatting
11 Peter Taylor	11 Graham Rix
Substitute	*Substitute*
12 Chris Jones	12 John Kosmina
Manager: Keith Burkinshaw	*Manager:* Terry Neill
	Scorers: Sunderland 1 minute, 38 minutes, 82 minutes; Stapleton 61 minutes; Brady 65 minutes

THE Seventies were a time of mixed fortunes for Arsenal's erstwhile rivals and indeed, apart from the start and end of the decade, for the Gunners too. The year (1971/72) that Arsenal lost in the FA Cup Final to Leeds United, they finished fifth, one place above Spurs. The next season, Arsenal finished runners-up to Liverpool in Division One, and Spurs came eighth, although they had the consolation of a League Cup win.

In 1973/74, Arsenal again finished above Tottenham in the league, and a defeat of Liverpool at Anfield handed the title to Leeds United. The following season, Spurs avoided relegation by one point. The season after that, Spurs improved and Arsenal just escaped the drop.

In Terry Neill's first season in charge, Arsenal finished a respectable eighth while Spurs propped up the other 21 clubs – their first relegation since 1935. Realising that he did not want to play football in a lower division, on 11 August 1977 Pat Jennings signed for Arsenal in a £45,000 deal, thus ending a 13-year association at White Hart Lane.

That season, Spurs just about managed to return to the top division, narrowly beating Brighton & Hove Albion to the top spot on goal difference. And so there was a return to the north London derbies that enthralled fans at both ends of the Seven Sisters Road. There were four ex-Spurs men representing Arsenal: Jennings, Steve Walford, Willie Young and manager Terry Neill.

Neill had signed defender Pat Howard from Newcastle United in September 1976 to replace Terry Mancini at centre-half, but barely had Howard settled into his new club than Young became available in March 1977 and Neill swooped for the tall Scot (for the second time, having brought him to London when he was at White Hart Lane), and Howard was jettisoned to Birmingham City for £40,000.

Spurs kicked off the 83rd league meeting between the two sides. John Pratt and Peter Taylor tried to impress upon the Arsenal goal, but Young was more than able to see the pair off. But then disaster struck for the Lilywhites. In the first minute, a back pass from Pratt was woefully underhit and caught John Lacy unawares; Alan Sunderland latched on to it and punted it past Mark Kendall, who could only get his left foot to it, and it went on into the Spurs goal.

Pratt tried to make amends with a shot facilitated by an attack from Colin Lee and Glenn Hoddle, but Jennings easily saved. Spurs had more of the play for about ten minutes, but could not penetrate the Arsenal defence. Steve Perryman got on the end of a Graham Rix pass and played an excellent ball to Lee, who got away from Young. But as Jennings advanced, Lee lost his nerve and hit the ball across the face of the six-yard line rather than putting it into the net or passing to Taylor.

Sunderland passed to Pat Rice, who gave the ball to David Price, who returned it to Sunderland going down the right wing. Perryman and Lee caught him, and Sunderland grabbed Lee around the waist after their legs became entangled. Losing his temper, Lee then pushed Sunderland in the face as he lay on the ground. The referee had words with Lee but not with Sunderland. In today's game, both would have been booked and Lee possibly sent off.

After Osvaldo Ardiles lost his temper with the referee for making him retake a free kick, having taken it while the ball was moving, Spurs mounted an attack. The Arsenal defence was somewhat chaotic, and Spurs appealed for a penalty after the ball appeared to strike Brady on the arm. Mr Spencer waved away the claims and nearly booked the Argentine after he gave the referee another verbal assault.

Brady laid on a marvellous pass to Sunderland, who advanced on the Spurs goal and let go a tremendous shot. As with the first, Mark

Kendall managed to touch the ball but could not stop it hitting the net.

Steve Perryman went in hard on a tackle on Steve Gatting, much to the Arsenal players' fury. Arsenal trainer Fred Street ran on with his magic sponge as the players argued. The loss of tempers was replicated on the terraces as the police went in to separate the rival fans and ejected a few.

At the start of the second half, Arsenal attacked through Price, who passed to Stapleton, who almost beat the 20-year-old Kendall – who knew nothing as the ball hit him and went out for a corner. From the resulting cross, Sunderland got his head to the ball and thought he had his hat-trick, only for the ball to hit the crossbar.

Kendall redeemed himself when Graham Rix made an excellent pass to Price, who headed what he must have thought was a goal only for the Spurs keeper to brilliantly defy him.

Rix and Brady combined to set up Arsenal's third as the curly-haired Yorkshireman passed to the Irishman, who took the ball up the left wing. In the Spurs area, Brady crossed and the ball was met by a diving header from Stapleton to make it 3–0.

Arsenal continued to pressure Spurs. Every Gunner seemed to want the ball, and passes flowed easily between the team-mates. Stapleton out to Rice, who passed up the line to Price, to Sunderland, back to Price, who crossed to Stapleton and Rice. Spurs tried to clear it, but Brady intercepted and scored one of the greatest goals White Hart Lane had ever seen. With his left foot, he curled it from the edge of the box into Kendall's top left-hand corner, giving him no chance. BBC television viewers later voted it the Goal of the Season.

Spurs had a couple of attacks in the last 15 minutes that came to nothing. From a resulting goal kick, Jennings punted the ball upfield to be met by Frank Stapleton, who passed to Sunderland, who ran on for his third and Arsenal's fifth.

In the closing minutes, Brady put Stapleton through for what was surely Arsenal's sixth, only to see his excellent shot bounce off the woodwork.

Arsenal went into Christmas ten games unbeaten in the league and promptly lost their next game. Their title challenge faltered, and they finished seventh, four places above Spurs. But there was still the FA Cup Final to come …

LAST-MINUTE WOBBLES

Arsenal 3 Manchester United 2

FA Cup Final. Saturday 12 May 1979, kick-off 3pm
Venue: Wembley Stadium, Middlesex, HA9 0WS
Arsenal: Yellow shirts with blue trim, blue shorts, yellow stockings
Manchester United: Red shirts, white shorts, black stockings
Referee: Ron Challis (Tonbridge, Kent)
Attendance: 99,219

Arsenal	Manchester United
1 Pat Jennings	1 Gary Bailey
2 Pat Rice (captain)	2 Jimmy Nicholl
3 Sammy Nelson	3 Arthur Albiston
4 Brian Talbot	4 Sammy McIlroy
5 David O'Leary	5 Gordon McQueen
6 Willie Young	6 Martin Buchan (captain)
7 Liam Brady	7 Steve Coppell
8 Alan Sunderland	8 Jimmy Greenhoff
9 Frank Stapleton	9 Joe Jordan
10 David Price (Walford, 83 minutes)	10 Lou Macari
11 Graham Rix	11 Mickey Thomas
Substitute	*Substitute*
12 Steve Walford	12 Brian Greenhoff
Manager: Terry Neill	*Manager:* Dave Sexton
Scorers: Talbot 12 minutes; Stapleton 43 minutes; Sunderland 89 minutes	*Scorers:* McQueen 86 minutes; McIlroy 88 minutes

FOUR teams enjoyed notable success in the FA Cup in the Seventies. Leeds United (1970, 1972 and 1973), Liverpool (1971, 1974 and 1977) and Manchester United (1976, 1977 and 1979) all appeared in three finals, but Arsenal outpaced them all with four appearances, winning two and losing the same number.

Under the managership of former player Terry Neill, Arsenal were the only team in the 20th century to reach three successive FA Cup finals. Six years to the day after they lost 1–0 to Leeds United, Arsenal returned to Wembley to meet Ipswich Town. A 100,000 crowd saw Paul Mariner and George Burley almost score for the Tractor Boys, but the woodwork and Pat Jennings saved Arsenal. After 76 minutes, Ipswich attacked and Willie Young mis-hit his clearance, the ball landing at the feet of Roger Osborne, who belted it past Jennings to take the cup by the now familiar scoreline of 1–0. Pat Rice was the only survivor from the 1972 final.

Neill had strengthened his side by signing Ipswich Town midfielder Brian Talbot for £450,000 in January 1979.

Arsenal were drawn against Sheffield Wednesday at Hillsborough in the third round of the FA Cup. The two teams played out a 1–1 draw on 6 January 1979, with Alan Sunderland scoring Arsenal's solitary goal. When the Arsenal coach arrived at the ground, Terry Neill said that the Wednesday pitch was the worst he had ever seen and that he was concerned for the safety of the players. Sheffield Wednesday manager Jack Charlton said that if the Arsenal boss thought it was bad, he should have seen it earlier in the season. The Arsenal players were bombarded with snowballs by Wednesday fans throughout the game, but the referee did nothing to protect the team.

Three days later, they played out another 1–1 draw at Highbury, with Liam Brady scoring for the Gunners in the 88th minute. Wednesday played a 4–5–1 formation, determined to stop Arsenal playing. In extra time, David Price almost won it for Arsenal but hit the post. Jack Charlton refused to toss for home ground for the next replay, so the teams decamped to Filbert Street, Leicester, for the second replay.

That match, on 15 January, saw Arsenal take the lead twice, first from Brady and then again from Sunderland, before Wednesday pulled it back.

Two days later, the clubs met in Leicester for a third replay and it ended three apiece. Wednesday twice came back from behind, David O'Leary, Steve Gatting and Sammy Nelson were booked and Liam Brady missed a penalty. Frank Stapleton scored twice, and Willie Young headed in a Brady corner. It was 2–2 at 90 minutes, and Wednesday were only rescued when Graham Rix fouled ex-Gunner Brian Hornsby and the ref pointed to the spot.

Finally, on 22 January, 16 days after the initial meeting, Arsenal triumphed, beating Wednesday 2–0 at Filbert Street. After nine hours and 16 goals, Arsenal went through to the fourth round. Frank Stapleton and Steve Gatting scored the goals in the first half, leaving Jack Charlton to rue the missed opportunities, saying, 'We gave them too much room.'

Five days after finally seeing off Sheffield Wednesday, Arsenal played Division Two side Notts County in the fourth round at Highbury. Goals from Brian Talbot and Willie Young saw off the minnows. In the entire 90 minutes, Notts County had just one shot, and Pat Jennings dismissively saved it with one hand.

Arsenal drew the other Nottingham side in the fifth round: Forest at the City Ground. Forest had not been beaten at home since April 1977, but they could not withstand the mighty Gunners. Viv Anderson fouled Alan Sunderland, and the referee awarded Arsenal a free kick.

Liam Brady took the kick, and Stapleton headed past Peter Shilton: 1–0 to the Arsenal.

On 19 March, Arsenal travelled to The Dell for the sixth round match against Southampton. David Price headed an Arsenal equaliser on 69 minutes, and the press responded with 'lucky Arsenal', which so annoyed Terry Neill he refused to speak to any journalists for the next five days.

Two days later, the Saints came to Highbury for the replay and played Charlie George in his first game in five months. However, if Lawrie McMenemy thought the former idol of the North Bank would inspire his players to victory, he was wrong. Alan Sunderland scored twice to take Arsenal through to the semi-final for the second year in a row. It also meant that Arsenal had lost only one cup tie at home in 15 years.

Arsenal went to Villa Park for the semi-final tie against Wolverhampton Wanderers. Liam Brady was absent, having been injured against Southampton in the quarter-final. It mattered little as Arsenal took the lead through Frank Stapleton on 15 minutes after a through ball from David Price. Wolves did not have a shot on the Arsenal goal until the 83rd minute, and almost immediately Alan Sunderland scored against his old club. It was Arsenal's ninth game in 34 days, but it took them to Wembley.

Arsenal wore their second-choice kit against Dave Sexton's Manchester United. Arsenal were determined to make up for their defeat the year before. There were 15 internationals on the pitch, but the game was hardly chock-full of skill and finesse. Arsenal had dispatched assistant manager Wilf Dixon and ex-Gunner George Male to compile a dossier to find United's weaknesses. They worked out that the United defence had a tendency to bunch together and did not defend the far post during crosses.

With 12 minutes on the clock, Liam Brady zoomed past his opponent, dribbled round Mickey Thomas and then made a long pass to Frank Stapleton, who had moved to the right touchline. He passed to David Price, who crossed with three Arsenal players in the box, but Brian Talbot muscled his way in and repaid Terry Neill's faith in him and Arsenal's outlay by opening the scoring.

In the Arsenal goal, Jennings was forced into making some good saves to keep the score at 1–0. Manchester United had much of the play, but the score remained 1–0 to the Arsenal, as they seemed unable to finish.

On 43 minutes, Brady crossed and Stapleton headed goal number two for Arsenal. Half-time came and went, and Arsenal seemed to be cruising to an easy win.

Then Terry Neill made what is still to some a surprising substitution – he pulled off midfielder David Price and sent on defender Steve Walford. The decision upset the balance of the Arsenal side, and suddenly Manchester United sniffed a chance. From a free kick from Steve Coppell, Joe Jordan pulled the ball across Arsenal's goal for Gordon McQueen to score in the 86th minute; and then, two minutes later, Sammy McIlroy made it 2–2.

It seemed that extra time would be needed, as with the 1971 game. Liam Brady said, 'When United pulled level I was dreading extra time because I was knackered and our substitute was already on.'

He needn't have worried – he and Arsenal had other ideas. Brady spotted Graham Rix on the left side of the pitch and passed to him, Rix took off and crossed the ball. Gary Bailey, in goal for United, misjudged the cross, and Alan Sunderland managed to connect with it with enough force to send it over the goal line and give Arsenal a last-minute victory.

It was the only major trophy won by Terry Neill in his seven years as manager, and the only final former Arsenal coach Dave Sexton took Manchester United to in his four years in charge at Old Trafford.

And Arsenal were to get to two finals in the next season – and lose them both.

Juventus 0 Arsenal 1

European Cup Winners' Cup semi-final, second leg. Wednesday 23 April 1980, kick-off 8.30pm
Venue: Stadio Comunale, Via Filadelfia, 96/b, 10134 Turin, Italy
Juventus: Black and white striped shirts, white shorts and stockings
Arsenal: Yellow shirts, blue shorts, yellow stockings with blue stripe at top
Referee: Erich Linemayr (Austria)
Attendance: 66,386

Juventus	Arsenal
1 Dino Zoff	1 Pat Jennings
2 Claudio Gentile	2 Pat Rice (captain)
3 Antonio Cabrini	3 John Devine
4 Giuseppe Furino (captain)	4 Brian Talbot (Hollins, 80 minutes)
5 Sergio Brio	5 David O'Leary
6 Gaetano Scirea	6 Willie Young
7 Franco Causio	7 Liam Brady
8 Marco Tardelli	8 Alan Sunderland
9 Roberto Bettega	9 Frank Stapleton
10 Claudio Cesare Prandelli (Marocchino, 67 minutes)	10 David Price (Vaessen, 77 minutes)
11 Pietro Fanna	11 Graham Rix
Substitutes	*Substitutes*
12 Luciano Bodini	12 John Hollins
13 Giampaolo Boniperti	13 Paul Vaessen
14 Roberto Salvalajo	14 Steve Walford
15 Domenico Marocchino	15 Steve Gatting
16 Antonio Pietro Paolo Virdis	16 Paul Barron
Manager: Giovanni Trapattoni	*Manager:* Terry Neill
	Scorer: Vaessen 87 minutes
	Booking: Young

HAVING beaten Manchester United in the FA Cup Final the previous May, Arsenal gained entry to the European Cup Winners' Cup. In the first round they were drawn against Turkish side Fenerbahçe, with the first leg at Highbury. Arsenal won 2–0, with the goals coming from Alan Sunderland on the half-hour mark and Willie Young with five minutes to go. They then played out a goalless draw in Istanbul to see them through to the second round.

Magdeburg were Arsenal's opponents – the only East German side to win a European trophy, taking the Cup Winners' Cup in 1974 over holders AC Milan – and the Gunners narrowly won the first leg at Highbury 2–1 before 34,375 fans on 24 October 1979. Young put Arsenal ahead after just four minutes. With five minutes to go to half-time, Jürgen Pommerenke equalised for the East Germans. On the hour mark, Alan Sunderland scored the winner.

On 7 November, Arsenal played the return behind the Iron Curtain. Midfielder David Price was unsettled at the club and the previous week had had a transfer request denied by Terry Neill. Price was named on the subs' bench, wearing the number 13. In the 27th minute, he came on for John Hollins, who had been hacked down off the ball by Wolfgang Steinbach. Hollins, blood dripping from his knee, tendons exposed, needed nine stitches in the gash.

Coming on for the man who had taken his place in the side, David Price gave Arsenal a well-deserved lead.

Five minutes into the second half, Magdeburg were awarded a controversial penalty. John Devine was penalised by Swedish referee Lars Bjoerck for bundling over Siegmund Mewes. Joachim Streich equalised from the penalty spot.

As Magdeburg seemed more concerned with kicking Arsenal off the park than playing football, the Gunners kept their composure. With six minutes left on the clock, Graham Rix jinked past two defenders to square for Brady to convert at the far post.

With two minutes to go, Pat Jennings failed to hold a free kick and Dirk Stahmann bundled home for the equaliser. Arsenal were through to the last eight, however.

In the quarter-finals, Arsenal were drawn against Swedish side Gothenburg. The Swedes took the lead against the run of play, when Pat Jennings rushed out but was unable to stop international striker Torbjörn Nilsson putting the ball past him. Alan Sunderland equalised within a minute, and Arsenal never looked back.

David Price put them ahead seven minutes later, and Sunderland scored his second – his 12th cup goal of the season – two minutes before half-time from a Price corner. Three minutes into the second half, he limped off to be replaced by Brian McDermott.

Fourteen minutes later, Liam Brady made it four, and seven minutes after that, Willie Young hit the fifth.

Gothenburg manager Sven-Göran Eriksson said, 'We knew Arsenal were a very good side. We will do our best in Sweden, but I don't think we have much hope.'

Alan Sunderland, Frank Stapleton and Liam Brady all came away with injuries, which was a worry for Terry Neill as Arsenal were due to face Watford in the FA Cup quarter-final at Vicarage Road on the Saturday.

He said, 'At least there is no deep-rooted structural damage to any of them. Sunderland has a bruised thigh and Brady and Stapleton collected knee injuries. It is too early to make judgements and we will see how they are tomorrow.'

In the end, all three players passed fitness tests, and Arsenal won the match 2–1 (Stapleton got them both) and moved into the semi-finals, where they were drawn against Liverpool and took four matches to get past them.

In the semi-final of the Cup Winners' Cup, they were drawn against Italian giants Juventus. The first leg was at Highbury on 9 April.

If the East Germans earlier in the competition had been vicious, then the Italians put them to shame. On 11 minutes, John Devine tried to head back to Pat Jennings, but his attempt was weak and Roberto Bettega jumped on to it. As he closed in on goal, Brian Talbot hauled him down inside the box. Jennings saved Antonio Cabrini's penalty, but the full-back scored on the rebound.

A brutal tackle by Roberto Bettega then put David O'Leary out of the game, causing Terry Neill to comment, 'We have taken the studs out of O'Leary's shin and handed them back to Bettega.

'That was one of the most vicious fouls I have seen in 20 years in this game.

'In one moment he has destroyed a reputation it has taken a career to build. I was only ten yards away and it really frightened me.

'It was disgraceful and has almost certainly put O'Leary out of the FA Cup semi-final on Saturday.' (It didn't. O'Leary played in all four games against Liverpool.)

Bettega escaped with only a yellow card as Pat Rice came on. Then Marco Tardelli was sent off in the 24th minute for a shocking foul on Liam Brady.

Arsenal began to make their extra man count, but Italy national goalkeeper Dino Zoff, 38, kept them at bay.

Then with five minutes to go, Brady sent over a free kick, which Willie Young got his head to – but, as the villain of the evening, Bettega, tried to clear it under pressure from Frank Stapleton, he managed only to head it into his own net.

Bettega, Cabrini, Sunderland and Franco Causio all found their way into Dutch referee Charles Corver's notebook.

Terry Neill said, 'It is not over yet. We tend to play better away from home and I'm sure we can still win it out in Italy.'

When Arsenal headed to the Stadio Comunale for the second leg a fortnight after the new Battle of Highbury, few gave them any hope of success. The match was hard fought, with neither side giving any quarter.

With 13 minutes remaining, Terry Neill pulled off the tired David Price and replaced him with Paul Vaessen. With two minutes to go, he scored the most important goal of his career. Graham Rix crossed and Vaessen jumped to head home. It was the first time any British team had beaten Juventus at the Italian club's home ground.

Terry Neill guided Arsenal to two cup finals that season and lost them both – the FA Cup Final to underdogs West Ham, and then the Cup Winners' Cup Final to Valencia, 5–4 on penalties – Liam Brady and Graham Rix both failing to convert.

Further glory was not to come Paul Vaessen's way. Injury forced him to retire from the game in the summer of 1983, aged just 21. He had scored nine goals in 39 games for Arsenal. The club did little for the ex-player after his retirement, and he worked in a number of menial jobs but, unable to cope, became a heroin addict. An attempt to train as a physiotherapist ended in failure and on 8 August 2001, he was found dead in his bathroom in Henbury, Bristol, a large amount of drugs in his bloodstream. He was 39.

Tottenham Hotspur 1 Arsenal 2

Football League Cup semi-final replay. Wednesday 4 March 1987, kick-off 7.30pm
Venue: White Hart Lane, 748 High Road, Tottenham, London N17 0AP
Tottenham Hotspur: White shirts, blue shorts, white stockings
Arsenal: Red shirts with white sleeves, white shorts, red stockings with white tops
Referee: Joe Worrall (Warrington, Cheshire)
Attendance: 41,055

Tottenham Hotspur	Arsenal
1 Ray Clemence	1 John Lukic
2 Danny Thomas	2 Viv Anderson
3 Mitchell Thomas	3 Kenny Sansom
4 Ossie Ardiles	4 Paul Davis
5 Richard Gough	5 Tony Adams
6 Gary Mabbutt	6 David O'Leary
7 Clive Allen	7 Martin Hayes
8 Paul Allen	8 David Rocastle
9 Chris Waddle	9 Michael Thomas
10 Gary Stevens	10 Charlie Nicholas (Allinson, 64 minutes)
11 Nico Claesen (Galvin, 72 minutes)	11 Niall Quinn
Substitutes	*Substitutes*
12 Tony Galvin	12 Ian Allinson
14 Mark Bowen	14 Gus Caesar
Manager: David Pleat	*Manager:* George Graham
Scorer: C. Allen 62 minutes	*Scorers:* Allinson 82 minutes; Rocastle 90 minutes
Booking: C. Allen	

I T was the one major domestic trophy that Arsenal had never won. They came close twice at the tail end of the Sixties, but lost to Leeds United and Swindon Town. As a player, George Graham had played in the first and had been a 71st-minute substitute (for Peter Simpson) in the second.

Graham had left for Manchester United and finished his playing career in America. On 6 December 1982, he became manager of Millwall, rescuing them from the bottom of Division Three. After Don Howe's resignation, the board turned to another ex-Arsenal player to take the helm. On 14 May 1986, George Graham became manager of Arsenal. The favourite to take over at Highbury had been Terry Venables, and he even signed a letter of agreement, but the story leaked and El Tel never came to Highbury. Other names such as Alex Ferguson, Howard Kendall, Graham Taylor and David Pleat were bandied about, but the Arsenal directors wanted Graham.

Known as 'Stroller' because of his languid playing style, he was to win a trophy in his first season in charge – and a trophy that the club had never previously won.

Graham was offered a three-year contract worth £60,000 a year, but was shocked to find that the club was £1 million in debt and almost a dozen players were nearly out of contract.

He appointed Theo Foley as his number two, and Steve Burtenshaw, who had had various stints as coach, became chief scout. Pat Rice returned to the club as youth team manager.

George Graham may have had a lazy side on the pitch as a player, but off it he was a stickler for discipline. He banned the card schools that the players had enjoyed on the coach to away games. He told Charlie Nicholas to take out his earring and insisted that the players wear a club tie and blazer on matchdays.

Graham's first league game in charge was against the side he had left Arsenal to join, Manchester United, on 23 August 1986, and a Charlie Nicholas strike separated the two teams.

Arsenal began their League Cup journey at home to Huddersfield Town, winning 2–0, before drawing 1–1 at Leeds Road in the second leg. In the third round on 28 October, Manchester City came to Arsenal but were soundly beaten 3–1.

On 15 November, Graham took Arsenal to The Dell in a league match, where they thrashed Southampton 4–0. The victory took Arsenal to the top of Division One for the first time under Graham.

In the fourth round, on 18 November, Charlton Athletic travelled from south London to Highbury but were unable to get a result, going down 2–0.

Arsenal then got the better of Nottingham Forest at home in the fifth round (quarter-finals), again by a 2–0 scoreline.

In the semi-finals, Arsenal drew arch-rivals Tottenham Hotspur. The first leg was at Highbury on 8 February 1987, and Spurs ran out winners by a solitary goal. Spurs manager David Pleat was furious when he overheard talk of T-shirts being printed to celebrate getting to Wembley.

Four days later, Arsenal went to White Hart Lane, where Spurs took the lead. At half-time, an announcement was made about how Spurs fans could get tickets for the final.

In the second half, Viv Anderson pulled a goal back and then Niall Quinn gave Arsenal a 2–1 victory, but, with no away goals rule in operation, the tie had to go to a replay. Referee Alan Gunn tossed a coin to decide who would play at home, and the first toss got stuck in the mud. A second toss decided the venue.

On 4 March, Arsenal returned to White Hart Lane. In those days, top-division teams took the competition seriously and played full-strength sides. Spurs' midfield general Glenn Hoddle, though, was ruled out of the game due to a stomach muscle problem.

As with all north London derbies, the match started at a fierce pace. Michael Thomas went in for a tackle on Clive Allen, which the Spurs man thought was unfair. His reaction landed him a place in referee Joe Worrall's notebook.

Chris Waddle came close to opening the scoring for Spurs, but instead his shot ended up in the side netting.

David Rocastle split the defence with a superb pass to Martin Hayes, but he was unable to finish.

In the 62nd minute, Thomas fouled Ossie Ardiles and Mr Worrall awarded Spurs a free kick.

Ardiles took it himself and put the ball deep into the Arsenal penalty area. Richard Gough got his head to the ball, and Clive Allen hit his 39th goal of the season.

Two minutes later, Charlie Nicholas was carried off with an injured ankle and Ian Allinson came on in his place.

Arsenal were determined not to lose to their north London neighbours, and, as the game moved into its final stages, Paul Davis passed to Allinson, who worked his way into the Spurs box. He took a shot that just beat Ray Clemence at the near post.

With very little time remaining and extra time beckoning, David O'Leary took a free kick about a yard outside the centre circle in the Arsenal half that floated into the Spurs area. Niall Quinn tried to get on the end of it, but the ball fell to Allinson – his shot was blocked. The ball bobbled into the Spurs area, and David Rocastle was on hand to score and put Arsenal ahead for the first time in the tie. With Arsenal leading as the referee played stoppage time, the Spurs fans began quickly leaving White Hart Lane.

After the match, Spurs manager David Pleat entertained George Graham, Theo Foley and Steve Burtenshaw in his office with a cup of tea and a sandwich before giving Graham a lift to his home in Cockfosters.

Graham commented, 'I am very proud of them and I must admit that I thought whoever scored first would win it. When they scored, I thought that was it but the players have shown a lot of resilience and I am absolutely delighted.

'We've built a platform hopefully for further success, a lot quicker than I'd thought.

'I was delighted for our players, who've all given me such a tremendous response this season. And I was delighted for our supporters, who gave us such fantastic backing. Even when we were behind, all the noise was coming from the Arsenal end.'

Match-winner David Rocastle commented, 'Some people might have written us off, but we always had that belief. It comes from the spirit that has built up at Highbury. We know we can build on it to achieve even greater things.

'It was an unbelievable feeling when I scored, but I must admit I first checked that the linesman's flag was down before I started to believe it.

'After Ian Allinson had equalised, I'd mentally prepared myself for extra time. I never dreamed the game would finish the way it did.'

David Pleat said, 'When they threw so many forward we only needed one goal to kill the tie. It was a gamble on their part which paid off.'

A NEW TROPHY AT LAST

Arsenal 2 Liverpool 1

Football League Cup Final. Sunday 5 April 1987, kick-off 3.15pm
Venue: Wembley Stadium, Middlesex, HA9 0WS
Arsenal: Red shirts with white sleeves, white shorts, red stockings
Liverpool: White shirts and stockings, black shorts
Referee: Lester Shapter (Devon)
Attendance: 96,000

Arsenal	Liverpool
1 John Lukic	1 Bruce Grobbelaar
2 Viv Anderson	2 Gary Gillespie
3 Kenny Sansom (captain)	3 Barry Venison
4 Steve Williams	4 Nigel Spackman
5 David O'Leary	5 Ronnie Whelan
6 Tony Adams	6 Alan Hansen (captain)
7 David Rocastle	7 Paul Walsh (Dalglish, 73 minutes)
8 Paul Davis	8 Craig Johnston
9 Niall Quinn (Groves, 73 minutes)	9 Ian Rush
10 Charlie Nicholas	10 Jan Molby
11 Martin Hayes (Thomas, 85 minutes)	11 Steve McMahon (Wark, 87 minutes)
Substitutes	*Substitutes*
12 Perry Groves	12 Kenny Dalglish
14 Michael Thomas	14 John Wark
Manager: George Graham	*Player-manager:* Kenny Dalglish
Scorer: Nicholas 30 minutes, 83 minutes	*Scorer:* Rush, 23 minutes

ARSENAL'S opponents in the final were Liverpool, the team they had beaten to win the Double in 1971. Liverpool had form in the League Cup, having won it in 1981, 1982, 1983 and 1984.

Arsenal stayed at the Noke Hotel in St Albans before the game, and George Graham gave his players a 20-minute team talk in the morning.

He went through the Liverpool team one by one, pointing out their weaknesses, saying that they were beatable and the Arsenal players in front of him could be the ones to do just that.

It was a very hot day at Wembley, and Liverpool, appearing in their eighth final in ten years, mostly dominated play in the first period.

Arsenal's Charlie Nicholas got the ball with just two minutes on the clock, but Alan Hansen was there to clear Liverpool's lines.

Niall Quinn blew a chance early on, and it was only John Lukic's athleticism that stopped Craig Johnston opening Liverpool's account.

An Arsenal free kick went nowhere as, having had the ball teed up for him by Paul Davis, Nicholas blasted the ball into the Liverpool wall. Jan Molby, at the other end, hit the ball over the bar. The ball reached Charlie Nicholas, and he headed towards the Liverpool goal, but the pass to Niall Quinn was poor and Liverpool recovered.

111

Ian Rush put the Merseysiders ahead in the 24th minute – his 36th goal of the season – and it looked certain that Liverpool would add another trophy to the Anfield boardroom. After all, in the 144 previous matches in which he had scored, Liverpool were unbeaten.

Molby started the move by sending Steve McMahon on his way. He moved on to the Arsenal goal from the right, and, as the defence moved to close him down, he passed to Rush, who was near the penalty spot. He side-footed it past Lukic in the Arsenal goal.

In previous years, Liverpool would have then parked the bus, but this time Arsenal began rattling the doors and windows. Six minutes later, Hansen fouled Quinn and Paul Davis took the free kick. The ball went into the Liverpool wall, but, in the mêlée, Charlie Nicholas got a foot to the ball, which hit the post. As it bobbled free, the Scotsman got on the end of it and put it past Bruce Grobbelaar to equalise.

From that moment on, Liverpool's grip on the game was loosened. Nicholas appealed for a penalty and missed a golden opportunity provided by Viv Anderson.

In fact, Anderson gave both sets of fans a laugh when, attempting an attack in the Liverpool goal area, he took a dive that would not have looked out of place in a production of *Swan Lake* at Covent Garden.

Seven minutes from the end, Perry Groves came on for Quinn. Alan Hansen later said, 'Our hearts sank when we saw a fresh Groves coming on. We were frightened to death of his pace.'

Groves played Nicholas through, and, thanks to a deflection off Ronnie Whelan, the Scotsman put it past Liverpool's Zimbabwean goalie to give Arsenal their second goal and first League Cup – and prize money of £75,000.

Arsenal finished fourth in the league, but unlike these days it did not guarantee European football, as English clubs were banned after the Heysel Stadium disaster.

The brace from Nicholas looked to have cemented his place at Highbury. Since signing from Celtic on 22 June 1983 for a fee of £750,000, Nicholas had been a regular on the front pages of newspapers for his nightclubbing lifestyle as much as the back for his sporting prowess.

George Graham thought Nicholas only occasionally reached the standard expected of him. When he arrived at Highbury, Graham called Nicholas into his office and told the player in no uncertain terms that he was unhappy with the 'Champagne Charlie' image.

'You're a super player,' Graham said, 'but you're letting yourself and the club down with your behaviour.'

In the summer of 1987, Celtic tried to re-sign their golden boy, but Nicholas, believing he had sufficiently impressed manager Graham to earn a first-team place, opted to stay in London. Graham had not changed his mind, and Nicholas was dropped after four matches in favour of Perry Groves. In January 1988, he went north of the border to join Aberdeen for £400,000. He had scored 54 goals in 184 matches for Arsenal.

Liverpool 0 Arsenal 2

Football League Division One. Friday 26 May 1989, kick-off 8.15pm
Venue: Anfield, Liverpool, L4 0TH
Liverpool: All red
Arsenal: Yellow shirts with blue sleeves, blue shorts, yellow stockings with white tops
Referee: David Hutchinson (Marcham, Oxfordshire)
Attendance: 41,718[15]

Liverpool	Arsenal
1 Bruce Grobbelaar	1 John Lukic
2 Gary Ablett	2 Lee Dixon
3 Steve Staunton	3 Nigel Winterburn
4 Steve Nicol	4 Michael Thomas
5 Ronnie Whelan (captain)	5 David O'Leary
6 Alan Hansen	6 Tony Adams
7 Ray Houghton	7 David Rocastle
8 John Aldridge	8 Kevin Richardson
9 Ian Rush (Beardsley, 32 minutes)	9 Alan Smith
10 John Barnes	10 Steve Bould (Groves, 76 minutes)
11 Steve McMahon	11 Paul Merson (Hayes, 73 minutes)
Substitutes	*Substitutes*
12 Barry Venison	12 Perry Groves
14 Peter Beardsley	14 Martin Hayes
Manager: Kenny Dalglish	*Manager:* George Graham
	Scorers: Smith 52 minutes; Thomas 90+2 minutes
	Bookings: Richardson, Rocastle

OFTEN the league title is decided long before the end of the season, as a team is so far ahead. Sometimes, it goes to the last day of the season and it hangs on the relative results of different matches. But, on 26 May 1989, it was decided, cup final-like, by the result of one game – the last of the season, between title contenders Liverpool and Arsenal. Except that, unlike a cup final, Arsenal had to win by at least two goals to claim the title at Anfield against a team that had recently beaten local rivals Everton in the FA Cup Final to set up the possibility of an unprecedented second Double.

'No one really fancies us outside Highbury,' said George Graham before the match. 'So we can relax and enjoy the game and hopefully get the goals we need. We had a tremendous first half of the season. Liverpool have had a terrific season since 1 January. It's an ideal finale to the season: number one and two going for the championship at Anfield. Tremendous. I hope football's going to be the winner. I keep reading in the papers that it's a waste of a journey to come up here.

---

15 Most sources give this as the attendance, but, commentating for ITV's *The Match* that night, Brian Moore said that there were 41,783 at Anfield.

It's a nice situation to be in. As long as we can keep a clean sheet for a long period of the game, there's always a good opportunity we can score some goals.'

Liverpool were clear favourites, having seen off West Ham United at Anfield 5–1 – a result that saw the Hammers relegated – three days earlier. And Arsenal's recent form had been poor. They struggled to beat Middlesbrough 1–0, lost 2–1 at home to Derby County and only managed a 2–2 draw at home to Wimbledon.

It was the sixth time the two teams were to meet that season – each team had won one game, and three had been drawn.

Liverpool had started the season poorly, and Kenny Dalglish was accused of making changes for changes' sake; he was not helped by injuries to key players like Alan Hansen, and Bruce Grobbelaar being in hospital with meningitis.

Arsenal went top of the league on Boxing Day 1988 after beating Charlton Athletic 3–2 at The Valley. They were rarely off the premier position for the rest of the season.

The match at Anfield had been due to be played on 23 April, which would have lost the drama, but, because of the Hillsborough disaster and various other postponements, it became the last match of the season. Then the kick-off was delayed for ten minutes because 24 coachloads of Arsenal fans were stuck in jams on the M6.

All the Arsenal team took to the pitch carrying bouquets of red roses, which they distributed among the crowd. Just before the kick-off, Arsenal chairman Peter Hill-Wood presented a cheque for £25,000[16] to the Hillsborough fund.

Arsenal went into the match not having won at Anfield since the 1974/75 season. Of the subsequent 13 games, they had drawn three and lost ten, scoring just seven goals while conceding 26. Liverpool had gone 24 games unbeaten since 2 January.

Considering that he had to get his team attacking, Graham surprised many by including three centre-backs – Tony Adams, Steve Bould and David O'Leary as a sweeper – in his side. Arsenal played a 5–3–2 formation.

When setting off for the match, David O'Leary had promised his son, celebrating his sixth birthday that day, that he would bring him back a winner's medal.

---

16 In his autobiography, George Graham says it was £30,000.

Graham began the game sitting in the directors' box, alongside his chairman and the vice-chairman, David Dein. By the start of the second half, he was down on the bench. Both teams wore black armbands in memory of Arsenal director Stuart McIntyre, who had died earlier that day. He had become a director in March 1962.

Arsenal kicked off. They had the best scoring record in the league with 71 goals and were averaging two goals a game away from home. Liverpool won the first two free kicks of the match, both from fouls by Steve Bould. David Rocastle won the first corner of the match when Steve Nicol put the ball out but Michael Thomas skied it over the Liverpool bar when Kevin Richardson crossed.

Arsenal won a free kick in the eighth minute when Alan Smith was brought down, and a minute later came close when Paul Merson headed the ball down for Rocastle, who got the ball to Thomas; he went down to the byline before crossing. Bould got his head to the ball, but it went just wide.

With ten minutes played, Arsenal had had the better of the chances, but it remained 0–0.

In the 18th minute, they won a free kick after a foul by McMahon, but Thomas drove into the wall. It bobbled out and Nigel Winterburn crossed, but Bruce Grobbelaar caught the ball.

With 23 minutes on the clock, a Liverpool attack was thwarted by Lee Dixon preventing John Barnes getting near the ball. The corner was Liverpool's first of the game, but it came to nothing as Rocastle got the ball. Ian Rush then smacked one from 30 yards, but John Lukic easily gathered.

Rush was pulled off after 32 minutes when it became apparent that he had injured himself taking the earlier shot against Lukic. It turned out to be a groin strain.

In the 39th minute, Liverpool mounted another attack and Whelan let fly with a cracker, only to see it turned over by Lukic. John Barnes took the corner and won another, but it was flicked away by Richardson. The score stayed goalless at half-time. In the Arsenal dressing room, assistant manager Theo Foley went around doling out words of advice to the players.

Both teams began the second half with an understandable sense of urgency. Arsenal had a chance after 49 minutes with a Paul Merson volley, but it went wide of Grobbelaar's right-hand post. With four minutes of the half gone, the chant 'Champions! Champions!' began to emanate from the Kop. Then Nigel Winterburn went down the left wing and crossed. Grobbelaar completely missed it, but so too did all the other players in the box, and it went out for a throw-in.

With seven minutes gone, captain Ronnie Whelan went in for a challenge on David Rocastle and was penalised for having his foot too high. Adams made a run as Winterburn floated the ball into the Liverpool box, and 26-year-old centre-forward Alan Smith headed the ball past Bruce Grobbelaar – his 25th goal of the season. The Liverpool players surrounded referee David Hutchinson, furiously protesting that the goal should have been disallowed. After consulting the linesman, Mr Hutchinson signalled the goal. He later said that he did not understand what the players were moaning about. Some time after, Ray Houghton confessed that none of his team-mates really knew what they were protesting about either – they were just so shocked by letting in a goal.

Not long after, Grobbelaar fumbled the ball as the pressure began to mount on the home side. In another attack, Merson got the ball to Thomas, and only a save by the Liverpool keeper stopped a second goal.

Liverpool began hustling the Arsenal players, but with 63 minutes gone the ball came in to Thomas in the Liverpool box; with only Grobbelaar to beat, he made it too easy for the keeper.

In the 69th minute, 30-year-old John Aldridge had an opportunity to score his 32nd – and 22nd league – goal of the season, but put the ball past Lukic's left upright.

With 11 minutes to go, Martin Hayes got on the end of a punt upfield and Grobbelaar had to come racing out of his goal to clear.

Eight minutes left on the clock and Houghton shook off the Arsenal defenders – now missing Bould after he was substituted – but blasted his shot over the top of Lukic's goal.

Arsenal had a number of opportunities in the last five minutes, but seemed unable to break down the Liverpool defence. Hayes went close but was denied by Grobbelaar.

In the 88th minute, John Lukic took a free kick after Liverpool were caught offside, but then Peter Beardsley broke away and rushed into the Arsenal half. He passed to Aldridge just outside the Arsenal box, but Aldridge overhit his first touch and Lukic was able to gather.

With 30 seconds of normal time remaining, John Barnes could be seen yelling encouragement to his team. As Gary Lewin administered treatment to Kevin Richardson, who had gone down with cramp, Steve McMahon went around telling the Liverpool players that there was a minute to go.

Liverpool attacked; Barnes, closing in on goal, looked unstoppable until Richardson tackled him and sent the ball back to Lukic. He passed to Dixon, who collected the ball and passed upfield to Alan Smith. Smith to Michael Thomas. Thomas outwitted Steve Nicol and Ray Houghton. Only Grobbelaar to beat. Grobbelaar came out to challenge Thomas, and Thomas flicked it to the Zimbabwean keeper's left for what has been called the most dramatic goal in Football League history.

Liverpool, from the kick-off, went on the attack again. Ronnie Whelan crossed, but it was Michael Thomas to Arsenal's rescue, passing back to Lukic. Another attack was not possible as Mr Hutchinson blew his whistle to send the trophy to north London.

The Liverpool players lay on the pitch, spent forces. David O'Leary attempted to help a crestfallen John Aldridge to his feet, but the Liverpool player was not interested in being helped.

Steve McMahon said, 'It hurts me. It hurts me. It hurts me so much. It was just unreal. It just flashed before you, the goal. It was like "Nah, is this really happening?"'

Churlishly, Liverpool's officials demanded that the trophy presentation be made in private, but Sir John Quinton, the chairman of Barclays – then sponsors of the competition – insisted it be made on the pitch. The Liverpool fans in the Kop and elsewhere in the ground showed the spirit for which they are rightly famed, and generously and sportingly applauded the Arsenal team that had stopped their club winning the Double.

Back in London, the Arsenal players went off to continue their celebrations at a club called Winners. George Graham went home alone, made himself a hot drink and climbed into bed to sleep the sleep of the victorious.

Nearly a quarter of a million people turned up to watch the team parade the league trophy through two miles of Islington streets from the ground to the Town Hall, where a civic reception awaited – the first time the trophy had been in London since 1971. Fans began gathering at 7am to be sure of a good vantage point. The journey took an hour.

The only player missing from the celebrations was David O'Leary, who was on international duty with the Republic of Ireland.

Islington Council leader Margaret Hodge (now Dame Margaret Hodge and Labour MP for Barking) called the victory a 'miracle'.

Asked how it compared to 1971, George Graham said, 'This is much nicer. It's great that the fans can join in as well.'

As well as being a remarkable footballing accomplishment, Arsenal's victory also had the unusual achievement of being made into two films.

The first was *Fever Pitch*, based on the 1992 book of the same name by Nick Hornby. The book, which sold more than a million copies in Britain, recounts Hornby's fan worship of Arsenal from his childhood to his early thirties. *Fever Pitch* won the 1992 William Hill Sports Book of the Year award.

Five years later, Channel 4 made the book into a fictionalised film featuring Colin Firth as teacher Paul Ashworth and his relationship with fellow teacher Sarah Hughes (Ruth Gemmell). Released on 4 April 1997, the film ends with Arsenal's victory at Anfield and Ashworth celebrating in the street with thousands of others.

Parts of the film were shot around Arsenal Stadium, but, because the ground was being redeveloped, the shots of fans on the terraces were filmed at Fulham's Craven Cottage. Sir Henry Norris would have been pleased.

The second was the 2017 documentary entitled simply *89*. Directed by David Stewart, it featured Lee Dixon, Michael Thomas, Tony Adams, Alan Smith, George Graham, Nigel Winterburn and authors Amy Lawrence and Nick Hornby. It features unseen footage plus interviews with key figures.

25

Arsenal 2 Sheffield Wednesday 1

Football League Cup Final. Sunday 18 April 1993, kick-off 5pm
Venue: Wembley Stadium, Middlesex, HA9 0WS
Arsenal: Red shirts with white sleeves, white shorts, red stockings
Sheffield Wednesday: Blue and white striped shirts, black shorts, blue stockings
Referee: Allan Gunn (Sussex)
Attendance: 74,007

Arsenal	Sheffield Wednesday
1 David Seaman	1 Chris Woods
22 David O'Leary	6 Viv Anderson (captain)
3 Nigel Winterburn	2 Roland Nilsson
14 Paul Davis	8 Chris Waddle
5 Andy Linighan	4 Carlton Palmer
6 Tony Adams (captain)	3 Phil King (Hyde, 83 minutes)
15 Steve Morrow	7 Danny Wilson (Hirst, 74 minutes)
10 Paul Merson	11 John Sheridan
8 Ian Wright	10 Mark Bright
7 Kevin Campbell	9 Paul Warhurst
11 Ray Parlour	15 John Harkes
Substitutes	*Substitutes*
4 Ian Selley	17 Graham Hyde
9 Alan Smith	5 David Hirst
Manager: George Graham	*Manager:* Trevor Francis
Scorers: Merson 20 minutes; Morrow 68 minutes	*Scorer:* Harkes 8 minutes
	Bookings: Palmer, Bright

I T was the trophy that Arsenal could apparently never win. That hoodoo was finally broken in 1987, although a return visit the following year ended in yet another defeat. It remains the one domestic trophy that Arsène Wenger has yet to win.

Arsenal's journey to their fifth League Cup Final began at home to south Londoners Millwall. The match ended 1–1, with Kevin Campbell getting Arsenal's goal. The return leg finished with the same result, and again Campbell got the Gunners' goal, although the matter was not helped by a Lee Dixon own goal eight minutes after Campbell's strike. Ian Wright hit the bar two minutes after Arsenal took the lead, as did Campbell later in the match, but the two teams could not be separated at 90 minutes and were still tied after 30 minutes of extra time. The match went to penalties, and Arsenal won 3–1. Both matches were marred by Millwall fans throwing coins at Arsenal players – Ian Wright was hit in the first leg, and Nigel Winterburn felled in the second with only four minutes on the clock.

Having given Millwall a lifeline, Dixon then provided them with another when he missed the first penalty. However, David Seaman

Sheffield United battle to stop Arsenal scoring in the 1936 FA Cup Final

The only FA Cup Final attended by HM King Edward VIII as monarch and Alex James holds the trophy, Eddie Hapgood carries the plinth and Joe Hulme and Arsenal manager George Allison in the grey hat look on

Arsenal captain Joe Mercer introduces his side to HM King George VI before the 1950 FA Cup Final. The King takes Peter Goring's hand

After the match, George VI presents the trophy to Joe Mercer, Arsenal's third FA Cup triumph

Arsenal captain Joe Mercer holds aloft the trophy as he is chaired on the shoulders of his team-mates for a lap of honour

John Radford equalises for Arsenal, beating Anderlecht goalkeeper Jean-Marie Trappeniers during the second leg of the 1970 Fairs Cup Final

Charlie George can't believe Arsenal have won and there won't be any extra time in the 1971 FA Cup Final

Ten years after another side from north London lifted the trophy, Frank McLintock is hoisted aloft by his team-mates as Arsenal do the Double for the first time

Charlie George and George Graham celebrate the FA Cup win that gave Arsenal their first Double

Arsenal fans celebrate the skill of Liam Brady at the 1979 FA Cup Final

Alan Sunderland turns as he scores the winning goal in the 1979 FA Cup Final just when it looked like Manchester United would take the match to extra time

Sunderland scores! Arsenal's Alan turns to celebrate after putting the ball past Gary Bailey in the Manchester United goal to give Arsenal the 1979 FA Cup Final

Cup winners – Pat Rice and Sammy Nelson hold the FA Cup while Frank Stapleton examines the base and Liam Brady holds the lid

Another European victory… Arsenal players and staff celebrate the 1-0 victory over Parma in the European Cup Winners' Cup Final at Copenhagen, Denmark on 4 May 1994

Arsenal's only (to date) Champions League Final line-up: back row Sol Campbell, Jens Lehmann, Gilberto, Emmanuel Eboué, Kolo Touré, Robert Pirès. Front row Alexander Hleb, Cesc Fàbregas, Freddie Ljungberg, Thierry Henry and Ashley Cole

Barcelona's Samuel Eto'o equalises, putting the ball past substitute goalkeeper Manuel Almunia in Paris in 2006

came to the rescue of his team-mate when he saved three out of four Millwall spot-kicks from Malcolm Allen, Don Goodman and Colin Cooper.

In the third round, Arsenal had to travel to Derby County, where they played out yet another 1–1 draw with that man Campbell getting on the scoresheet. In the replay at Highbury, Arsenal won 2–1, with who else but Kevin Campbell getting a goal – his fourth in four League Cup ties – and Ian Wright got the second goal.

In the fourth round, Arsenal travelled to the McCain Stadium (the Athletic Ground on Seamer Road until they sold naming rights), Scarborough – locally known as the Theatre of Chips – to play the minnows from the Third Division (which had been the Fourth before the advent of the Premier League). Scarborough had already beaten Bradford City, Coventry City and Plymouth Argyle to get this far.

On 6 January 1993, 6,261 fans crowded in to watch a full-strength Arsenal side with three centre-halves narrowly win through a Nigel Winterburn goal. It would be fair to say that the pitch was not up to Arsenal's usual standard. It was rain-soaked and with large patches of mud dotted around. Scarborough wore red shirts with white sleeves, while Arsenal donned their 'psychedelic' change kit of yellow shirts with blue chevrons. It was to be the only meeting between the two clubs, as Scarborough fell out of the Football League on 8 May 1999, and out of existence with debts of £2.5 million on 20 June 2007 after 128 years as a club.

In the fifth round, Nottingham Forest came to Arsenal Stadium, where Ian Wright saw them off with two goals.

Wright's old team Crystal Palace were drawn against Arsenal in the semi-final. The first leg was played at Selhurst Park, and Alan Smith got a brace with Wright popping one in.

At Arsenal Stadium, the Gunners ran out comfortable 2–0 winners, with goals from Andy Linighan and Ian Wright, to win 5–1 on aggregate.

Arsenal met Trevor Francis's Sheffield Wednesday in the final – the first of three Wembley finals between the two sides that season.

It was the first occasion that a team in Europe wore squad numbers with the players' names on their backs.

Steve Morrow said, 'George had pulled me aside a few days before and told me I was going to be starting. We had a good week of preparation for that game and George was very much opposition analysis focused. Sheffield Wednesday had a talented team in those days, a good midfield, with players like Chris Waddle and John Sheridan, so we were very much focused on what we would do to stop them playing.'

Arsenal kicked off. Wednesday had an early opportunity when a flick-on from Mark Bright played the ball to Paul Warhurst, who hit the post.

In the eighth minute, Wednesday were awarded a free kick outside the Arsenal box after a foul on American John Harkes by Ray Parlour. Rather than floating a cross in, John Sheridan played a dinky pass to Phil King, who crossed, and when the ball came to the edge of the box off David O'Leary's foot, Harkes smashed the ball past David Seaman in the Arsenal goal.

Twelve minutes later, Paul Merson's shot gave Chris Woods no chance and the scores were level. Kevin Campbell almost gave Arsenal the lead when, on a thrilling run down the left-hand side, his shot beat Woods but hit the post and rebounded into the grateful goalie's arms.

Merson crossed in the 68th minute for Steve Morrow to hit the winning goal – only his third goal in 87 appearances for the club. Wright put the ball in the net, but it was ruled out after a trip on Viv Anderson, Arsenal's former right-back, who finished the match with a bloodied bandage on his head – but a worse injury was to come.

As Arsenal celebrated their victory, Tony Adams tried to hoist match-winner Steve Morrow on to his shoulders, but succeeded only in dropping the 22-year-old Irishman. Morrow landed awkwardly, breaking his arm and having to be taken to hospital.

Once he had recovered, Morrow recalled being told at half-time by George Graham to push forward. 'I didn't score many goals, especially not with my right foot either. George had said to me at half-time, "There are opportunities for you to get forward, so by all means take the chance."'

Of scoring the winner, Morrow said that it was 'amazing. My thoughts for the next 20 minutes were, "please, hang on". We fought hard. It was backs against the wall for the last 15 or 20 minutes. We had to defend very well. To score a winning goal in a game like that was an amazing feeling that I'll never forget.'

He also will not forget the Adams event. 'What can I say about that incident? I look back on the game and I remember the positive aspects, the winning goal, getting the winner's medal from it eventually, but it was just a bizarre incident and a painful one at the time. I could tell there was something badly wrong. Tony, bless him, saw my arm was in a very unnatural position and went to lift it and put it back. The doctor stopped him, thankfully. I believe it's a quiz question these days – because it's such an unusual incident.'

Chris Waddle later remembered, 'It wasn't a classic match. It was a game where they stopped us playing and we stopped them playing. It was a slog and was just down to whoever got the chance to nick it. They did, and fair play to them.

'It's a very different type of Arsenal now to the side they had then. George Graham had them organised, strong and powerful. The current Arsenal team is obviously a lot of finesse, lovely on the eye, pass, pass, pass. The Sheffield Wednesday side I played for in 1993 would have enjoyed playing against the Arsenal side they have at the minute.'

Arsenal 2 Sheffield Wednesday 1 (aet)

FA Cup Final Replay. Thursday 20 May 1993, kick-off 8.30pm
Venue: Wembley Stadium, Middlesex, HA9 0WS
Arsenal: Red shirts with white sleeves, white shorts, red stockings
Sheffield Wednesday: Blue and white striped shirts, black shorts, blue stockings
Referee: Keren Barratt (Warwickshire)
Attendance: 62,267

Arsenal	Sheffield Wednesday
1 David Seaman	1 Chris Woods
2 Lee Dixon	2 Roland Nilsson (Bart-Williams, 118 minutes)
3 Nigel Winterburn	3 Nigel Worthington
14 Paul Davis	8 Chris Waddle
5 Andy Linighan	4 Carlton Palmer (captain)
6 Tony Adams (captain)	9 Paul Warhurst
7 Kevin Campbell	7 Danny Wilson (Hyde, 62 minutes)
17 John Jensen	11 John Sheridan
8 Ian Wright (O'Leary, 81 minutes)	5 David Hirst
9 Alan Smith	10 Mark Bright
10 Paul Merson	15 John Harkes
Substitutes	*Substitutes*
22 David O'Leary	14 Chris Bart-Williams
4 Ian Selley	17 Graham Hyde
Manager: George Graham	*Manager:* Trevor Francis
Scorers: Wright 34 minutes; Linighan 119 minutes	*Scorer:* Waddle 68 minutes
Booking: Smith	

I T was the third time Arsenal and Sheffield Wednesday had met in Wembley finals in the same season – a record that is unlikely to be beaten now that matches go to penalties rather than replays.

Arsenal began their trip to Wembley away at Yeovil Town in the third round, where George Graham chose to play three centre-halves – Tony Adams, Steve Bould and David O'Leary. Yeovil sported a fetching kit of green and white striped shirts, green shorts and stockings in only their second meeting with Arsenal, almost 22 years to the day after their first encounter – also in the third round of the FA Cup – a match that George Graham played in. Thick fog threatened to halt the game, but it cleared 90 minutes before kick-off.

In the first half, Anders Limpar took a corner that Steve Bould tipped on for Ian Wright to smash home for his 13th goal of the season.

On the stroke of half-time, a chip from the edge of the box gave Ian Wright and Arsenal their second of the match. Midway through the second half, Wright got his hat-trick. Then Bould fouled Micky Spencer in his own penalty area and John Lloyd, the referee, pointed to the spot. Paul Batty, who was on the transfer list at the time, made no mistake and pulled one back with ten minutes to go.

Yeovil player-manager Steve Rutter said, 'Arsenal had to come good again at some point and it was a pity it happened today. There was a big gap in class and we couldn't overcome it.'

Ian Wright said, 'When the goals don't go in I just concentrate on doing the things I am good at. There is so much quality in the side that it is always a matter of time before I get another scoring chance. They create so much and I'm grateful to be the one there to tuck them away.'

Of Wright's finishing, Steve Rutter said, 'You know he is not going to become a bad player overnight just because he's had a run without goals.

'He was always going to score again sooner or later and he just needed a performance like that to get his confidence going. It will do him as much good scoring a hat-trick here as it would have done at Aston Villa or Manchester United.

'If you are a goalscorer, a goal is a goal.'

Only 26,516 fans turned up to Highbury on 25 January 1993 to see Arsenal's fourth round tie with Leeds United. Wright was suspended. Gary Speed opened the scoring to put the all-yellow-clad Yorkshiremen into the lead. Lee Chapman made it 2–0 to Leeds, and that was the way it stayed until half-time. In the second half, Nigel Winterburn gave the ball to Ray Parlour, who, on a dinking run, pulled one back for Arsenal despite several attempts to bring him down. Paul Merson equalised for Arsenal on the same side as Parlour, but hit from a distance rather than dribbling into the box.

In the replay on 3 February before 26,490 people at Elland Road, Arsenal were without Bould, Anders Limpar, John Jensen, David Hillier and Mark Flatts, so George Graham drafted in 18-year-old Ian Selley and Steve Morrow, 22.

Lee Chapman almost gave Leeds an advantage, but a double save by David Seaman meant the Yorkshire club had only a corner. They put pressure on Arsenal but seemed unable to get past Seaman, making his 134th consecutive appearance for the club.

Against the run of play it seemed, Ian Wright went down the wing and managed to cross from the touchline. Alan Smith got on the end of it to give Arsenal the lead. It was his third of the season and first in ten matches after returning from an injury that had seen him miss five games.

In the 70th minute, Carl Shutt got into Arsenal's box and equalised for Leeds. Eleven minutes later, Andy Linighan gave away a foul about

30 yards out. Gary McAllister took the free kick and blasted it past Seaman to give Leeds the advantage.

To their dismay, Ian Wright equalised for Arsenal in the 83rd minute. At 90 minutes, the two teams were still level, so extra time was needed. In the first period, Tony Dorigo knocked the ball into the path of Paul Merson and it took a great save from David Seaman to prevent a goal. At half-time in the first period of extra time, the teams were still deadlocked. George Graham sent on David O'Leary to replace Nigel Winterburn.

Merson managed to get the ball to Ian Wright, who shot, and although John Lukic was able to get his hands to the ball, the kick was too powerful to stop it going into his goal, giving Arsenal a 3–2 lead. The final few minutes were played in a frenzy, with former Arsenal favourite David Rocastle fighting to get an equaliser against his old club.

The cup seemed the only route to glory that season for either club – Leeds were in 15th and Arsenal four places above them when referee Joe Worrall blew his whistle to send Arsenal through to the fifth round.

Nottingham Forest were the visitors to Highbury, but two superb goals from Wright before a boarded-up North Bank (prior to an all-seated area being built) put Arsenal through to the quarter-finals.

Arsenal travelled east to Portman Road in Ipswich for the tie. Chris Kiwomya gave the Tractor Boys the lead in a scramble in the Gunners' six-yard box. Tony Adams headed Arsenal back into the game. When John Wark upended Ian Wright, Arsenal were awarded a penalty. Wright made no mistake, hitting his 50th goal for Arsenal in only 68 games. Wright put another one away, although there was a suspicion that the ball may have come off Phil Whelan. Whoever's boot made the last contact was irrelevant (except perhaps to Ian Wright): Arsenal were 3–1 up. Kevin Campbell hit the fourth in a 4–2 win.

Ipswich boss Mick McGiven was not about to make excuses: 'If you give a team like Arsenal time and space you will get punished for it. We were playing a side who on their day are one of the best in the country. This is our first season in the Premier League and we are learning.'

Both semi-finals were local derbies. On 3 April, Sheffield Wednesday met Sheffield United, and the following day it was an all-north-London affair. Both matches were played at Wembley Stadium. Wednesday took extra time to beat their local rivals, but Arsenal overcame Spurs by a goal to nil, the goal being headed in by Tony Adams with 11 minutes to spare.

The victory made Arsenal fans forget their disappointment in the first Wembley semi-final when Spurs ran out winners in 1991. Arsenal hung on despite having Lee Dixon sent off and six minutes of stoppage time, to win what Graham called a 'fascinating tactical battle'.

The Arsenal boss criticised referee Phil Don of Middlesex for showing Dixon the red card for a second bookable offence. 'I don't think he deserved to be sent off,' said Graham. 'It was unnecessary.'

The right-back echoed his manager, 'I don't think I deserved to be sent off and at the time didn't realise it would rule me out of the Coca-Cola Final.

'It was only when we were celebrating that someone mentioned it. I'm sure it will sink in tomorrow.'

Dixon was one of five players booked by Mr Don. The defender's first yellow card came just before half-time following a clash with Nayim. His second was for a body check on Justin Edinburgh.

Indeed, Spurs had much the better of the play in the 20 or so minutes leading up to the break. In the second half, whatever George Graham had said in the dressing room, it worked, because Arsenal immediately put goalkeeper Erik 'the Viking' Thorstvedt under pressure.

Arsenal's goal came after Justin Edinburgh had fouled Ray Parlour, who needed extended treatment with the magic sponge. Adams and Andy Linighan trotted into the box, where Neil Ruddock was left to mark both of them. Paul Merson took the kick, and Adams rose to put the ball across Thorstvedt and into the Spurs net.

Adams said, 'It's been a fabulous week for me and that was the most important goal I have ever scored.

'I got on the end of Paul Merson's free kick but it wasn't one we had particularly been working on. I just got free.

'There are three things to win each season and we are now in with a chance of two of them.'

The FA Cup Final turned out to be a repeat of the League Cup Final (see page 124) a month earlier. Steve Morrow received the League Cup winner's medal he had been unable to accept on the day. 'It was a great moment for me,' he said. 'But just to have that moment as the teams were coming out, to collect my medal and get a great reception from the Arsenal fans, was fantastic.'

On 15 May, the Gunners and the Owls met again at Wembley. This time, 79,347 fans watched the two teams play out a 1–1 draw (after extra time), with Arsenal's solitary goal coming from Ian Wright, who was playing with a broken toe. Luckily, he scored with his head. This was the first FA Cup Final in which squad numbers had been used, having been trialled in the League Cup Final. Players from both clubs used the same numbers for all three matches. The Premier League adopted the system for the following season.

The match was not a thrilling final. As the teams had played in the League Cup only a month before and in the league a fortnight before, when Wednesday won 1–0 at Hillsborough, if the expression 'familiarity breeds contempt' has any meaning, it could be assigned to this match (or series of matches).

One report suggested that both managers had served up a dish of 'tactical gruel'.

Wednesday's Chris Waddle was supposed to be the star of the match, whose brilliance would outshine Arsenal. John Jensen had other ideas and marked him out of the game.

On 20 minutes, Ian Wright opened Arsenal's account, receiving the ball and making a run that ended with him putting the ball past Chris Woods.

It was 16 minutes into the second half when David Hirst pulled one back for Wednesday.

Wright almost won the game for Arsenal in the last minute of the match but was denied by Woods.

And so they all had to traipse back to Wembley for the following Thursday.

Owls manager Trevor Francis was confident his team could triumph in the replay: 'We do have enough in our team to beat Arsenal,' he said. 'I tipped them to win the championship at the start of the season, so that gives you an idea of what I think about them. They are a very strong team.

'You have to play well to beat them and anything less than a good performance won't be enough. We will just have to do better than we did today.'

George Graham opined, 'We can play a lot better than that. Our passing could certainly improve. But sometimes sides cancel each other out and that happened today.

'I would have loved a match that ended with Arsenal winning 4–3.'

Both FA Cup semi-finals were staged at Wembley, so the Gunners and the Owls each played there four times in six weeks – FA Cup semi-final, League Cup Final, FA Cup Final and replay. The replay attracted the smallest crowd for an FA Cup Final at Wembley. The kick-off was put back half an hour because a crash on the M1 had delayed thousands of Wednesday fans. It was the first time a Wembley match had not kicked off on time since the White Horse final in 1923. It was also raining heavily.

After three minutes, a tackle by John Jensen left Chris Waddle writhing on the ground. Andy Linighan remembered, 'It was getting tasty, Tony [Adams] had gone through the back of someone and John Jensen put Chris Waddle up in the air. Then I jump with Mark Bright – elbow on the nose.

'All I'm thinking is, "I don't want to come off".'

Bright's challenge on Linighan broke the Arsenal man's nose.

Ian Wright opened the scoring on 34 minutes, putting Arsenal ahead as he had done in the first game, but after 61 minutes Waddle equalised for Wednesday, his shot rebounding off Lee Dixon.

David O'Leary came on for Wright in the 81st minute, marking his last appearance for the club. Wright limped off in agony from his broken toe.

When referee Keren Barratt blew his whistle at 90 minutes, the two teams were deadlocked and extra time beckoned for the second time in five days.

It was during the added-on period that Alan Smith was booked – the only yellow card in his 13-year professional career.

With just a minute of extra time remaining, Andy Linighan won the game for Arsenal with a header. It made Arsenal the first side to win the League Cup and FA Cup in the same season, and George Graham became the first football professional to win all three domestic trophies as a player and as a manager.

Of Linighan, Graham said, 'I always had faith in him and that's why I turned down his transfer request about 18 months ago.

'He has had a very difficult time. He didn't win the fans over but Steve Bould's injury gave him his chance and football is always learning about good times and bad times.

'I never looked back – my belief in him from the time I signed him remained. It's strange that the two heroes from our cup wins are similar. Steve Morrow scored the winner in the Coca-Cola and Linighan the one here. Both were unsung heroes.'

After he retired, Linighan went back to the job he had before football: plumbing. He recalled, 'People sometimes ask about it and, yeah, I don't mind talking about it. I'll go to someone's house to work and they'll say, "Did you?"'

He remembered the match vividly. 'John Jensen took a shot and it went for a corner, a minute left. John says to me, "Big man, it was going for the top corner." This is John Jensen who scored one goal for Arsenal.

'Paul Merson takes the corner, plenty of pace on it. We did this corner at Norwich before I joined where I'd stand on the edge of the D with Ian Butterworth. He'd spin round and I'd attack the middle. I headed it flush and that was that.

'That night we went to Sopwell for a big party. I left with some friends at 2am and we got pulled over. The bobby put his head in the car, saw me sleeping in the back and said, "He scored the winning goal tonight. On you go son." That was a good night.'

Arsenal were the first but not the only double cup winners – Liverpool repeated this feat of winning both league and FA Cup in 2001, as did Chelsea in 2007.

Standard Liège 0 Arsenal 7

European Cup Winners' Cup second round, second leg. Wednesday 3 November 1993, kick-off 8.15pm
Venue: Stade Maurice Dufrasne, Rue de la Centrale 2, 4000 Liège, Belgium
Standard Liège: White shirts and shorts with two diagonal red stripes, white stockings with red stripe at top
Arsenal: Yellow shirts with three diagonal blue stripes, blue shorts with three diagonal yellow stripes, yellow stockings with three blue hoops
Referee: Kaj Natri (Finland)
Attendance: 13,276

Standard Liège	Arsenal
1 Jacky Munaron	1 David Seaman
2 Regis Genaux	2 Lee Dixon
3 Philippe Leonard	3 Nigel Winterburn
4 Roberto Bisconti	4 Paul Davis
5 André Cruz	5 Martin Keown (Bould, 82 minutes)
6 Thierry Pister	6 Tony Adams (captain)
7 Guy Hellers (captain)	7 John Jensen
8 Patrick Asselman	8 Ian Selley
9 Michaël Goossens	9 Alan Smith (McGoldrick, 46 minutes)
10 Frans van Rooij	10 Paul Merson
11 Marc Wilmots	11 Kevin Campbell
Substitutes	*Substitutes*
12 Tim Nuyens	12 Steve Bould
13 Yves Soudan	13 Alan Miller
14 Didier Ernst	14 David Hillier
15 Axel Smeets	15 Anders Limpar
16 Daniel Kimoni	16 Eddie McGoldrick
Coach: René Vandereycken	*Manager:* George Graham
Booking: Bisconti	*Scorers:* Smith 3 minutes; Selley 20 minutes; Adams 36 minutes; Campbell 42 minutes, 80 minutes; Merson 72 minutes; McGoldrick 81 minutes

ARSENAL had finished fourth in the Premiership in 1993/94 (and modern football fans think Arsène Wenger is the master of the fourth-place finish), conceding just 28 goals but drawing 17 matches. George Graham was worried by a lack of firepower in front of the opposition goal. Attempts to sign Roy Keane had failed because of Arsenal's wage structure, and so the Irishman went to Manchester United.

In the first round of the European Cup Winners' Cup, Arsenal were drawn against Odense from Denmark. The first leg was played away on 15 September 1993 before 9,580 spectators, and Arsenal got off to a terrible start when Odense were awarded a penalty in the third minute after a lumbering tackle by Andy Linighan. Jess Thorup stood up to take the kick but smashed the ball against the post. In the 18th minute, the home side attacked and the ball went in off Martin Keown's knee from a cross by Brian Skaarup. Nigel Winterburn took a shot from 25 yards, and goalkeeper Lars Høgh was unable to hold it; Paul Merson was quick to follow up, but his shot was blocked and Ian Wright got on to the rebound to score.

The scores remained level at half-time, and Graham laid into his side in the dressing room: 'You will be disgusted if you lose this to a team not fit to tie your bootlaces.' Graham's words galvanised the Gunners, and in the 68th minute Kevin Campbell put Paul Merson through to score what was to be the winning goal.

For the second leg at Highbury on 29 September – Arsenal's fourth match in 11 days – Graham was able to return Tony Adams and Lee Dixon to the back four. It was 0–0 at half-time, but Kevin Campbell put Arsenal into the lead seven minutes into the second half. Allan Nielsen pulled one back for Odense with four minutes to go.

In the second round, Arsenal faced Standard Liège of Belgium, with the first leg to be played at Arsenal Stadium on 20 October 1993. It was somewhat one-way traffic, with Arsenal overwhelming the Belgian side with 17 shots to Liège's three and 14 corners to the opposition's two. Arsenal striker Ian Wright had an eventful game – he was booked in the first half, scored twice (in the 39th and 63rd minutes) and was substituted in the second half with a possible hamstring injury. Merson scored Arsenal's second five minutes into the second half, and the final first leg score was 3–0.

Two days before Bonfire Night, Arsenal travelled to Belgium for the second leg and played Standard Liège off the park – even without Ian Wright, who was left out in case he picked up a second booking and missed the quarter-final. In between the two legs, the Belgians had sacked their coach, Arie Haan. Alan Smith opened Arsenal's account after just 122 seconds. Ian Selley passed to Paul Merson, who crossed and Smith, having lost his marker, put the ball beyond Jacky Munaron for only his second goal of the season.

Eighteen minutes later, Selley scored his first goal for the club. Lee Dixon passed to Kevin Campbell, who went down the wing with Smith and Merson waiting in the middle. The cross came in, but Merson was unable to control it. Selley came running in and smashed the ball into the Standard Liège net.

Goals from Tony Adams and Kevin Campbell before half-time put the game beyond the Belgians' reach. In the 36th minute, Paul Davis took a corner that Campbell got his head to but Munaron managed to stop, before Adams followed up to score. Six minutes later, Campbell made it four. David Seaman took a goal kick that went deep into the Standard half, and Campbell got on to the end of it and gave the advancing Munaron no chance.

At half-time, George Graham replaced Smith with Eddie McGoldrick. The newcomer played Merson through to make it five before Campbell made it six, getting on the end of a McGoldrick shot.

McGoldrick scored the goal of the match nine minutes from time, making a solo run and then hitting a shot that went in off the crossbar.

The Londoners ran out 7–0 winners, 10–0 on aggregate.

George Graham called the display 'probably the best in my time at the club. If it had gone wrong and we had lost 4–0 no doubt I would have been crucified for leaving Ian out but there was never much danger of that, was there?

'It was a breathtaking performance, especially by the three lads up front. Every time we went forward it looked like we would score.'

There was a tragic postscript to the match, as Liège defender Regis Genaux died on 8 November 2008 from a pulmonary embolism. He was just 35.

RECORD BREAKERS ... AGAIN

Arsenal 1 Torino 0

European Cup Winners' Cup quarter-final, second leg. Tuesday 15 March 1994, kick-off 7.30pm
Venue: Arsenal Stadium, Avenell Road, London N5 1BU
Arsenal: Yellow shirts with red collars and two blue diagonal stripes, blue shorts, yellow stockings
Torino: Claret shirts, white shorts, claret stockings
Referee: John Blankenstein (De Bilt, Holland)
Attendance: 34,678

Arsenal	Torino
1 David Seaman	1 Giovanni Galli
2 Lee Dixon	2 Enrico Annoni
3 Nigel Winterburn	3 Angelo Adamo Gregucci
4 Paul Davis	4 Roberto Mussi
5 Steve Bould	5 Daniele Fortunato
6 Tony Adams	6 Luca Danilo Fusi
7 David Hillier (Selley, 15 minutes)	7 Sandro Cois
8 Ian Wright	8 Marco Sinigaglia (Poggi, 72 minutes)
9 Alan Smith	9 Giorgio Venturin (Jarni, 26 minutes)
10 Paul Merson	10 Enzo Francescoli
11 John Jensen (Keown, 87 minutes)	11 Andrea Silenzi
Substitutes	*Substitutes*
12 Ian Selley	12 Paolo Poggi
13 Martin Keown	13 Robert Jarni
14 Kevin Campbell	14 Luca Pastine
15 Anders Limpar	15 Danielle Delli Carri
16 Alan Miller	16 Sottil
Manager: George Graham	*Manager:* Emiliano Mondonico
Scorer: Adams 65 minutes	*Bookings:* Fortunato, Gregucci
	Sending-off: Gregucci

AFTER disposing of Odense and Standard Liège in the first two rounds, Arsenal were drawn against Torino in the quarter-finals. On 2 March 1994, the sides played out a goalless draw in the first leg in Turin.

It was a result that George Graham had hoped for, and he restructured the team to try to close down the Italians. When the Serie A outfit arrived in London 13 days later, there was all to play for. Graham did not announce his team until just before the kick-off in a bid to keep the Italians guessing.

Steve Bould and especially Tony Adams were immense in defence. David Hillier had to go off in the 15th minute with a serious ankle injury that required eight stitches. Andrea Silenzi had raked his studs down the Arsenal man's leg.

His replacement was Ian Selley, who, five minutes after coming on, was a little too enthusiastic and went into the referee's book for a foul on Daniele Fortunato, who was in turn booked for chopping down

Paul Merson. Angelo Gregucci had his name taken for a foul on Ian Wright.

At half-time the score was still 0–0, and in the dressing room George Graham told his side to make the most of set pieces, insisting that Adams and Bould come up at every opportunity. It was a ploy that worked. Adams broke the deadlock and sent Arsenal through to the semi-finals. Alan Smith had been fouled and Arsenal awarded a free kick. Paul Davis took it, and Adams jumped to head the ball past Giovanni Galli.

To add to the Italians' woes, defender Angelo Gregucci was sent off for a foul on Ian Wright.

John Jensen, who was yet to score after nearly two years at the club, was given a standing ovation by the Highbury crowd when he was replaced in the 87th minute by Martin Keown.

David Seaman had just one save to make from a Torino attack, and the Arsenal defence kept Torino limited to just three attacks over both legs.

George Graham said, 'After England's performance against Denmark last week it shows we have a lot to offer at club level.

'We were patient and proved we can beat top-class opposition.'

His captain commented, 'It was a great win from England's point of view at Wembley last week, but this is our bread and butter.

'We showed we can be patient and not always revert to the long ball. We stuck to our guns and played to feet. I could not see Torino creating a chance and it would have been an injustice had they nicked it.'

Torino manager Emiliano Mondonico complained, 'We only played to 50 per cent of our potential but I was not impressed by Arsenal.'

Gunners boss Graham, however, thought, 'Our goalkeeper David Seaman didn't have to make a save all night. Torino were a formidable outfit, yet we always looked comfortable.

'[Tony Adams] was outstanding for England at Wembley. On the ball he was superb. I've said that Frank McLintock was the best Arsenal skipper, but Tony now has more silverware than him.

'The best thing I can say about Tony is that he is a winner.'

Arsenal 1 Parma 0

European Cup Winners' Cup Final. Wednesday 4 May 1994, kick-off 8.15pm
Venue: Parken Stadium, Per Henrik Lings Allé 2, DK-2100 Østerbro, Copenhagen, Denmark
Arsenal: Red shirts with white sleeves, white shorts, red stockings
Parma: Yellow shirts with blue sleeves, yellow shorts and stockings
Referee: Václav Krondl (Czech Republic)
Attendance: 33,765

Arsenal	Parma
1 David Seaman	1 Luca Bucci
2 Lee Dixon	2 Antonio Benarrivo
3 Nigel Winterburn	3 Alberto Di Chiara
4 Paul Davis	4 Lorenzo Minotti (captain)
5 Steve Bould	5 Luigi Apolloni
6 Tony Adams (captain)	6 Roberto Sensini
7 Kevin Campbell	7 Tomas Brolin
8 Steve Morrow	8 Gabriele Pin (Melli, 71 minutes)
9 Alan Smith	9 Massimo Crippa
10 Paul Merson (McGoldrick, 86 minutes)	10 Gianfranco Zola
11 Ian Selley	11 Faustino Asprilla
Substitutes	*Substitutes*
12 Andy Linighan	12 Marco Ballotta
13 Alan Miller	13 Roberto Maltagliati
14 Eddie McGoldrick	14 David Balleri
15 Ray Parlour	15 Daniele Zoratto
16 Paul Dickov	16 Alessandro Melli
Manager: George Graham	*Manager:* Nevio Scala
Scorer: Smith 20 minutes	*Bookings:* Crippa, Asprilla
Bookings: Adams, Selley, Campbell	

PARIS St Germain, who had beaten Real Madrid in the previous round, were Arsenal's semi-final opponents. They were on an unbeaten run of 35 games, and Graham played mind games by letting it be known that Ian Wright would not be playing, when he knew all the time that he would be. The first leg took place on 29 March 1994 in the French capital. Wrighty gave the Gunners the lead in the 35th minute with a header before David Ginola equalised for the Frenchmen five minutes into the second half.

A fortnight later, Paris St Germain came to Arsenal Stadium having suffered their first defeat in 38 games. The Gunners won by a solitary goal, scored by Kevin Campbell in the seventh minute, but disaster struck when Ian Wright was booked for a silly foul on Alain Roche and would thus be ineligible for the final. The striker was in tears.

In the second half, a mistake by Ian Selley let Ginola through on goal, but surprisingly the Frenchman shot wide from 12 yards. Arsenal held on to win 1–0, and 2–1 on aggregate, to face Parma in the final in Copenhagen.

Having beaten Antwerp in the same competition in the previous year, Parma were aiming to become the first side to win consecutive finals and consequently were favourites; five sides had previously failed to do so after reaching the final for a second consecutive year. The final was the first time that Parma had come up against English opposition.

George Graham was confident that Arsenal could win with a full-strength squad, but he had to compete with injury and suspension. The club were without leading goalscorer Ian Wright, who was suspended, and John Jensen, Martin Keown and David Hillier, who were all out injured. David Seaman had a cracked rib, but Graham was forced to play his first-choice keeper.

Arsenal had practised a number of set plays at their training ground, London Colney, in the run-up to the final.

It was the first time any European competition's final had been held in Denmark. The venue had only opened two years before, at a cost of DK640 million (£76 million). The home of Copenhagen and the Danish national football team, it had taken two years to build and was constructed on the site of the national team's previous home, Idrætsparken.

Arsenal had a narrow escape early on when Tomas Brolin hit the post. In the 20th minute, emulating a London Colney move, Lee Dixon aimed a throw-in at Alan Smith in the Parma half. Smith, as practised, passed back to Dixon, who crossed into the Parma box. Lorenzo Minotti, the captain, tried a scissor kick to clear and managed to make a mess of it. Smith was on to the loose ball in a flash and from 20 yards hit a left-footed volley. It smashed into Luca Bucci's post and went in. It was Smith's seventh goal of the season.

Without Wright, Smith was the lone striker as Arsenal played a 4–5–1 formation. Tony Adams played out of his skin, encouraging the team. Adams, Campbell and Ian Selley all went into the referee's notebook.

Parma had their chances, and a superb sliding tackle by Steve Bould deprived Faustino Asprilla of a certain goal.

Brolin assisted Gianfranco Zola's run and pass, and he shot firmly against the base of David Seaman's right-hand post.

A Paul Merson corner was met by Kevin Campbell's head, but he was unable to send the ball home.

In the film *The Arsenal Stadium Mystery*, then manager George Allison said, 'It's 1–0 to the Arsenal and that's the way we like it.'

Modern manager George Graham was also happy with that scoreline, as Arsenal became the fourth London club to win the trophy.

The first European trophy of his eight-year reign completed a full set for the Scot, who had won everything the domestic game had to offer. It seemed that Graham's position at Arsenal was rock solid and only further consolidated by the European victory.

Little did anyone know that nine months later, Graham would be sacked over accusations that he had taken a bung – a bribe in layman's terms – two bundles of cash, totalling £482,205, from Rune Hauge, a Norwegian football agent, for buying John Jensen and Pal Lydersen. Graham said that he believed the money was an unsolicited gift. The FA banned him from football for a year before he returned as manager of Leeds United and then Tottenham Hotspur in October 1998. In his time out, Graham lost money in legal fees, plus around £2 million in earnings.

'I regret it, of course I do. I was wrong to accept the money. I concede that greed got the better of me. I should not have done it. But, really, is it any different from big business? It's commonplace in the commercial world for such gifts to be given – and received,' said Graham later.

When the Arsenal board became aware of the money, Graham said that he had made arrangements to leave the club at the end of the season with a compensation package. However, on 21 February 1995, he was told to clear his desk and leave – without a penny.

'I don't want to talk about it. I never do, if I can help it. It's in the past. I have to be positive. What I did has made me grow up as a person,' he said in an interview five years later. 'I could very well have collapsed. It's how you conduct yourself after such things have happened, that's what matters. I did not run away from it. I faced it, have overcome it, and like to think I am stronger by it.'

Graham was known for his discipline as a manager and commented, 'Perhaps I have got a bit softer than I was, compared with my Arsenal days. There, I was probably a bit hard on people such as Martin Keown, who can be a bit hypersensitive and nervous. I was probably a bit too tough on him at times, put too much pressure on him. I still wouldn't hug a player, but I think I'm more understanding of their feelings than I used to be. My basic belief, however, is still the same. I'm not interested in this idea of pressure. The man in the street has just as many pressures as footballers. I don't sympathise with those players who can't take the strain.'

Arsenal 4 Everton 0

FA Premiership. Sunday 3 May 1998, kick-off 4pm
Venue: Arsenal Stadium, Avenell Road, London N5 1BU
Arsenal: Red shirts with white sleeves, white shorts, white stockings with red tops
Everton: All blue
Referee: Gerald Ashby (Worcestershire)
Attendance: 38,269

Arsenal	Everton
1 David Seaman	31 Thomas Myhre
2 Lee Dixon	28 Slaven Bilić (Oster, 46 minutes)
3 Nigel Winterburn	12 Craig Short
4 Patrick Vieira	25 Michael Ball
14 Martin Keown	32 John O'Kane (Farrelly, 46 minutes)
6 Tony Adams	5 Dave Watson
15 Ray Parlour	23 Carl Tiler
17 Emmanuel Petit (Platt, 44 minutes)	8 Nick Barmby
9 Nicolas Anelka (Wright, 72 minutes)	9 Duncan Ferguson
12 Christopher Wreh (Bould, 80 minutes)	10 Don Hutchison
11 Marc Overmars	15 Peter Beagrie (Madar, 46 minutes)
Substitutes	*Substitutes*
13 Alex Manninger	13 Paul Gerrard
7 David Platt	22 Gavin McCann
8 Ian Wright	7 Mickaël Madar
5 Steve Bould	19 John Oster
18 Gilles Grimandi	17 Gareth Farrelly
Manager: Arsène Wenger	*Manager:* Howard Kendall
Scorers: Bilić (o.g.) 5 minutes; Overmars 28 minutes, 57 minutes; Adams 89 minutes	*Bookings:* Barmby, Ferguson, Hutchison, O'Kane, Oster
Booking: Dixon	

DESPITE his taking the team to the final of the European Cup Winners' Cup as caretaker manager in 1994/95, the Arsenal board overlooked the chance to name Stewart Houston as full-time manager. In June 1995, Arsenal appointed Bruce Rioch to restore the club's fortunes. Earlier that year, during the George Graham fiasco, Arsenal chairman Peter Hill-Wood, following in the footsteps of his father and grandfather in the role, gave dinner to Arsène Wenger at Zianis, his favourite restaurant and close to his London home. Hill-Wood was uncertain about hiring Wenger: 'I think at that moment we were nervous of hiring a foreign manager. We hadn't the nerve to do it.'

Wenger was under contract to Grampus Eight in Japan and would not break the deal. In his year in charge, Rioch took Arsenal to fifth in the Premiership, the third round of the FA Cup and the semi-finals of the League Cup. Tony Adams said, 'The timing wasn't great for Bruce. For a start he lost his captain for six months. I had gone AWOL and that's never a good thing ... I had several injuries which were all alcohol-induced and I couldn't get on the playing field.'

Rioch always referred to the club as 'the Arsenal' and sought to strengthen the side with his first signing, Dennis Bergkamp (bought from Inter Milan for £7.5 million in June 1995), and then David Platt (from Sampdoria for £4.75 million the following month).

'Arsenal made it clear that they really wanted me,' Platt said. 'My talks with Bruce Rioch were exceptional. We hit it off straight away. He is a great communicator with some exciting ideas on tactics and a definite view on how he sees me fitting into his plans.'

The manager, who had cut short his holiday, was equally enthusiastic. 'I'm delighted to sign a player of David's calibre. I have admired him for a long time and through these discussions with him I have been very impressed by his knowledge, ambition and desire.'

There were some departures – Kevin Campbell to Nottingham Forest, Stefan Schwarz to Benfica after just one season at Highbury, and Alan Smith's knees forcing him into retirement.

Rioch had a spiky relationship with Ian Wright, and in February or early March 1996 the striker put in a transfer request, but the board refused to accept it.

Arsenal qualified for the UEFA Cup under Rioch, but when he refused to sign his contract the board lost patience.

They had a Frenchman lined up, so the embarrassment of sacking a manager was short-lived. They gave Rioch a year's salary as compensation.

Of the new man, Peter Hill-Wood said, 'I believe Arsène Wenger is going to be a great success and drag football in this country into the 20th century. There is no doubt in my mind we are blinkered and backward as a sporting nation. Look at the British results in Europe, they were not good, including ours. We keep telling ourselves we have the best league in Europe, but it is not true. We need to catch up with the Continentals and we think Arsène is the man to help us.'

Wenger could not start until October, so Stewart Houston – known by the players as the Coneman because he arranged the traffic furniture in training sessions – was asked to resume his managerial caretakership. He stayed for six games, winning, drawing and losing in equal numbers. Realising he was never going to get the top job, he resigned on 13 September 1996, and Pat Rice took charge of the side.

George Graham, recently appointed manager of Leeds United after serving his ban, asked Houston to join him at Elland Road. However, Houston wanted to manage a club, so he took over at Queens Park Rangers and appointed Bruce Rioch as his assistant. The pair could not bring success to Loftus Road, though, and on 10 November 1997 Houston and Rioch were sacked by QPR, with the club sitting 13th in the First Division.

Rioch complained, 'I was at home watching the Louise Woodward case on television when I turned on Ceefax and read that I had been sacked.

'I am bitterly disappointed they didn't have the courtesy to let the manager phone me or that they didn't phone me themselves before I read it on television. That tells you a lot about the people [at Loftus Road]. I think my record as a manager stands up to scrutiny and I have always had a hankering to get back to a hands-on job as a number one.

'I think the directors at QPR may have been concerned that I have been linked with so many jobs since I went there and decided they wanted to clear up the position.'

In Wenger's first season in charge, Arsenal finished third in the Premiership and were knocked out of the League Cup in the fourth round, the FA Cup at the same stage, and the UEFA Cup in the first round.

The next season, Wenger's first full season in charge, Arsenal did the Double for the second time in their history.

Many pundits believed that Arsenal would wobble and Manchester United's greater experience would see them through the finishing line. It was United who wobbled when they failed to see off Newcastle United at Old Trafford while Arsenal beat Wimbledon by five goals to nil. Arsenal then travelled to Barnsley where they won thanks to goals from the Dutch duo of Dennis Bergkamp and Marc Overmars. A victory over Derby County at home meant Arsenal needed one win from their last three matches to take the championship. The title arrived with two games to spare thanks to a 4–0 walloping of relegation-threatened Everton at Highbury.

Arsenal got off to a bright start when Christopher Wreh forced a diving save from Thomas Myhre within two minutes.

Three minutes later, they opened their account. Emmanuel Petit took a free kick, which floated towards the far post. Tony Adams claimed the goal, but TV replays showed that it was Everton defender Slaven Bilić who gave Arsenal the lead.

Patrick Vieira and Petit marshalled the midfield, while Wreh, Overmars and Nicolas Anelka kept the Everton defence busy.

Overmars netted either side of half-time. His first was a fantastic solo effort. Referee Gerald Ashby played the advantage as John O'Kane cut down Petit, but not before the Frenchman passed the ball to his Dutch colleague. Overmars bore down on the Everton defence, went past Dave Watson and shot. Myhre got a hand to the ball, but the strength of the shot took it into the goal.

Wreh and Vieira missed two chances each, and Ray Parlour brought a nimble save from Myhre with a firm downward header.

Mr Ashby booked Don Hutchison for a two-footed tackle on Petit, which saw the Frenchman go off with a severe shin injury. David Platt was the replacement.

Everton manager Howard Kendall took off John O'Kane, Slaven Bilić and Peter Beagrie and sent on Mickaël Madar, Gareth Farrelly and John Oster in their stead.

In the 57th minute, Overmars made it 3–0 with a shot that gave Myhre no chance, ending up in the far corner.

Ian Wright, out injured since January, came on for Nicolas Anelka with 18 minutes to go.

With ten minutes left, Wenger pulled off Wreh and replaced him with Steve Bould.

It meant that the back four who had played when Arsenal won the title in 1988/89 at Anfield – Adams, Bould, Dixon and Winterburn – were all on the pitch when Arsenal won it in 1997/98.

Tony Adams made it four with a minute on the clock. A pass from Bould was chested down by Adams before he smacked it past Myhre. The method of Adams's celebration was later made into a statue outside the Emirates.

It was just as well that Arsenal won the title with two games to spare, because they lost their final pair of games – both away – 4–0 to Liverpool and by a solitary goal to Aston Villa.

The match was the last officiated by Gerald Ashby. He took charge of the 1995 FA Cup Final, the year after he reached FIFA's mandatory retirement age. After retiring from the Premier League, he became a referees' assessor. However, three years after his retirement he died of a heart attack on 17 December 2001. He was 52.

Arsenal 2 Newcastle United 0

FA Cup Final. Saturday 16 May 1998, kick-off 3pm
Venue: Wembley Stadium, Middlesex, HA9 0WS
Arsenal: Red shirts with white sleeves, white shorts, white stockings with red tops
Newcastle United: Black and white striped shirts, black shorts, black and white hooped stockings
Referee: Paul Durkin (Dorset)
Attendance: 79,183

Arsenal	Newcastle United
1 David Seaman	1 Shay Given
2 Lee Dixon	23 Alessandro Pistone
3 Nigel Winterburn	12 Stuart Pearce (Andersson, 73 minutes)
4 Patrick Vieira	2 Warren Barton (Watson, 76 minutes)
14 Martin Keown	34 Nikos Dabizas
6 Tony Adams (captain)	6 Steve Howey
15 Ray Parlour	7 Rob Lee (captain)
17 Emmanuel Petit	4 David Batty
9 Nicolas Anelka	9 Alan Shearer
12 Christopher Wreh (Platt, 62 minutes)	14 Temuri Ketsbaia (Barnes, 86 minutes)
11 Marc Overmars	11 Gary Speed
Substitutes	*Substitutes*
13 Alex Manninger	15 Shaka Hislop
5 Steve Bould	19 Steve Watson
7 David Platt	27 Philippe Albert
18 Gilles Grimandi	10 John Barnes
8 Ian Wright	40 Andreas Andersson
Manager: Arsène Wenger	*Manager:* Kenny Dalglish
Scorers: Overmars 23 minutes; Anelka 69 minutes	*Bookings:* Shearer, Barton, Dabizas, Howey
Booking: Winterburn	

I T took Bertie Mee five years to do it. Terry Neill and George Graham never did it, and Bruce Rioch was never given the chance to do it, but Arsène Wenger won the Double for the club in his first full season in charge, thus becoming the first foreign manager to win the Premiership and the only foreigner to do the Double. His first match in charge was a 2–0 victory over Blackburn Rovers on 12 October 1996. The Premiership title came with a convincing 4–0 win over Everton at Highbury. A fortnight later, they beat Newcastle United 2–0 in the FA Cup Final, which was the last with commentary by ITV's Brian Moore.

Arsenal's FA Cup journey did not get off to the greatest of starts when they were drawn against Port Vale at Arsenal Stadium. They only managed a goalless draw before going to Vale Park for the replay 11 days later. Even then it took penalties before Arsenal could progress to the fourth round. At 90 minutes, the score was 1–1, and Arsenal finally went through by four penalties to three. Lee Dixon missed the first before Ray Parlour, Dennis Bergkamp, Luis Boa Morte and Steve Hughes sank theirs to put the Gunners through.

In the fourth round, Arsenal were drawn away to Middlesbrough at the Riverside Stadium. Goalie David Seaman was out with a broken finger, so Alex Manninger made his FA Cup debut. After 68 seconds, Bergkamp put Marc Overmars through and he hit the ball into the bottom far corner, from just outside the area. Before 20 minutes were up, Ray Parlour made it two for Arsenal, and that was the way it stayed until half-time. Former Gunner Paul Merson pulled one back for Boro in the 67th minute, but Arsenal held on to progress to the fifth round.

It took two tries for Arsenal to see off Crystal Palace in that round. A goalless draw at home was followed by a 2–0 win at Selhurst Park – the goals coming from Nicolas Anelka and Bergkamp. The club stayed in London for the quarter-final when they were drawn against West Ham. The Gunners went behind when Ian Pearce got on the end of a Frank Lampard corner, but managed to reply with a Bergkamp penalty.

A replay nine days later also ended with each team scoring one – former Gunner John Hartson equalising for the Hammers after Nicolas Anelka had scored for Arsenal. Bergkamp was sent off for elbowing Steve Lomas in the face, and Luis Boa Morte, Remi Garde, Steve Hughes and Nigel Winterburn were all booked. Penalties again, and Arsenal went through 4–3.

In the semi-final, Arsenal were drawn against Wolverhampton Wanderers and a Christopher Wreh goal was enough to separate the teams and send the Gunners to the final.

The match was an opportunity for Arsenal to achieve a second league and cup Double. It was Wenger's first cup final in English football.

The night before the match, the Arsenal team stayed at a hotel in Chelsea Harbour. On the morning of the final, they walked around the complex for 15 minutes, followed by 15 minutes of stretching. At 12.55pm, Wenger gave his team talk, but it lasted just five minutes. He announced the team and said that Wreh would play instead of the fit-again Ian Wright. The sun shone on Wembley as the teams came out – the temperature rose to the 90s. The Magpies were understandably the underdogs, having finished in 13th place in the league under Kenny Dalglish while Arsenal had become the champions.

Newcastle's last final had ended in a defeat to Liverpool in 1974.

After an uninspiring start, Arsenal began to gain momentum. Nicolas Anelka missed a header that he should certainly have scored – Parlour crossed and, with Newcastle goalkeeper Shay Given nowhere,

Anelka saw the ball go over. In the 23rd minute, Emmanuel Petit passed to Marc Overmars, who shrugged off a tackle by Alessandro Pistone to nutmeg Given and give Arsenal a lead that would last until half-time.

Newcastle weren't afraid to get stuck in, and Stuart 'Psycho' Pearce played on despite suffering a head wound. Alan Shearer was booked for a foul on Adams, but the Arsenal skipper 'saw him coming and rode the challenge'. On 62 minutes, Nikos Dabizas got his head to a free kick but watched in vain as the ball clipped the top of the bar.

Two minutes later, Arsenal defender Martin Keown trod on the ball, and the Premier League's leading goalscorer, Alan Shearer, pounced – but this time his left-foot effort did not bear fruit as the ball struck Seaman's upright.

With 21 minutes left on the clock, Parlour – the man of the match – found Anelka, and the teenager put it away to become the third-youngest player to score in an FA Cup final, and to ensure the cup went to north London and not the North East.

Wenger said of Overmars, 'All Europe thought Overmars was dead because of his damaged knee, but in every important game we have had this season, he has scored. He has got great mental strength. He is a world-class player.'

Arsenal 2 Chelsea 0

FA Cup Final. Saturday 4 May 2002, kick-off 3pm
Venue: Millennium Stadium, Westgate Street, Cardiff, CF10 1NS
Arsenal: Red shirts with white sleeves, white shorts, red stockings
Chelsea: Blue shirts and shorts, white stockings
Referee: Mike Riley (West Yorkshire)
Attendance: 73,963

Arsenal	Chelsea
1 David Seaman	23 Carlo Cudicini
12 Lauren	15 Mario Melchiot (Zenden, 76 minutes)
3 Ashley Cole	3 Celestine Babayaro (Terry, 45 minutes)
11 Sylvain Wiltord (Keown, 89 minutes)	30 Jesper Grønkjær
23 Sol Campbell	13 William Gallas
6 Tony Adams (captain)	6 Marcel Desailly (captain)
4 Patrick Vieira	8 Frank Lampard
15 Ray Parlour	17 Emmanuel Petit
14 Thierry Henry (Kanu, 81 minutes)	9 Jimmy Floyd Hasselbaink (Zola, 68 minutes)
10 Dennis Bergkamp (Edu, 72 minutes)	22 Eiður Guðjohnsen
8 Freddie Ljungberg	14 Graeme Le Saux
Substitutes	*Substitutes*
24 Richard Wright	1 Ed de Goey
2 Lee Dixon	26 John Terry
5 Martin Keown	10 Slaviša Jokanović
17 Edu	11 Boudewijn Zenden
25 Nwankwo Kanu	25 Gianfranco Zola
Manager: Arsène Wenger	*Manager:* Claudio Ranieri
Scorers: Parlour 70 minutes; Ljungberg 80 minutes	*Bookings:* Le Saux, Terry, Guðjohnsen
Bookings: Vieira, Henry	

I N 120 FA Cup finals, this was Arsenal's 15th appearance, and their second in a row. Opponents Chelsea had appeared in fewer than half that number – it was their seventh trip to the final.

Arsenal drew Division One Watford in the third round, travelling to Vicarage Road. They won the match relatively easily, 4–2. Thierry Henry opened the scoring after eight minutes, before Freddie Ljungberg hit the second two minutes later. Although Arsenal dominated, it was Watford who scored the next goal, with Gifton Noel-Williams pulling one back for the Hornets. The Gunners squandered numerous chances before Nwankwo Kanu and Dennis Bergkamp put the tie beyond Watford's grasp. Marcus Gayle scored a consolation goal in stoppage time, but it was the Gunners who progressed to the fourth round.

Liverpool were the visitors on 27 January 2002, in a rainy, bad-tempered match in which the two teams were separated only by a Bergkamp header. Liverpool had the first opportunity to break the deadlock on 12 minutes when Arsenal alumnus Nicolas Anelka sent Michael Owen clear, but his shot was well handled by Richard Wright in the Arsenal goal. Not long after, John Arne Riise almost set up Emile Heskey. Robert Pirès had to be substituted after a clash with Sami Hyypiä.

Ashley Cole's cross was almost sent home by Sylvain Wiltord as the Gunners poured forward. Then Thierry Henry played a one-two with Giovanni van Bronckhorst before crossing for Bergkamp to head home. Arsenal very nearly doubled their lead, but the Dutchman failed to send home an Ashley Cole cross.

In the second half, Martin Keown saw red for a professional foul on Owen after 66 minutes. Then Bergkamp and Jamie Carragher got into an argument after a late challenge from the Dutchman that had referee Mike Riley reaching for his red card again.

In the end, Arsenal did just enough to progress into the fifth round. Arsène Wenger said, 'It was a real cup tie, but not a dirty game – we were outstanding mentally.'

Gillingham were the visitors to Highbury for the fifth round and, unsurprisingly, no one gave the Gills a chance. Tony Adams was back for the Gunners after a four-month layoff. Lee Dixon and Francis Jeffers also came back from long spells out of the first team.

Brazilians Edu and Juan Maldonado also came into a new-look side. It was Juan's second and final game for Arsenal – his career at Highbury was cut short when he suffered a cruciate injury. A brief spell on loan at Millwall followed before he returned to his homeland.

On 38 minutes, Sylvain Wiltord put Arsenal into the lead after ex-Gunners goalie Vince Bartram had parried Francis Jeffers's 15-yard shot, and the Gunners went in at half-time a goal to the good.

Two minutes into the second half, Marlon King equalised for the visitors. On the 50th minute, Kanu gave the lead back to Arsenal before former Gunner Ty Gooden beat off the challenges of Patrick Vieira and Wiltord to put the Gills level with a sensational 20-yard lob four minutes later.

The match stayed level until Arsenal's class finally began to show. In the 67th minute, skipper Adams scored with his head to rescue his side. Wiltord and Ray Parlour both scored to make the final score look lopsided.

'I always believed we would win the game in the end but we needed to go up a gear and put some fresh legs on,' said Wenger.

On 9 March, Arsenal met Newcastle United at St James' Park in the quarter-finals. It was the second meeting in a week between the two sides, and although Arsenal won the league encounter, the Magpies had enough in the tank to hold them to a 1–1 tie. A fortnight later, Arsenal comfortably eased past Newcastle in the replay by a 3–0 scoreline, with strikes coming from Robert Pirès, Dennis Bergkamp and Sol Campbell. Pirès suffered an injury to his medial knee ligament in the match and was forced to miss the rest of the season.

In the semi-finals, Arsenal drew Middlesbrough in a match at Old Trafford, and an own goal from Gianluca Festa, who had been on the losing side for Middlesbrough in both the FA Cup and League Cup finals five years earlier, put paid to Boro's hopes.

The final was an all-London affair – north versus west, although it was played in south Wales rather than Middlesex. Both teams hired six planes to fly their supporters to Wales. Flights cost £135. There were warnings of lengthy traffic delays on the M4 leading to the Severn Bridge, and although the motorway was busy, there were few significant delays.

A South Wales Police spokesman said, 'The motorways are clear, despite the predictions. People seem to have taken our advice and left early.'

Chelsea were given the south dressing room, which had a reputation for being unlucky. The last nine teams to use it had lost. As the players examined the pitch, Arsenal's players wore Hugo Boss suits, while Giorgio Armani clothed Chelsea. Both teams wore their first-choice kit, with Arsenal being sponsored by Dreamcast and Chelsea by future Gunners sponsors Emirates.

The two finalists received £1 million in prizes, with the winners getting a further million from television fees.

Wenger was confident that Arsenal would win. 'We have been facing cup games in the league every week for a long time and this is just another.

'Chelsea will be a difficult team to beat if they are at their best on Saturday, but such is the confidence in this squad, we just feel we can win every game.'

In the ongoing war with Sir Alex Ferguson, Wenger had another skirmish when the Manchester United boss had said that his side played the best football in England. '[Arsenal] are scrappers who rely on belligerence – we are the better team.' Wenger annoyed him with his response, 'What do you want me to say? Everyone thinks they have the prettiest wife at home.'

Sir Alex was very upset, and Wenger rang him to say that the remark had not been a dig at Lady Ferguson – but the Scot would not be placated, and their animus went up a notch.

Back in Wales, Wenger dropped goalie Wright in favour of David Seaman. For Chelsea manager Claudio Ranieri, there was good and bad news. Graeme Le Saux and Jimmy Floyd Hasselbaink were deemed fit after calf injuries, but John Terry was dropped to the bench having woken up feeling poorly.

He said, 'It was a tough decision but he did what he felt was right. It seems like somebody up there doesn't like me.' Ranieri said of Chelsea's appearance in the final, 'We are building something. It gives the young players confidence. Winning the FA Cup would make up for missing out on the Champions League. If the team can win, they will believe in themselves, but if they don't, it won't be the worst setback to the building process.'

On a fabulously sunny day, Roberto Di Matteo, who had been forced to retire earlier in the season due to a serious injury, led a pre-Roman Abramovich Chelsea on to the pitch.

After the cup final hymn, 'Abide with Me', the sextet Tenors and Divas performed the national anthem.

Both managers chose a 4–4–2 formation. Chelsea kicked off, and within a minute Le Saux was booked for fouling Lauren. In the ninth minute, Arsenal won the first corner of the match. It came to naught as Adams fouled Mario Melchiot.

There was little to write home about in the first half hour, and neither side looked especially like scoring. Guðjohnsen had an attempt in the 12th minute that was ruled a foul. A minute later, Desailly saved an effort from Wiltord. After a Vieira error in the 17th minute, Seaman was forced to save from Lampard. The Arsenal goalie was forced into action again when Campbell's mistake left Guðjohnsen clean on goal, but he hit his shot straight at Seaman.

Celestine Babayaro came off during the half-time break and was replaced by Terry. Gallas moved to left-back.

Carlo Cudicini stopped Henry from opening Arsenal's account. And in the 57th minute, Seaman was forced to tip Guðjohnsen's effort over the bar. Ten minutes later, Ranieri pulled off Hasselbaink for Zola.

On the 70th minute, Parlour shot from 25 yards and Cudicini could not stop it going into the top right-hand corner, giving Arsenal the lead. It was one of the best goals of his career.

'That was probably the most important goal of my career,' he said later. 'It was a really tough game against Chelsea. They were buying good players.

'It was a weird week … To be honest, the lads were getting a bit tired, feeling a bit of fatigue. You never get tired when you're playing in an FA Cup Final. But we knew if we lost, that would make us feel tired.

'To play in my first FA Cup Final was a real honour; then to score in one was a dream come true. I remember making a run. Thierry Henry made a great run, he took two defenders away from me, and then it was me and Desailly and all I really did was get the opportunity to bend it round him and hope for the best.'

Wenger substituted Bergkamp for Edu. In the 75th minute, Henry and Terry both went into the referee's notebook for unsporting behaviour.

With ten minutes left on the clock, Ljungberg hit a second to send the FA Cup to north London. The Swede avoided Terry's challenge and then, from the edge of the penalty box, put the ball past Cudicini.

The Arsenal fans sang of Ljungberg, 'We love you Freddie, cos you've got red hair.'

Lampard commented, 'They can win when they are not playing particularly well. We need to find that consistency and if we can do that, I believe we will be up there with them soon.'

Wenger, in his post-match interview, said, 'We were very frustrated last year. We have shown a lot of strength to come back here – beating Liverpool and Newcastle on the way.'

Arsenal had to go and win at Old Trafford to take the Double, and Wenger was confident. 'This team knows how to win. I said three or four months ago that we will win the championship and the FA Cup. They really want to do it. And we will do it.'

Parlour remembered, '[Chelsea] were such a good team even in that final and to beat them, then go to Old Trafford and win the league with one of our best performances away from home was fantastic.'

The team celebrated with a parade with both trophies through the streets of Islington, finishing at the Town Hall.

Manchester United 0 Arsenal 1

FA Premier League. Wednesday 8 May 2002, kick-off 7.45pm
Venue: Old Trafford, Sir Matt Busby Way, Stretford, Manchester M16 0RA
Manchester United: Red shirts, white shorts, black stockings with red and white tops
Arsenal: Gold shirts, black shorts and stockings
Referee: Paul Durkin (Dorset)
Attendance: 67,580

Manchester United	Arsenal
1 Fabien Barthez	1 David Seaman
12 Phil Neville	12 Lauren
6 Laurent Blanc	3 Ashley Cole
4 Juan Sebastián Verón (van Nistelrooy, 58 minutes)	4 Patrick Vieira (captain)
24 Wes Brown	5 Martin Keown
27 Mikaël Silvestre	23 Sol Campbell
18 Paul Scholes	17 Edu
16 Roy Keane (captain)	11 Sylvain Wiltord
21 Diego Forlán (Fortune, 68 minutes)	25 Nwankwo Kanu (Dixon, 89 minutes)
20 Ole Gunnar Solskjær	15 Ray Parlour
11 Ryan Giggs	8 Freddie Ljungberg
Substitutes	*Substitutes*
13 Roy Carroll	24 Richard Wright
30 John O'Shea	2 Lee Dixon
25 Quinton Fortune	26 Igors Stepanovs
22 Ronnie Wallwork	10 Dennis Bergkamp
10 Ruud van Nistelrooy	9 Francis Jeffers
Manager: Sir Alex Ferguson	*Manager:* Arsène Wenger
Bookings: Scholes, Neville, Keane, Blanc	*Scorer:* Wiltord 56 minutes
	Bookings: Edu, Lauren

FOUR days after winning the FA Cup, what better place to capture the third Double of the club's history than at the Theatre of Dreams and against bitter rivals Manchester United, managed by Arsène Wenger's long-term nemesis Sir Alex Ferguson? At the start of the season, Sir Alex had announced that he would step down as United manager in May. But on 2 February he told Maurice Watkins, a United director, that he had changed his mind and had decided to stay. He wanted to sign for two more years, but the board insisted that he sign a three-year contract. Sir Alex was given a £10,000-a-week pay rise, increasing his salary to £70,000 a week (£3.6 million a year, although not the £4 million that he had asked for). In time, he would always insist that the manager was the best-paid employee at any football club, but then midfielder Juan Sebastián Verón was being paid more.

That season was disappointing for the Red Devils. United finished third in the league, went out of the League Cup in the third round, exited the FA Cup in the fourth and reached the semi-final of the Champions League. Sir Alex considered that the announcement of his retirement at the start of the season had unsettled the team – Wenger would give a similar excuse when he hesitated over signing a new Arsenal contract at the end of the 2016/17 season and Arsenal failed to qualify for the Champions League for the first time in 20 years. Remarkably, the United board had the very same man in mind to replace their manager, but Wenger decided to stay at Arsenal. They turned their attentions to England manager Sven-Göran Eriksson, and hands were shaken and deals agreed before Sir Alex decided he was going nowhere, or – in his words – his wife decided that he was going nowhere.

In the run-up to the title-winning match, Arsenal beat Sunderland at Arsenal Stadium and then victory against Charlton Athletic sent Arsenal to the top of the table. Liverpool and Manchester United were hoping for a slip-up from the Gunners but Wenger's men were resolute. Victory against deadly rivals Spurs and West Ham United put Arsenal in the driving seat. United dropped out of the race leaving Liverpool to compete with Arsenal after beating Spurs at the Lane. Victory against Bolton Wanderers meant Arsenal needed one win out of their last two games. But first, there was the small matter of the FA Cup. (See Match 32).

Wenger made changes from the cup-winning side, bringing in Martin Keown, Edu and Nwankwo Kanu for Thierry Henry, Tony Adams and Dennis Bergkamp. For United's part, Sir Alex dropped Ruud van Nistelrooy to the bench, and Nicky Butt was missing with a knee injury. The match began at a furious tempo, and several United players who saw red were lucky not to see a red card in the first half. Paul Scholes was fortunate not to be dismissed for a wild challenge on Edu, and Phil Neville was shown leniency by Paul Durkin, the referee, for a stupid lunge at Sylvain Wiltord. Roy Keane got in on the act by flattening Patrick Vieira, his midfield rival, as temperatures threatened to boil over – but, for all United's bullying, Arsenal were rarely in danger of losing.

Diego Forlán was busy rushing around but did little constructive. On 48 minutes, Wiltord nearly found Edu with a cross, but the Brazilian's stretch was in vain. Fabien Barthez almost let in Wiltord, but the Arsenal player was not quick enough to take advantage.

Future Arsenal player Mikaël Silvestre carelessly gave the ball away to Wiltord, who saw Freddie Ljungberg on a run from the middle. Ljungberg beat Laurent Blanc, but his shot was saved by Barthez; the United goalie could not hang on to the rebound, though, and Wiltord was there to pounce. It was his 100th goal for the club.

Despite Sir Alex sending on van Nistelrooy for the limping Juan Sebastián Verón, United could not avoid their sixth home defeat of the season.

The Double was won for the third time – the second under Wenger. Ray Parlour remembered, '[Chelsea] were such a good team even in that final and to beat them, then go to Old Trafford and win the league with one of our best performances away from home was fantastic.' The team celebrated with a parade with both trophies through the streets of Islington, finishing at the Town Hall.

Arsenal had also equalled Manchester United's record of 12 consecutive Premier League wins, created a club record of eight away wins on the bounce, extended their unbeaten record to 28 matches and scored in their 38th consecutive Premier League match. They also became the first team since Preston North End in 1888/89 to go an entire season unbeaten away from home.

Tony Adams announced his retirement at the end of the season; his back could finally take no more, and Wenger did not ask him to reconsider his decision, much to Adams's disappointment. Goalkeeping coach Bob Wilson and Lee Dixon also left the club, as did goalkeepers Alex Manninger, Richard Wright and Guillaume Warmuz (who had joined on a short-term contract and never made an appearance), and Matthew Upson.

Wenger was named Manager of the Year and League Managers' Association Manager of the Year. Ljungberg was made Player of the Year. Pirès was named the Football Writers' Association Footballer of the Year. Henry earned the Premier League Golden Boot, scoring 24 league goals. Behind the scenes, Paul Burgess was named Premier League Groundsman of the Year.

At the start of the next season, Wenger was asked if he thought a team could go undefeated for an entire season. The Frenchman hesitated before saying that, yes, it could be done, and other managers thought so but were too scared to say it publicly.

KING HENRY REIGNS IN ROME

AS Roma 1 Arsenal 3

European Champions League Phase 2 Group B (group of 16). Wednesday 27 November 2002, kick-off 8.45pm
Venue: Stadio Olimpico, Viale dei Gladiatori, 00135 Rome, Italy
AS Roma: Red shirts with yellow sleeves, black shorts and stockings
Arsenal: Pale and dark blue shirts, white shorts and stockings
Referee: Ľuboš Micheľ (Stropkov, Slovakia)
Attendance: 49,860

AS Roma	Arsenal
1 Francesco Antonioli	24 Rami Shaaban
2 Cafu	22 Oleg Luzhny
32 Vincent Candela	3 Ashley Cole
11 Emerson	19 Gilberto Silva
23 Christian Panucci	23 Sol Campbell
19 Walter Samuel	18 Pascal Cygan
5 Jonathan Zebina	8 Freddie Ljungberg (Edu, 90 minutes)
18 Antonio Cassano (Montella, 64 minutes)	7 Robert Pirès (van Bronckhorst, 78 minutes)
24 Marco Delvecchio (Guigou, 57 minutes)	14 Thierry Henry
10 Francesco Totti (captain)	11 Sylvain Wiltord (Keown, 84 minutes)
8 Francisco Lima (Batistuta, 73 minutes)	4 Patrick Vieira
Substitutes	*Substitutes*
22 Ivan Pelizzoli	13 Stuart Taylor
13 Leandro Cufré	5 Martin Keown
20 Davide Bombardini	26 Igors Stepanovs
28 Pep Guardiola	29 Moritz Volz
25 Gianni Guigou	17 Edu
33 Gabriel Batistuta	16 Giovanni van Bronckhorst
9 Vincenzo Montella	9 Francis Jeffers
Manager: Fabio Capello	*Manager:* Arsène Wenger
Scorer: Cassano 4 minutes	*Scorers:* Henry 6 minutes, 70 minutes, 75 minutes
Bookings: Samuel, Emerson, Batistuta	

I N their bid to win the European Champions League, Arsenal were drawn in Group A against Auxerre, Borussia Dortmund and PSV Eindhoven. Three wins and a draw helped them to top the group on goal difference from the Germans, who they beat 2–0 at home and lost 2–1 to in Dortmund.

In the second group stage they faced Ajax, AS Roma and Valencia. Arsenal began their attempt in Rome.

Roma had failed to win any of their three home matches in the first group stage, so Arsenal went into the match with a certain optimism, even if they were missing key players including goalkeeper David Seaman.

Oleg Luzhny and Sol Campbell, not used to playing together, were to make a number of errors, but it was thanks to Pascal Cygan, playing his best game for Arsenal, that Roma were mostly unable to exploit the weakness.

154

Near the start, a Cygan last-ditch tackle rescued Rami Shaaban, but Roma continued to attack.

Ashley Cole had failed to move up, and Francesco Totti placed the ball between Luzhny and Campbell to find Italian under-21 international Antonio Cassano, who opened Roma's account with a fourth-minute shot that beat Shaaban, bouncing off his right-hand post. Head coach Fabio Capello had chosen Cassano over Vincenzo Montella, and his gamble appeared to pay off. Capello had paid £19 million to take him from Bari in 2001.

Arsenal were not deterred, and within two minutes Thierry Henry levelled the scores with an excellent finish. Receiving the ball from Gilberto Silva, who beat Christian Panucci, Henry gave Francesco Antonioli in the Roma goal no chance.

Both teams carried out a strategy of swift counter-attacks.

Just before the 30-minute mark, Cafu outpaced Ashley Cole and crossed to Totti, who only had Shaaban to beat. The Roma captain hit the ball on the volley and it shot past the Arsenal goalie, but, running back, Cygan managed to deflect the ball off the line with his knee.

The sides went into the break on level terms, and Arsenal ran the match when the players returned to the pitch. Roma rarely posed any threat until the 64th minute, when the Arsenal defence was put under pressure. Totti released substitute Gianni Guigou, who fell under the challenge of Shaaban; in today's game Roma would probably have been awarded a penalty, but referee Ľuboš Micheľ waved away Roma's calls and signalled for a corner.

In the 70th minute, Oleg Luzhny crossed from the right and the ball dropped for Henry between Cafu and Christian Panucci. The Arsenal striker gave Roma no chance as he blasted it past Antonioli.

Five minutes later, Henry completed the club's first Champions League hat-trick. Arsenal were awarded a free kick five yards outside the penalty area after Sylvain Wiltord was brought down, and again Henry left Antonioli cold as he hit it into the net. It was his sixth goal in seven Champions League appearances.

'Henry had a exceptional night with three different, but three great goals,' Arsène Wenger said. 'But it was also an exceptional team performance. We have a great squad and I wouldn't change any of them.'

'Thankfully we had Thierry today who changed the course of the game,' commented Arsenal goalkeeper Rami Shaaban.

'We played well but we wasted opportunities,' Roma coach Fabio Capello said, 'just as we have been doing in the Italian league, and the second goal ended that spell. With Arsenal, as with all great teams, they punish you for every mistake. Arsenal are a very well organised squad full of top players, and as I have said, they are the best side in Europe in the moment.'

'In the second half we dominated with 60 per cent of the possession,' Wenger said, 'and we just had to find the way to get behind their defence. We are in a strong position now, but every game in this round will be massive.'

And massive they were – so massive in fact that Arsenal never won another match in Group B, drawing their next four games and losing the final one to Valencia, which brought their European dreams to an end for another season.

Arsenal 1 Southampton 0

FA Cup Final. Saturday 17 May 2003, kick-off 3pm
Venue: Millennium Stadium, Westgate Street, Cardiff, CF10 1NS
Arsenal: Red shirts with white sleeves, white shorts and stockings
Southampton: Yellow shirts with blue trim, blue shorts with yellow trim, yellow stockings
Referee: Graham Barber (Hertfordshire)
Attendance: 73,726

Arsenal	Southampton
1 David Seaman (captain)	14 Antti Niemi (Jones, 66 minutes)
12 Lauren	32 Chris Baird (Fernandes, 86 minutes)
3 Ashley Cole	3 Wayne Bridge
7 Robert Pirès	33 Paul Telfer
5 Martin Keown	5 Claus Lundekvam
22 Oleg Luzhny	11 Michael Svensson
15 Ray Parlour	8 Matthew Oakley
19 Gilberto Silva	12 Anders Svensson (Tessem, 75 minutes)
14 Thierry Henry	36 Brett Ormerod
10 Dennis Bergkamp (Wiltord, 77 minutes)	9 James Beattie
8 Freddie Ljungberg	4 Chris Marsden (captain)
Substitutes	*Substitutes*
13 Stuart Taylor	1 Paul Jones
28 Kolo Touré	6 Paul Williams
16 Giovanni van Bronckhorst	19 Danny Higginbotham
11 Sylvain Wiltord	29 Fabrice Fernandes
25 Nwankwo Kanu	21 Jo Tessem
Manager: Arsène Wenger	*Manager:* Gordon Strachan
Scorer: Pirès 38 minutes	*Bookings:* Beattie, Telfer, Marsden, M. Svensson
Bookings: Keown, Henry	

THE new Wembley Stadium was still being built, so for the third year the FA Cup moved to Wales and Cardiff's Millennium Stadium; and for the third year Arsenal appeared in the final.

Of the two in the Welsh capital, Arsenal had won one and lost one. The road to Arsenal's 16th appearance in an FA Cup final had begun at Arsenal Stadium against Oxford United on 4 January 2003. Dennis Bergkamp's 100th goal for the Gunners and an own goal by defender Scott McNiven guaranteed Arsenal's progress to the fourth round.

In that round they were drawn against non-league side Farnborough Town, but since their Cherrywood Road ground was not considered suitable, the match was moved to London. Arsenal dispatched the non-leaguers with ease, running out 5–1 winners.

In the fifth round, Arsenal met Manchester United at Old Trafford on 15 February. It was expected to be a tough match, as were nearly all contests between Alex Ferguson's and Wenger's sides. Arsenal had lost 2–0 in the league in December and were seeking revenge. Wenger dropped Bergkamp and put Thierry Henry on the substitutes' bench.

Sylvain Wiltord started up front alongside Francis 'Fox in the Box' Jeffers, and veteran Ray Parlour returned on the right. Within the first seven minutes, Paul Scholes, Ruud van Nistelrooy and Patrick Vieira all found their names in referee Jeff Winter's book. Ryan Giggs missed a sitter for the Red Devils: having got the better of David Seaman and Sol Campbell, he managed to miss an open goal from the edge of the area and hit the ball over the bar.

On 35 minutes, Edu opened Arsenal's account thanks to a deflection off David Beckham's shoulder, leaving goalkeeper Fabien Barthez helpless.

Seven minutes after the interval, Wiltord side-footed home from 15 yards to make it 2–0 to the Arsenal. That was the way it stayed. Arsenal captain Vieira said, 'We knew when we lost here in the league that we had lost the battle in midfield. We had to put that right, and we did.'

The quarter-final saw a home tie against Chelsea, the beaten finalists the previous year and with future Gunner William Gallas and ex-Gunner Emmanuel Petit in the side. The Blues' John Terry opened the scoring with a header before Jeffers and Henry equalised and then put the Reds ahead. Frank Lampard scored a late equaliser to send the match to a replay at Stamford Bridge on 25 March. Terry opened the scoring once again, but this time in his own net, before Wiltord gave Arsenal a second. Terry managed to get one in the right end to give Chelsea a slim hope, but Lauren made it three with eight minutes to go. Pascal Cygan was sent off, but Arsenal did not give in and made it through to the FA Cup semi-final for the fifth time in six years: Wolverhampton Wanderers in 1998, Manchester United in 1999, Tottenham Hotspur in 2001 and Middlesbrough in 2002, with Sheffield United to look forward to at Old Trafford on 13 April. Goalie Seaman, making his 1,000th career appearance, had little to do in the first half, and Freddie Ljungberg scored after 34 minutes to take Arsenal back to Wembley for a hat-trick of consecutive appearances.

Nine days before the final, the two clubs played each other in the league at Highbury – Arsenal's last home fixture of the season. Thanks to earlier results, Arsenal were unable to win the title. So Wenger dropped several regulars, as did Southampton manager Gordon Strachan, whose team began without six of their first-choice eleven. In spite of the youngsters, Arsenal ran out 6–1 winners, with both Pirès and full debutant Jermaine Pennant hitting a hat-trick. Unknown to Wenger, Pennant had not expected to play, so had gone out on the lash the night before. Despite his hangover, he had a brilliant first start for the senior side, hitting three inside ten minutes in the first half.

Arsenal were favourites to lift the cup, causing Strachan to say, 'There is little pressure on Southampton to lift the trophy. We were not expected to reach the final and have already clinched a place in the UEFA Cup.'

Wenger expected 'Southampton to be at their best against us because it will be a different team than the one we faced in the championship recently.'

South London opera singer Tony Henry sang cup final hymn 'Abide with Me'. There were 73,726 spectators at the final, and due to poor weather the game was played indoors as the roof was closed – the first FA Cup final played indoors. David Seaman, in his last appearance for the club, donned the captain's armband instead of Patrick Vieira, who was out with a knee injury. Campbell was suspended, and Cygan not playing thanks to a thigh strain.

Arsenal wore their usual red and white strip, but, as with the game against Liverpool two years earlier, their opponents wore what had been Arsenal's normal away strip of yellow and blue. Chris Marsden skippered the Saints in the absence of Jason Dodd, the injured club captain.

Arsenal opened more brightly than Southampton and had their first chance within 24 seconds, when Ljungberg put Henry through down the right-hand side, but Southampton goalkeeper Antti Niemi saved his shot. After eight minutes, Chris Baird cleared Bergkamp's effort off the goal line. Pirès scored what was to be the winning goal for the Gunners in the 38th minute, hitting home from eight yards after Freddie Ljungberg's shot had been blocked and rebounded into his path.

In the second half, Niemi strained his calf muscle and had to be replaced by Paul Jones. With a minute or so to go, James Beattie thought he had equalised with a header, but Ashley Cole cleared it off the line.

Arsenal's victory marked the first time a team had retained the trophy since Tottenham Hotspur in 1982. Former England manager Sir Bobby Robson presented the trophy to Seaman.

36

Inter Milan 1 Arsenal 5

European Champions League Group B. Tuesday 25 November 2003, kick-off 8.45pm
Venue: San Siro, Via Piccolomini 5, 20151, Milan, Italy
Inter Milan: Blue and black striped shirts, black shorts and stockings
Arsenal: Red shirts with white sleeves, white shorts and stockings with red trim
Referee: Wolfgang Stark (Bavaria, Germany)
Attendance: 85,400

Inter Milan	Arsenal
1 Francesco Toldo	1 Jens Lehmann
2 Iván Córdoba	28 Kolo Touré
23 Marco Materazzi	3 Ashley Cole
6 Cristiano Zanetti	8 Freddie Ljungberg
17 Fabio Cannavaro (Pasquale, 59 minutes)	23 Sol Campbell
4 Javier Zanetti (captain)	18 Pascal Cygan
8 Sabri Lamouchi (Almeyda, 57 minutes)	15 Ray Parlour (captain)
31 Jeremie Brechet	25 Nwankwo Kanu (Silva, 73 minutes)
32 Christian Vieri	14 Thierry Henry (Aliadière, 89 minutes)
30 Obafemi Martins	17 Edu
7 Andy van der Meyde (Cruz, 69 minutes)	7 Robert Pirès
Substitutes	*Substitutes*
12 Alberto Fontana	33 Graham Stack
26 Giovanni Pasquale	5 Martin Keown
11 Luciano	30 Jérémie Aliadière
25 Matías Almeyda	22 Gaël Clichy
15 Daniele Adani	32 Michal Papadopulos
18 Kily González	45 Justin Hoyte
9 Julio Cruz	19 Gilberto Silva
Head coach: Alberto Zaccheroni	*Manager:* Arsène Wenger
Scorer: Vieri 33 minutes	*Scorers:* Henry 25 minutes, 85 minutes; Ljungberg 49 minutes; Edu 87 minutes; Pirès 89 minutes
	Bookings: Cygan, Edu

T was the game that only diehard Arsenal fans gave the team any chance of winning. Two months earlier, Inter Milan had come to Highbury and comprehensively beaten Arsenal 3–0.

Arsenal needed to win to keep their faint hopes of qualifying for the next round alive. Both sides were missing key players through injury or suspension – Arsenal were without Patrick Vieira, Sylvain Wiltord, Martin Keown and Lauren, although Keown managed to get on to the bench.

Inter had sacked their coach, Héctor Cúper, in October after a string of poor domestic results, although they went into this game having beaten Perugia 6–0 the previous weekend.

Arsenal fans have complained in the past (and, no doubt, will do so again in the future) about having to traipse up to Burnley or Stoke on a wet Wednesday. Well, here they travelled to Milan on a wet Tuesday. It had been raining for days in the second richest city in the European

Union after Paris, but the rain had eased off to a drizzle by the time the match kicked off.

The match got off to a slowish start, although Arsenal showed some nice touches. A third-minute corner taken by Thierry Henry swung in, but Inter goalie Francesco Toldo played to the crowd by clearing with a one-handed punch rather than taking the ball.

On nine minutes, Inter swept the ball up the field and won a free kick, but Christian Vieri wasted the opportunity by hitting it high and wide, miles past Jens Lehmann's right upright.

Around the ten-minute mark, Arsenal began to string passes together and looked like a team that possibly believed in themselves. Still, the Nerazzurri peppered Lehmann's goal with shots, but nearly all of them went wide, few testing the German.

Then, on the 25th minute, the game changed and Arsenal swung into action. To boos from the San Siro – well, the blue and black section at any rate – Arsenal moved seamlessly upfield. From Robert Pirès to Ashley Cole, who cut inside and slid the ball to Henry, who, from ten yards out, slotted it past Toldo into the bottom corner of the net. One-nil to the Arsenal! Henry had scored a hat-trick against AS Roma the last time the Gunners played in Italy.

The lead was short-lived. On 32 minutes, after Edu lost possession to Cristiano Zanetti, the Milan captain passed to Vieri, who hit the ball from 20 yards out, and it deflected off Sol Campbell before heading goalwards. The 6ft 3in Lehmann was only able to tip the ball on to the bar, whence it went into the goal to give the Milanese the equaliser. Vieri, unhappy at Inter Milan, refused to celebrate his goal.

After that, the match changed into a high-octane end-to-end contest. Pirès was unable to control the ball and it went nowhere near Toldo's net, before Lehmann saved a 25-yard free kick by Marco Materazzi. On 42 minutes, a free kick from Henry 35 yards out went over the bar. It was honours even when German referee Wolfgang Stark blew for half-time.

Four minutes after the restart, Arsenal attacked again. Henry jinked past Materazzi, cut inside from the left and found Freddie Ljungberg. The Inter players appealed for offside, but keeper Toldo came out, and after he had committed himself, Ljungberg put the ball into the middle of the net – his third goal in three games.

Arsenal had another chance in the 52nd minute. Nwankwo Kanu found Henry, but, with Toldo stranded in no man's land, the

Frenchman's effort was poor. Back up the field, Zanetti went close with an effort from 25 yards. Three minutes later and the Italians continued their pressure. Lehmann's attempt to clear Andy van der Meyde's corner was less than impressive, and the Italians won another corner. Fortunately for the Londoners, Materazzi's effort came to naught.

With just over an hour played, Milan threatened the Arsenal goal, and defender Pascal Cygan, no favourite of the Highbury faithful but who had played well so far, cynically hacked down Obafemi Martins 20 yards out and received a yellow card for his troubles. Herr Stark blew his whistle for the free kick to be taken, and van der Meyde narrowly put the ball over Lehmann's goal. The Dutch winger was convinced that Lehmann had got a touch on the ball, but Herr Stark disagreed with him.

Henry shot down the wing and beat Iván Córdoba to cross the ball, but there were no Arsenal forwards on hand to finish the job. Then the Frenchman did it again, beating Zanetti, but Ljungberg needed to be about four inches taller to reach the ball.

With 17 minutes of normal time to play, Arsène Wenger sent on Gilberto Silva for Kanu, leaving Henry as the sole striker and packing the midfield with five players. Inter Milan began to pile on yet more pressure, and Lehmann's goal came under constant attack. Yet Arsenal held on and began counter-attacks.

On the 77th minute, Henry again made his move down the left, cut inside and headed towards goal. He watched Toldo – regarded by pundits as one of the greatest goalkeepers of his generation – and attempted to put it into the corner, but the 6ft 5in Paduan-born stopper tipped it wide.

With five minutes to play, Henry got the ball in his own half and headed towards Toldo's goal. Zanetti attempted to stop Henry, but the Frenchman was too tricksy, and with three men in the Italian defence, Henry put it into the bottom-right corner to give Arsenal a comfortable lead. Arsenal were far from finished, and two minutes later Edu gave them their fourth. He also went into the referee's notebook for taking his shirt off while celebrating the goal, which was and is against UEFA rules.

Wenger sent on Jérémie Aliadière for Henry in the 89th minute, and with virtually his first touch of the game he found himself in space in the box after beating Jeremie Brechet. Toldo came out, but Aliadière passed it to Pirès, who eventually put it in the net to round off a thrilling Arsenal victory.

The triumph put the Gunners one win away from qualifying for the Champions League round of 16. It was the Milan club's heaviest home defeat in 47 years of European football. 'Not in my wildest dreams could we have predicted that sort of result,' said Arsène Wenger.

'I am very proud of the players and the spirit they showed. Our character came out. We were persistent and we took our chances.'

Arsenal needed to beat Lokomotiv Moscow at Highbury in their final match to qualify. And on 10 December, that is exactly what they did, dispatching the Russians 2–0 with strikes by Pirès and Ljungberg. That same night, Inter Milan could only share two goals with Dynamo Kiev, meaning that Arsenal topped Group B, two points clear of Lokomotiv Moscow.

In the round of 16, Arsenal met Spanish side Celta Vigo and saw them off 5–2 on aggregate. They came a cropper in the quarter-finals, though, losing to Chelsea – the only other English side remaining in the competition – and lost 3–2 on aggregate.

Tottenham Hotspur 2 Arsenal 2

FA Premier League. Sunday 25 April 2004, kick-off 4.05pm
Venue: White Hart Lane, 748 High Road, Tottenham, London N17 0AP
Tottenham Hotspur: White shirts, blue shorts, white stockings
Arsenal: Red shirts with white sleeves, white shorts, red stockings
Referee: Mark Halsey (Bolton)
Attendance: 36,097

Tottenham Hotspur	Arsenal
13 Kasey Keller	1 Jens Lehmann
30 Anthony Gardner	12 Lauren
34 Stephen Kelly (Poyet, 79 minutes)	3 Ashley Cole
26 Ledley King (captain)	19 Gilberto Silva
3 Mauricio Taricco (Bunjevčević, 90 minutes)	23 Sol Campbell
6 Michael Brown	28 Kolo Touré
29 Simon Davies	7 Robert Pirès
32 Johnnie Jackson (Defoe, 46 minutes)	15 Ray Parlour (Edu, 67 minutes)
15 Jamie Redknapp	14 Thierry Henry
9 Frédéric Kanouté	10 Dennis Bergkamp (Reyes, 80 minutes)
10 Robbie Keane	4 Patrick Vieira (captain)
Substitutes	*Substitutes*
33 Lars Hirschfeld	33 Graham Stack
5 Goran Bunjevčević	5 Martin Keown
14 Gus Poyet	17 Edu
18 Jermain Defoe	22 Gaël Clichy
27 Rohan Ricketts	9 José Antonio Reyes
Manager: David Pleat	*Manager:* Arsène Wenger
Scorers: Redknapp 62 minutes; Keane 90 minutes (penalty)	*Scorers:* Vieira 3 minutes; Pirès 35 minutes
Bookings: Redknapp, Keane	*Bookings:* Lehmann

IT was something that was beyond the dreams, never mind the abilities, of any team in the modern era – to go a whole season unbeaten. It just could not be done – or could it? It had been done – 115 years earlier in 1888/89 – by Preston North End, and they had to remain undefeated for only 22 games.

In 2001/02, the season of Arsène Wenger's second Double, Arsenal were unbeaten away from home, although they lost three games at Highbury. In 1990/91, George Graham's side lost just one game when they won the title.

Two of the great disappointments of Wenger's tenure at Arsenal are that although he has transformed the club, he has never been able to win the Premier League title in successive seasons – and indeed not at all since 2003/04, nor has he been able to win the Champions League.

It was a title that they won at the home of deadly north London rivals Tottenham Hotspur, who finished in a lowly but well-deserved 14th position.

The season opened on 16 August 2003 with a 2–1 home victory against Everton, followed by wins against Middlesbrough, Aston Villa and Manchester City before they dropped their first points at home to Portsmouth. Two more were dropped in the next match, a goalless draw at Old Trafford. Arsenal were top of the league from their second game until their 14th – a 0–0 draw against Fulham – when they dropped to second. Until match 21 – a 4–1 victory over Middlesbrough – Arsenal were in first or second. Then they climbed to the top of the tree and stayed there for the rest of the season.

By the end of February Arsenal were nine points clear of Chelsea and Manchester United at the head of the table. Off the pitch the club announced that they would be leaving Arsenal Stadium for a new stadium a few hundred yards away at Ashburton Grove. Arsenal were aiming for a treble that season but were seen off by Chelsea in a Champions League Quarter Final. When in the next league game they went in two-one down at half-time against Liverpool, some fans feared their season could implode. Thierry Henry had other thoughts and thanks to him Arsenal won by four goals to two. Arsenal needed just a point to take the league title.

The title could be won at, of all places, White Hart Lane – echoes of 1971 – and, if achieved, it would mean that Arsenal had won twice as many league titles in Tottenham as Spurs had.

It would also make Wenger the first manager to win three league titles – Herbert Chapman having died before his team could achieve that hat-trick, although he did win consecutive titles.

Spurs would do their best to stop Arsenal taking the title at the Lane, but it was beyond their capabilities.

With just three minutes on the clock, Patrick Vieira, Arsenal's talismanic captain, opened the scoring. Amazingly, the goal had come from a Spurs attack. Having won a corner, Johnnie Jackson crossed and saw Anthony Gardner head the ball – straight to Thierry Henry's feet.

The Frenchman took off on a lightning 50-yard run deep into Tottenham territory before finding Dennis Bergkamp on the wing. He put the ball in, and Vieira got a long leg to it to push it past Kasey Keller.

Frédéric Kanouté and Mauricio Taricco went close for Spurs, but Jens Lehmann was equal to their efforts.

With ten minutes to go to half-time, Robert Pirès doubled Arsenal's lead. The title was in the bag and so too, it would appear, was the unbeaten record. Then, in the second half, Arsenal decided to relax and enjoy themselves. Big mistake. Spurs scored twice to force a draw and might have got a third.

As it turned out, Arsenal held on for a draw and the title at the Lane.

They very nearly lost the unbeaten record twice in the last four games. Against Portsmouth on 4 May, they went in at half-time 1–0 down. Fortunately, José Antonio Reyes scored to equalise and preserve the then unbeaten record.

The last game of the season, ten days later, was at home to Leicester City. The visitors arrived and went to their dressing room, where they got changed and waited for their team talk. Instead, Micky Adams, the manager, just wrote down the names of the Arsenal team on a flipchart, said 'Good luck with this lot', and walked out of the room.

Arsenal again found themselves a goal adrift at half-time. But goals from an Henry penalty and Vieira saw Arsenal through to victory and an unbeaten season as the Invincibles.

Wenger used 20 players in that season, and Lehmann was the only ever-present. Henry missed one match and Kolo Touré two.

Arsenal 0 (5) Manchester United 0 (4) (aet)

FA Cup Final. Saturday 21 May 2005, kick-off 3pm
Venue: Millennium Stadium, Westgate Street, Cardiff, CF10 1NS
Arsenal: Red shirts with white sleeves, white shorts, red stockings
Manchester United: Black shirts and shorts, white stockings with black tops
Referee: Rob Styles (Hampshire)
Attendance: 71,876

Arsenal	**Manchester United**
1 Jens Lehmann	13 Roy Carroll
12 Lauren	22 John O'Shea (Fortune, 77 minutes)
3 Ashley Cole	27 Mikaël Silvestre
4 Patrick Vieira (captain)	24 Darren Fletcher (Giggs, 91 minutes)
28 Kolo Touré	5 Rio Ferdinand
20 Philippe Senderos	6 Wes Brown
7 Robert Pirès (Edu, 105 minutes)	16 Roy Keane (captain)
15 Cesc Fàbregas (van Persie, 86 minutes)	18 Paul Scholes
10 Dennis Bergkamp (Ljungberg, 65 minutes)	10 Ruud van Nistelrooy
19 Gilberto Silva	8 Wayne Rooney
9 José Antonio Reyes	7 Cristiano Ronaldo
Substitutes	*Substitutes*
24 Manuel Almunia	1 Tim Howard
23 Sol Campbell	2 Gary Neville
8 Freddie Ljungberg	25 Quinton Fortune
17 Edu	11 Ryan Giggs
11 Robin van Persie	14 Alan Smith
Manager: Arsène Wenger	*Manager:* Sir Alex Ferguson
Penalties	*Penalties*
(2) Lauren – scored	(1) Van Nistelrooy – scored
(4) Ljungberg – scored	(3) Scholes – missed
(6) Van Persie – scored	(5) Ronaldo – scored
(8) Cole – scored	(7) Rooney – scored
(10) Vieira – scored	(9) Keane – scored
Bookings: Cole, Lauren, Reyes, Vieira	*Bookings:* Silvestre, Scholes
Sending-off: Reyes	

O N what was becoming an annual trip to Cardiff for either Arsenal or bitter enemies Manchester United, the teams lined up in front of 71,876 fans. Arsenal began their latest journey to the final with a match at Arsenal Stadium against Stoke City. Things did not immediately go to plan as the Potters scored just before half-time. Fortunately, José Antonio Reyes and Robin van Persie scored in the second half to give the Gunners a victory and a place in the fourth round.

Another home draw saw Wolverhampton Wanderers come to Highbury. Goals from Patrick Vieira and Freddie Ljungberg saw Arsenal comfortably into the fifth round.

The third home draw in a row brought Sheffield United to London. Arsenal made hard work of the tie, not helped by Dennis Bergkamp being sent off on 35 minutes for an apparent push on Danny Cullip. On the 79th minute, Robert Pirès scored for Arsenal, but the Blades won a late penalty, which Andy Gray put away. A replay at Bramall Lane on 1 March 2005 also ended goalless, as did extra time. The tie was decided by a penalty shoot-out. Manuel Almunia was the hero of the night, saving two penalties to win the match.

Bolton Wanderers played host to Arsenal in the quarter-final at the Reebok Stadium. Three minutes in, Ljungberg scored what was to be the only goal of the game. In stoppage time, the Swede had the chance to double Arsenal's lead but managed to hit the ball over the bar from just six yards out. A BBC Sport reporter said that it was the 'most glaring miss of the match, if not the entire season'.

In the semi-finals, both of which were played at the Millennium Stadium, Arsenal played Blackburn Rovers on 16 April. The match was hard fought, with seven players (three from Arsenal and four from Rovers) going into referee Steve Dunn's notebook. Pirès opened the scoring three minutes before half-time, and substitute van Persie (on for Bergkamp) hit the net in the 84th and 90th minutes to see Arsenal safely through 3–0. Manchester United easily saw off Newcastle United in the other semi-final by a 4–1 scoreline.

Beginning with the Community Shield in August 2004, Arsenal and Manchester United met five times in the 2004/05 season. First blood went to Arsenal as they won the Community Shield 3–0. That was the last victory until May – United were victorious in both league matches and also dispatched Arsenal from the fifth round of the League Cup by a solitary goal, although neither manager took that competition very seriously and both played junior footballers.

The FA Cup Final – the first one between the two clubs since 1979 (see page 99) – was a little overshadowed by behind-the-scenes machinations at Old Trafford, where American businessman Malcolm Glazer was attempting to take over Manchester United, and fans opposed to the deal threatened to demonstrate in Cardiff. In the end, the protests fizzled out when only about 100 people turned up to stand in the rain and sing anti-Glazer songs.

Both sides were appearing in their 17th FA Cup final, with United having won 11 and Arsenal nine. United were the holders, and Arsenal had won the previous year to that.

As was and indeed is his wont, Wenger took the press to task for what he regarded as their bias or, perhaps, unfairness. 'What is good in football is that it is not predictable,' he said. 'You act now like it is a decade that we haven't beaten Manchester United – it's not true. It's two games.'

Sir Alex discounted suggestions that his team were too physical when it came to matches against Arsenal. 'We committed three fouls on Reyes, for instance, but that hardly constitutes *The Texas Chainsaw Massacre*, does it?' he asked of the October 2004 match. 'There were six by them on Cristiano Ronaldo.'

With Thierry Henry ruled out with an Achilles injury, Wenger went for a 4–5–1 formation with Bergkamp his solitary forward. Gilberto Silva moved into the place vacated by Henry, while José Antonio Reyes and Pirès got the nod ahead of Ljungberg and Van Persie on the wings. Wenger chose Philippe Senderos in defence and left the experienced Sol Campbell on the bench.

Sir Alex Ferguson left the veteran Ryan Giggs warming his bench, and United skipper Roy Keane appeared in his seventh FA Cup Final, having played in 1991, 1994, 1995, 1996, 1999 and 2004.[17] Most neutral observers, and quite a few biased ones, would admit that United had much the better of the match and took four times as many shots as Arsenal, with Jens Lehmann performing heroics to repel all boarders.

As the rain poured down, Reyes went close, but Roy Carroll managed to prevent the attack being completed. In the 60th minute, Ashley Cole became the first player to be booked, for a foul on Wayne Rooney. Five minutes later, Mikaël Silvestre joined him in Rob Styles's notebook.

On the 27th minute, Rooney's shot was saved by Lehmann, only for Rio Ferdinand to put the rebound into the net – but the linesman ruled it offside and Arsenal escaped. The non-goal seemed to have galvanised Rooney, and he forced Lehmann into another fine save after a great effort from Ruud van Nistelrooy down the right. Rooney then went close to scoring a miracle goal when he volleyed just over from a Paul Scholes corner.

As the half came to an end, Van Nistelrooy tricked Senderos but scuffed his shot to allow Lehmann to make an easy save. After he was fouled, Rooney took the free kick but hit the ball over Lehmann's bar.

United began the second half with the same sense of urgency that epitomised their first-half efforts. Rooney went close in the 48th

---

17 Ashley Cole would go on to appear in eight finals.

minute, but his shot was blocked. Then Roy Keane had an effort averted by Kolo Touré before Ronaldo shot wide from 25 yards.

Lauren kept niggling at Ronaldo before going into the referee's book for persistently fouling the Portuguese in the 62nd minute. Three minutes later, Wenger made a tactical substitution, sending on Ljungberg for Bergkamp.

United continued to pile on the pressure, but Arsenal's back four managed to hold on, defending yet more efforts from Ronaldo, van Nistelrooy, Darren Fletcher and the ubiquitous Rooney.

In the 76th minute, Reyes was booked for a late tackle on Silvestre and then Quinton Fortune came on for John O'Shea, who seemed to have a calf injury. In the 84th minute, United won a corner. Lehmann came out to meet it and missed the ball completely. It ended up on van Nistelrooy's head, but, luckily for Arsenal, Ljungberg was on the line to head it on to the crossbar and away to safety.

Mr Styles blew to end the 90 minutes and start 30 minutes of extra time. In the first minute, Fletcher went off and Sir Alex sent on the experienced Ryan Giggs. It was the seventh minute of extra time before Arsenal got their first shot on target. A free kick by van Persie – awarded for a foul by Silvestre – forced Carroll into making a diving save. In the 11th minute, United appealed for a penalty, claiming that Cole had handled, but replays showed the ball struck him amidships. Another handball claim was made against Touré, but Mr Styles waved away the shouts. The second period of extra time began as was expected, with United on the attack. Reyes fouled Silvestre and Mr Styles warned him to watch his behaviour. Scholes was then booked for a tackle on Reyes.

The game threatened to boil over when Ljungberg went down after colliding with Fortune, who then tackled Gilberto forcefully. Mr Styles was well placed and quickly calmed things down. The referee added two minutes of stoppage time, and, with just seconds left, Ronaldo set off towards the Arsenal goal, only for Reyes to bring him down. Mr Styles waved a second yellow card before producing a red, making the Spaniard the second player to be sent off in an FA Cup Final, after United's Kevin Moran in 1985. Immediately after the dismissal, Mr Styles blew for full time – it was the first final without goals since 1912.

As the rain continued to pour, the teams lined up to take penalties – the first time the FA Cup would be decided that way.

Van Nistelrooy took the first penalty for Manchester United, in front of the United faithful, and put the ball to Lehmann's right while sending the Arsenal keeper left: 1–0 to Manchester United.

Lauren gave the slightest of hesitations in his run-up before thumping the ball past Roy Carroll, who also went the wrong way: 1–1.

Scholes made a very fast run-up and hit the ball low and hard to Lehmann's right, but the German was more than equal to it and saved. Still 1–1.

Ljungberg gave Carroll no chance, with his spot-kick sending the Irishman the wrong way: 2–1 to the Arsenal.

Ronaldo stopped on his run-up and then coolly placed the ball in the bottom-right corner as Lehmann dived to his bottom left. No celebrations from the Portuguese as he returned to his team-mates: 2–2.

Van Persie took his time in placing the ball on the spot. Carroll almost got a hand to the shot, but it was out of his reach: 3–2 to the Gunners.

Rooney took a very short run-up to blast the ball into Lehmann's net: 3–3.

Cole gave Carroll no chance and pumped his fists in celebration after his penalty gave Arsenal the lead: 4–3.

Keane took the potential last penalty kick for United. He gave Lehmann no chance and then calmly walked away before turning to applaud the United fans.

It was all down to Patrick Vieira – to win the FA Cup for Arsenal or miss and go to sudden death. The Arsenal captain stepped up, and although Carroll guessed correctly, he was unable to get his gloves on the ball.

It was Vieira's last kick for the Gunners before leaving Highbury for a new life in Italy with Juventus.

And then the long drought began …

THE YOUNGSTERS DID GOOD

39

Real Madrid 0 Arsenal 1

European Champions League round of 16, first leg. Tuesday 21 February 2006, kick-off 7.45pm
Venue: Santiago Bernabéu Stadium, Avenue de Concha Espina, 1, 28036 Madrid, Spain
Real Madrid: All white
Arsenal: Yellow shirts, dark blue shorts and stockings
Referee: Stefano Farina (Ovada, Italy)
Attendance: 80,000

Real Madrid	Arsenal
1 Iker Casillas	1 Jens Lehmann
3 Roberto Carlos	27 Emmanuel Eboué
11 Cicinho	16 Mathieu Flamini
16 Thomas Gravesen (Júlio Baptista, 76 minutes)	15 Cesc Fàbregas (Song, 90 minutes)
4 Sergio Ramos	28 Kolo Touré
18 Jonathan Woodgate (Mejia, 9 minutes)	20 Philippe Senderos
10 Robinho (Bravo, 63 minutes)	13 Alexander Hleb (Pirès, 76 minutes)
5 Zinédine Zidane	19 Gilberto Silva
9 Ronaldo	14 Thierry Henry (captain)
14 Guti (captain)	8 Freddie Ljungberg
23 David Beckham	9 José Antonio Reyes (Diaby, 80 minutes)
Substitutes	*Substitutes*
42 David Cobeño	24 Manuel Almunia
2 Michel Salgado	2 Abou Diaby
19 Antonio Cassano	7 Robert Pirès
21 Carlos Diogo	17 Alexander Song
24 Álvaro Mejia	32 Theo Walcott
8 Júlio Baptista	36 Johan Djourou
7 Raúl Bravo	41 Arturo Lupoli
Head coach: Juan Ramón López Caro	*Manager:* Arsène Wenger
Bookings: Cicinho, Casillas	*Bookings:* Silva, Reyes
	Scorer: Henry 47

ARSENAL joined the 2005/06 Champions League in the group stage after finishing runners-up in the Premier League, and were drawn in Group B along with Ajax from Holland, Sparta Prague from the Czech Republic and Thun from Switzerland, who had still been playing amateur football as recently as 1998.

They began their challenge at home to Thun on 14 September and only won narrowly. The previous weekend, they had lost 2–1 to Middlesbrough, and Arsène Wenger had said, 'We missed our chances and we gave them presents for their two goals. We were good enough to win this game.' Wenger made five changes to the starting line-up against Thun. Two of them were enforced: Jens Lehmann began a two-match UEFA suspension, so Manuel Almunia deputised between the sticks, and Cesc Fàbregas replaced the injured Mathieu Flamini. Sol Campbell was back from injury for the first time since May. Henry was missing with a groin strain and was expected to be out for six weeks, but, despite the absence of their talismanic striker, Arsenal attacked and went close twice inside the opening quarter of an hour. Robin van Persie shot straight at Eldin Jakupovic, and the Thun keeper did well to save a free kick from Kolo Touré. The opening half's drama came just before half-time, when referee Gregorz Gilewski showed van Persie a straight red after he caught Alen Orman with a boot in the face.

Six minutes after the restart, Gilberto nodded a cross from José Antonio Reyes beyond 20-year-old Jakupovic and into the corner. Nelson Ferreira pulled one back for the visitors two minutes later lobbing the ball over Almunia, and it seemed as if the match was heading for a draw. Wenger pulled off Fàbregas in the 73rd minute and sent on Dennis Bergkamp, who was scared of flying and would only go abroad by car. With two minutes of stoppage time gone, Bergkamp wrong-footed Thun's defence with a sublime back-heel from six yards.

Arsenal's next match was away to Ajax, who had beaten the Gunners 3–1 on aggregate in the quarter-finals of the same competition in 1971/72, the year after Arsenal's Double triumph. After just 80 seconds, Freddie Ljungberg, playing as a makeshift striker, collected Reyes's pass before clipping a clever finish past Hans Vonk to open the scoring. In the second half, Vonk brought down Reyes and Robert Pirès calmly slotted home to give Arsenal a two-goal lead.

Almost immediately, Ajax's Markus Rosenberg tapped in after Tomas Galasek had hit the post, but Arsenal stood firm. A comparatively easy couple of matches against Sparta Prague were up next, with Arsenal winning 2–0 away on 17 October (a brace from Henry made him the club's highest scorer, overtaking Ian Wright's tally of 185 goals) and 3–0 at home (one from Henry and two from van Persie).

With a solitary goal away to Thun and a goalless draw at home to Ajax, Arsenal topped their group, five points clear of second-placed Ajax. Thun finished third and went into the group of 32 in the UEFA Cup.

On 21 February 2006, Arsenal faced a tough challenge after being drawn against Real Madrid in the round of 16, the first leg at the Bernabéu. Real had never lost at home to an English club, so the odds were against the north Londoners, who were not helped by injuries to eight regular first-team players.

Few gave the Gunners any chance, and many were thus surprised when Arsenal nearly took the lead after just two minutes. Thierry

Henry put through José Antonio Reyes, and it was only a fine one-handed save from Iker Casillas that stopped it being 1–0 to the Arsenal.

Then Arsenal pressed forward again. It was only an excellent tackle from Roberto Carlos that stopped Freddie Ljungberg opening the Arsenal account. On nine minutes, Real's Englishman Jonathan Woodgate limped off with a hamstring strain. Reyes played it in and Henry headed wide, but Arsenal could have scored three times in the opening ten minutes.

Madrid's best chance fell to David Beckham, his hair prettily kept out of his eyes with an Alice band, but he headed a yard wide. A second opportunity was also missed, and Jens Lehmann saved. A miskick by Alexander Hleb left Robinho free to shoot, but Lehmann got down to save.

Both teams had chances to score, but excellent goalkeeping or poor finishing denied them. The first half ended 0–0.

Not long after the second half began, Henry jinked past four Real players and with a left-foot finish put the ball beyond Casillas to give Arsenal a thoroughly well-deserved lead.

Beckham nearly pulled Madrid level, but his finishing was poor. With ten minutes to go, Wenger pulled off Reyes and sent on Abou Diaby, who nearly marked his Champions League debut with a goal after 89 minutes with his first touch, but Casillas saved at his feet. After 95 minutes, Italian referee Stefano Farina, who died in May 2017 aged 54, blew for full time and Arsenal became the first English team to beat Real Madrid at the Bernabéu.

At the time, the future of Henry was in doubt, and it seemed that he was in his last season at Highbury. Henry said, 'You see that as soon as Arsenal is not scared to play, we can play good football. We have only won one game. We are not there yet so we have to stay calm and focus. In some games recently we have been kicking the ball up front for no reason. Here we played football. We were tremendous at the back – amazing.'

Arsène Wenger hoped that the result in Madrid could convince Henry that Arsenal were a big club and could compete for major trophies. 'I hope the quality that our young team has shown will persuade Thierry to stay,' said the Arsenal chief. 'I think this will help convince him he has a future here because the young boys have shown they can produce the results he wants. We needed big nights from

Henry, Kolo Touré and Gilberto Silva but the young players did well. There was not a single player who wasn't outstanding. We started well and that may have made Real insecure. I'm happy in every department. In fact, my only regret, if there is one, is that we did not add one or two more goals. I still think they will turn up [in the second leg] and give everything; to sit on our lead at Highbury would be a major mistake.'

'That's what happens when you don't work hard and tackle back. I'm bitterly disappointed,' said Beckham. 'I knew after five minutes we were going to lose, but we have got away with it, we could have lost by more.

'I said before that if we didn't perform we wouldn't win the game and we didn't perform. Arsenal played well but we didn't play like we have done for the last two months. I don't know what happened. They got the space to enjoy themselves and they did well, but it was a really bad performance from our whole team.'

Real coach Juan Ramón López Caro said that Arsenal deserved to win. 'We suffered an important setback out there, but they played a great game. We never really managed to find any clarity or precision in midfield and didn't show our usual personality. It certainly wasn't our best performance, but we still have got a chance of getting through.'

Arsenal drew the second leg 0–0 at Highbury on 8 March to go through. Wenger said, 'To play two games against Real and not concede a goal shows remarkable spirit. Something is happening with this team. They are gelling together. They have shown character, and that is very good. I feel we have grown as a team during these last two months. We have shown character and solidarity and always maintained the basic values of our club. I feel sometimes this season we have been kicked off the park without protection, maybe because we were a bit young and we couldn't face up to that. We tried to be faithful and sometimes we even looked naive because we tried to play football but I prefer that type of game, the type we have seen.'

Wenger praised his opponents, saying: 'They went at it, and so did we. Everybody wanted to score when they got the ball, and it was a great football game. Both teams tried to attack every time they could.'

Henry added: 'We are going through maybe not in the Arsenal way – but we are through. It was a proper game. It had everything, a bit of tension at the end. It was not a boring 0–0. We didn't concede a goal home or away against Real Madrid – that is something special.'

Arsenal 4 Wigan Athletic 2

FA Premier League. Sunday 7 May 2006, kick-off 3pm
Venue: Arsenal Stadium, Avenell Road, London. N5 1BU
Arsenal: Redcurrant shirts, white shorts and redcurrant stockings
Wigan Athletic: Blue and white striped shirts, blue shorts, white stockings
Referee: Uriah Rennie (South Riding of Yorkshire)
Attendance: 38,359

Arsenal	Wigan Athletic
1 Jens Lehmann	12 Mike Pollitt
27 Emmanuel Eboué	26 Leighton Baines
3 Ashley Cole	2 Pascal Chimbonda
15 Cesc Fàbregas	4 Matt Jackson
28 Kolo Touré	18 Paul Scharner
23 Sol Campbell	23 Reto Ziegler (Francis, 66 minutes)
13 Alexander Hleb (van Persie, 78 minutes)	11 Graham Kavanagh
9 José Antonio Reyes (Bergkamp, 78 minutes)	7 Henri Camara (Connolly, 82 minutes)
12 Thierry Henry (captain)	27 David Thompson (Johansson, 73 minutes)
19 Gilberto Silva	10 Lee McCulloch
8 Robert Pirès (Ljungberg, 73 minutes)	30 Jason Roberts
Substitutes	*Substitutes*
24 Manuel Almunia	15 David Wright
20 Johan Djourou	6 Stéphane Henchoz
7 Freddie Ljungberg	17 Damien Francis
10 Dennis Bergkamp	8 Andreas Johansson
20 Robin van Persie	22 David Connolly
Manager: Arsène Wenger	*Manager:* Paul Jewell
Scorers: Pirès 8 minutes; Henry 35 minutes, 56 minutes, 76 minutes (pen)	*Scorers:* Scharner 10 minutes; Thompson 33 minutes
Booking: Fàbregas	*Booking:* Jackson
	Sending-off: Johansson

FTER almost 93 years, Arsenal played their 2,010th and last game at Highbury, the venue that they had moved to in 1913 from south of the Thames. The first game played at Arsenal Stadium was a Division Two match on Saturday 6 September 1913 against Leicester Fosse. Tommy Benfield of Leicester scored the first goal at the new ground, and George Jobey scored the first Arsenal goal as the Gunners ran out 2–1 winners (see page 19). The last game played there was on 7 May 2006 against Wigan Athletic.

Arsenal needed to get a better result than rivals Spurs (who were playing West Ham United at the Boleyn Ground) to guarantee a place in the Champions League for the next season, so there was a double incentive to end with a good finish.

Arsène Wenger made three changes from the side that had beaten Manchester City four days earlier. Cesc Fàbregas, Alexander Hleb and Robert Pirès came in for Alex Song, Freddie Ljungberg and Robin van Persie.

First blood went to Arsenal when Pirès, standing near the goal, got on the end of a Sol Campbell header and put the ball past Mike Pollitt after the Latics keeper had saved his initial effort. News filtered through that Spurs had gone behind at Upton Park thanks to Carl Fletcher's goal, so things were going according to plan.

Then it all went wrong.

Arsenal only held the lead for two minutes, until David Thompson whipped over a free kick from 20 yards, Gilberto left it at the near post and Paul Scharner pulled one back for the visitors in the unguarded area between Jens Lehmann and his near post as the Arsenal defence fell asleep.

Then it almost got worse.

Jason Roberts bettered Sol Campbell, who then brought him down in the area, but referee Uriah Rennie turned down Wigan's appeals for a penalty.

Then it did get worse.

Wigan were awarded a free kick from 40 yards out, and Lehmann decided it was too far out for him to need a wall. Thompson saw the potential. The space allowed the little Liverpudlian to angle his drive just inside Lehmann's disregarded right-hand post: 2–1 to the visitors.

Just two minutes more had elapsed when a neat through ball from Hleb found Henry in clear space, and Arsenal were again level as the Frenchman put away his 135th Highbury goal.

When Thompson tried the same trick of aiming for the unprotected post two minutes before the break, Lehmann was wise to it.

In the second half, there were two further scares for the Gunners, with Lee McCulloch and Henri Camara both going close to adding to Wigan's tally.

The news filtered through to Highbury that Spurs had pulled one back at Upton Park, so Arsenal needed to win.

Then there was a break.

For reasons that probably still keep him awake at night, Thompson tried to pass back to Pollitt but underhit the ball. His manager, Paul Jewell, described it as a 'ridiculous' move.

It ended up at the feet of Henry, who went round the Wigan keeper and put it in the back of the net.

Then Pollitt was forced to save on the line from Fàbregas's header. Jewell sent on Andreas Johansson for the unfortunate Thompson in the 73rd minute. Without even touching the ball, Johansson pulled

Ljungberg down. Referee Mr Rennie pointed to the spot and produced a red card for Johansson, who had only been on for seconds.

Henry took the penalty to complete the last hat-trick at Highbury. He knelt down and kissed the famous Highbury turf.

Dennis Bergkamp came on for his final Arsenal performance – the opening match at the new Emirates Stadium would be his testimonial.

When Mr Rennie blew his whistle for the final time, the old clock on the South Stand read 4.54pm.

The match ended Arsenal 4 Wigan Athletic 2, and there was more good news from east London, where West Ham had beaten Spurs 2–1. It was enough to give Arsenal fourth place.

Henry said, 'That was the perfect send-off. We are fourth in the league and the table does not lie after 38 games, so we deserve to be in this position. We've missed so many players this season and we did it the hard way. When I kissed the ground after my third, I was saying goodbye to this stadium.

'It's not normally what we do, finish fourth, but we will take that this season. However, we still have to play qualifying games so we are not quite in the Champions League yet.'

Wigan manager Jewell said, 'Uriah Rennie likes to make history, something was bound to happen. We just don't get penalties at Arsenal. And to send off Andreas Johansson was nonsense really. When you look back in years to come, Rennie's name will be in the record books and he'll like that.

'But I want to say how proud I am of my team. We have had a fantastic time, we've done exceptionally well.'

Wenger said that he would have been disappointed if Arsenal had not won their final game at Highbury.

'For the history of the club and for this building here, to finish on a high I am very proud.

'We would all have felt guilty to have walked out of here on a low after what has happened here for years.

'There was fantastic excitement, strength of character and quality as well.'

Midfielder Gilberto Silva revealed he thought it was essential for Arsenal to be playing in the Champions League in their new stadium.

'It's very important for this club to be in that competition,' said the Brazilian, who had signed a new four-year contract and said he would stay at Arsenal for life.

'With this season it was different because we weren't playing for the title but we definitely deserve fourth place.'

There was a parade of Arsenal legends after the game, with helpful signs identifying the old heroes and when they played for the club, in case younger fans were bewildered. Then there were fireworks and it was all over.

It was the final season at Arsenal for Bergkamp, Pirès, Sol Campbell, Pascal Cygan, Reyes and Ashley Cole.

That summer, the bulldozers moved in to turn the stadium into Highbury Square, a series of 711 small and costly apartments, with the pitch area becoming a communal garden. The East and West Stands have been preserved in the new development, which topped out on 6 March 2008.

Barcelona 2 Arsenal 1

European Champions League Final. Wednesday 17 May 2006, kick-off 8.45pm
Venue: Stade de France, 93216 Saint-Denis, France
Barcelona: Red and blue striped shirts, red shorts, blue stockings
Arsenal: Yellow shirts, black shorts and black stockings with yellow backs
Referee: Terje Hauge (Bergen, Norway)
Attendance: 79,610

Barcelona	**Arsenal**
1 Víctor Valdés	1 Jens Lehmann
23 Oleguer (Belletti, 71 minutes)	27 Emmanuel Eboué
12 Giovanni van Bronckhorst	3 Ashley Cole
15 Edmílson (Iniesta, 46 minutes)	19 Gilberto Silva
4 Rafael Márquez	28 Kolo Touré
5 Carles Puyol (captain)	23 Sol Campbell
17 Mark van Bommel (Larsson, 61 minutes)	7 Robert Pirès (Almunia, 18 minutes)
8 Ludovic Giuly	15 Cesc Fàbregas (Flamini, 74 minutes)
9 Samuel Eto'o	14 Thierry Henry (captain)
20 Deco	13 Alexander Hleb (Reyes, 85 minutes)
10 Ronaldinho	8 Freddie Ljungberg
Substitutes	*Substitutes*
25 Albert Jorquera	24 Manuel Almunia
2 Juliano Belletti	20 Philippe Senderos
16 Sylvinho	22 Gaël Clichy
3 Thiago Motta	16 Mathieu Flamini
6 Xavi	9 José Antonio Reyes
24 Andrés Iniesta	10 Dennis Bergkamp
7 Henrik Larsson	11 Robin van Persie
Manager: Frank Rijkaard	*Manager:* Arsène Wenger
Scorers: Eto'o 76 minutes; Belletti 80 minutes	*Scorer:* Campbell 37 minutes
Bookings: Oleguer, Larsson	*Bookings:* Eboué, Henry
	Sending-off: Lehmann

IT was to Paris and the Stade de France in Saint-Denis that Arsenal travelled in the spring of 2006 to compete in their first (and so far only) European Cup Final (renamed the European Champions League Final in 1992/93). It was also the first occasion when a team from London had made the ultimate match. Their opponents, Barcelona, had appeared in 1961, 1986 and 1994, when they were runners-up; and in 1992, when they won the last European Cup final before the Champions League was inaugurated, beating Sampdoria.

The Spaniards were favourites to take the title for a second time, although Deco was keen to dispel any complacency, 'Milan were winning 3–0 last year against Liverpool and ended up losing in the end. We need to be serious, calm and fully concentrated so that we don't make any errors.'

The Stade de France had hosted the final six years previously, when Real Madrid had beaten Valencia 3–0 – the first time two clubs from the same country had met in the final. Barcelona went into the match as champions of La Liga, while the Gunners had the record for the longest time in the Champions League without letting in a goal – 919 minutes since conceding against Ajax in the group stage. In fact, they had let in only two goals in their 12 matches to the final, including ten successive matches without conceding, a Champions League record. It was also six years to the day since Arsenal had last been in a European final – they lost to Galatasaray in the UEFA Cup 4–1 on penalties after the match had finished goalless after 90 minutes and extra time. Thierry Henry and Dennis Bergkamp were the two survivors from that game, and Sylvinho was now wearing Barcelona's colours.

With Liverpool, Chelsea and Rangers all losing in the round of 16, Arsenal had been the sole carriers of the British flag into the quarter-finals.

They were drawn against the most successful side in Italian football, Juventus, with the first leg at Highbury. Arsenal's European form had been excellent, but few among the 35,472 crowd could have anticipated the ease with which they saw off the Old Lady.

Fàbregas gave Arsenal the lead with a low strike from 20 yards and later passed for Henry to convert into an empty net from 12 yards out. It was due to Juventus goalie Gianluigi Buffon that Henry, Fàbregas and Alexander Hleb did not score in the second half. Juventus were eight points ahead at the top of Serie A, but you would never have known it by their poor performance. Mauro Camoranesi and Jonathan Zebina were both sent off late in the match, meaning the Turin side finished it with nine men. Arsenal's clean sheet meant that they had gone seven matches without conceding in the Champions League – equalling the record set by AC Milan in the previous season.

Arsenal old boy Patrick Vieira was given a warm welcome by the Highbury faithful, but a yellow card in the second half meant that he, Camoranesi and Zebina missed the return leg. 'I believe we will finish the job in the second leg in Italy but there is still a lot to come,' said Wenger in his post-match interview. 'We have to keep our feet on the ground and keep our football simple. That is what the boys do and they can do better. They are not inhibited. There is quality in this team and they are good to watch.'

Juventus manager Fabio Capello kept the faith. 'What annoyed me were the two expulsions. The tie is still alive and my team need a big game in Turin. In the first half we played as well as Arsenal until we conceded the goal but after the goal they got better. It's difficult to play against a team with ten players behind the line of the ball. There was no space for us.'

When Arsenal travelled to the Stadio delle Alpi in Turin for the second leg, they took the rain with them. Juventus put on a poor performance, and Arsenal never looked like losing. Discipline problems came back to haunt the Italians, who had Pavel Nedved sent off. Jens Lehmann made an excellent save from Zlatan Ibrahimović, who, had the circumstances been different, might have been playing in a yellow shirt that night. The story has it that Arsène Wenger wanted Ibrahimović to have a trial at Highbury but the Swede replied, 'Zlatan doesn't do auditions.'

In the semi-final, Arsenal faced another Spanish side in Villarreal, with the first leg at Highbury. Wenger named his expected line-up, with Reyes out through suspension and Fàbregas shaking off an injury, and only one Englishman – Theo Walcott – in the squad.

The Spaniards were missing their two first-choice centre-backs, Gonzalo Rodríguez and Juan Manuel Pena, and joining them on the sidelines was suspended goalie Sebastien Viera. *The Guardian* described his replacement, Mariano Barbosa, as possessing 'the handling of Massimo Taibi, the agility of Peter Shilton *circa* 1990, and the concentration of David James. An accident waiting to happen.'

Highbury was not used as a 1966 World Cup venue because the pitch was too small, but on this night Arsenal made that an advantage as their speed and agility on the grass was too much for Villarreal. The Arsenal also had a twelfth man on the pitch, making his appearance after ten minutes – a squirrel.

In the next minute, Henry had a goal disallowed for offside when the linesman flagged, but television replays showed that the Arsenal centre-forward was level and the goal should have stood. By the 18th minute, the squirrel had worn his legs out and took shelter behind an advertising hoarding.

It was in the 41st minute that Kolo Touré gave Arsenal the lead when he slotted home Aleksander Hleb's pass. It turned out to be the only goal of the game, meaning another clean sheet for Lehmann. The French boss was pleased. 'I believe it is a good result but we will know after the second game,' he said. 'We wanted a second goal but sometimes we were too nervous. We faced a good team, very strong in the midfield, and we couldn't impose enough to create more chances. At home you never know what is enough in a semi-final and it is difficult to go forward. We want to keep a clean sheet in the second leg, and we have proved we can do that, but it is not enough to just go there and defend. We want to play our game and score goals.'

Unlike Juventus in their second leg, Villarreal brought their A-game to the return match. They dominated the first half. Campbell, as expected, was recalled in place of the injured Philippe Senderos, for his first Champions League appearance since November; and after nine minutes Mathieu Flamini limped off with a hamstring injury to be replaced by Gaël Clichy.

Lehmann was Arsenal's hero throughout the match, making save after save to stop the Spaniards. Then, just as it seemed Arsenal were going through, Clichy fouled José Mari and gave away a penalty. The German keeper was again the Gunners' saviour. He dived to his left to save Juan Roman Riquelme's spot-kick and send Arsenal through.

Villarreal coach Manuel Pellegrini said, 'It is difficult to explain how one feels after this. We were even better than Arsenal at Highbury. We deserve to be in the final. I thought from the first minute we could make it. We had three shots in the first half, two headers in the second and then the penalty. Until the last minute I thought it was possible. The players are very sad; they are gutted. I'm proud of the way they played but we also have a feeling of frustration because we played so well and we just couldn't make it.'

The Arsenal manager was full of praise for his at times eccentric shot-stopper. 'I said to myself that if it is our year, Jens will save it. I knew he had strength of character, and I knew he would not be beaten easily. It comes down to psychological reason and Jens guessed right. It was more of a poker game than good training. I am pleased because when a guy shows professionalism and a winning attitude, you always want him to be rewarded.'

Lehmann said, 'We deserved it because we fought very hard. We didn't think it was a penalty, but I thought about Riquelme putting one to his right last week and decided to go there. It's a great night, but right now I want to win that final. It was a gift of a penalty, but fortunately he chose the same side as me. If you want to reach the final you have to make saves like these.'

Campbell, back in the side after a season almost wrecked by injury, commented, 'Jens is in fantastic form now and I had every confidence in him. It's been a tough road but I've kept going. The lads have been fantastic for me. I got my chance here and I've done a job.'

Henry also paid tribute to Lehmann, saying, 'Jens had an amazing game and not only the penalty. Throughout he was magnificent. Once you are in the final anything can happen. We have shown we can play with flair and with desire. This result was about desire and commitment – we worked hard and everyone was chasing.'

Neither side had been beaten en route to the final, with Arsenal conceding only two goals in their 12 matches before the final – Lehmann went a Champions League record 853 minutes without conceding a goal. Barcelona, on the other hand, had scored 114 goals in all competitions before the Stade de France.

As well as the glory of another European trophy – a new cup, since having won the title five times, Liverpool were allowed to keep it – to put into the boardroom cabinet, there was also the small matter of the financial rewards that came with winning. Arsenal would receive revenue of around €37.3 million if they won or €34.7 million if they lost; the Spaniards would get around €31.5 million or €28.9 million respectively.

Barcelona coach Frank Rijkaard was unable to name his team too far in advance, as Lionel Messi had injured a thigh muscle during the second leg of the match with Chelsea and had not been able to play since. Rijkaard included the talented Argentinian in the 22-man squad he announced for the final. As it turned out, Messi missed the match.

There was much discussion in the media and among fans whether Wenger would pick Reyes over Pirès, who would be playing his last game for Arsenal, having agreed to join Villarreal for the 2006/07 season after rejecting a one-year rolling contract. In the end, the Frenchman, who had started only two of the previous eight games, was selected and Reyes relegated to the bench, although between them they would spend less than half an hour on the pitch.

There was official controversy even before the match kicked off when it was revealed that Ole Hermann Borgan, one of the linesmen, had posed for the Norwegian newspaper *Drammens Tidende* wearing a Barcelona shirt. After appearing to stick by him, and despite the support of referee Terje Hauge, UEFA caved in and replaced him with fellow Norwegian Arild Sundet. 'It was both insensitive and stupid of me. I did not think deeply enough about the situation and the consequences when I was asked to dress up in the shirt,' Borgan said.

The Spanish giants went for a 4–3–3 formation, while Wenger chose a 4–5–1 arrangement with Henry as the lone striker. Arsenal made some defensive changes. For the first time since the second match of the competition the previous September, Arsenal fielded their two current England internationals – Sol Campbell and Ashley Cole, who returned at left-back, making only his third appearance in the competition because of injury. At right-back, Emmanuel Eboué replaced the injured Lauren.

Arsenal played in their change strip of yellow shirts, which had seen them win cup finals in 1950, 1971 and 1979 but lose in 1969, 1978, 1980 (twice) and 2000. Referee Hauge tossed the coin, Arsenal won the decision, and Henry chose which side to attack, meaning Barcelona would kick off.

It was the Gunners who had the first scoring opportunity as, at the two and a half minute mark, Thierry Henry, on the edge of the Barcelona six-yard box, received a cross from Eboué but shot straight at goalkeeper Víctor Valdés, who conceded a corner. Valdés was furious that he had been left undefended. Henry took the corner and, in a move with Pirès, had a crack from outside the area, which almost opened Arsenal's account. Only a punt away by Valdés kept the score at 0–0.

Arsenal had much of the opening play and should have been in the lead. Barcelona's first proper attack came in the seventh minute, when Lehmann saved from Ludovic Giuly after he shot from a narrow angle. In the 11th minute, Barcelona were awarded a free kick 35 yards from goal, but Ronaldinho subsequently shot wide.

Then, in the 18th minute, disaster struck for the north London side. Barcelona attacked after Hleb lost the ball on the halfway line to Samuel Eto'o. Ronaldinho played the ball through to his Cameroonian team-mate, who only had Lehmann to beat. The German rushed out and brought down Eto'o outside the box as the ball bobbled to Ludovic Giuly, who put the ball into the back of the Arsenal net.

Confusion reigned as referee Hauge was surrounded first by Arsenal players, then Barcelona ones. Then, after what seemed an age, the man in black reached into his back pocket and produced a red card for the Arsenal goalkeeper, the first man to be sent off in a European Cup Final. Commentating for Sky, Andy Gray expressed confusion at Mr Hauge's decision: 'I've no idea what the referee is doing here. Let play go. 1–0 Barcelona. Game carries on. Oh dear, you cannot believe it. I have no idea what this referee was doing.'

Jens Lehmann took more than 40 seconds to leave the pitch as a disbelieving Manuel Almunia, who had not played a game in four months, put on his grey jersey over his singlet, with van Persie standing to encourage his team-mate. As Almunia stood on the touchline to go on, Lehmann came up behind him to wish him good luck. The two keepers had rarely seen eye to eye during their time at Highbury. Wenger pulled off Pirès for his reserve goalie to come on.

Ronaldinho took the free kick and hit it wide. The sending-off seemed to encourage the Spaniards, and the game became more physical. In the 22nd minute, Eboué went into the referee's notebook for a high tackle on former Gunner Giovanni van Bronckhorst, whose shirt bore the name 'Gio', presumably because the manufacturers could not fit 'van Bronckhorst' on the back.

By the 36th minute, Barcelona had had 59 per cent of possession. Then Eboué made a run down the right flank and was brought down by Carles Puyol, Barcelona's extravagantly haired captain. Henry took the free kick, and Campbell rose above the Catalans and headed the ball into the right-hand side of the net to give the Gunners the lead. In the second minute of the four added for stoppage time, Eto'o came close to equalising for Barcelona, but Almunia made a brilliant save to push the shot on to his right post. The half ended with Arsenal in the lead 1–0 against all the odds.

Arsenal kicked off the second half. Barcelona had brought on Andrés Iniesta for the more defensively minded Edmílson. The change seemed to make sense, for, after eight minutes of play, Iniesta forced an excellent save by Almunia. In the 51st minute, the Arsenal captain performed a perfect sliding tackle on Mark van Bommel, only for referee Hauge to show Henry a yellow card. Henry was amazed by the decision, as van Bommel had kicked him; Wenger was furious, remonstrating with fourth official Tom Henning Øvrebø, and having to be ordered back to his technical area.

In the 55th minute, Ronaldinho was brought down on the edge of the Arsenal box. His free kick was hit into the Arsenal wall, and he hit the rebound into Eto'o for an Arsenal goal kick. As the rain poured down, Barcelona attacked more and more. In the 63rd minute, Hleb almost made it two for Arsenal but his shot went wide.

Despite the disparity in men and the weather, Arsenal pushed forward, and Henry and Freddie Ljungberg both saw shots saved – Henry's when he was clear with only the goalkeeper to beat. Disaster struck when Iniesta passed to Henrik Larsson (on for van Bommel), who put the ball through to Eto'o, who easily beat Almunia at the near post to level the scores – although some believed that the Cameroonian was offside.

As the rain fell more heavily, Arsenal's limbs began to feel heavier. Then, with 80 minutes on the clock, Juliano Belletti scored the goal that finally broke Arsenal hearts. The ball went through Almunia's legs, hitting his right calf and going into the net. Commentator Andy Gray said, 'It's probably going wide if it doesn't hit Almunia's leg.'

Arsenal could not find the strength to come back, and Barcelona took their second European Cup title. After the match, Henry said, 'I think we can be proud of ourselves, more than proud. I don't want to start any arguments but I don't know if the referee had a Barcelona shirt on or something. They kicked me all over the place in the first half and … I got a yellow card. Maybe they are not used to the speed of the Premiership but I thought that was harsh. After Jens, I am sorry but the ref did not want us to win it … Some calls in the game were a bit strange. Next time I may learn how to dive. They tried to kick me in my knee, kick my ankle from behind, but I am not a woman, so I will stay on my feet. I expected the referee to do his job but I don't think he did. No disrespect to Barcelona but we were the better team when it was eleven v eleven.

'People always talk about Ronaldinho, Eto'o, Giuly and everything, but I didn't see them today, I saw Henrik Larsson. He came on, he changed the game, that is what killed the game. Sometimes you talk about Ronaldinho and Eto'o and people like that; you need to talk about the proper footballer who made the difference, and that was Henrik Larsson tonight. I would like to have seen a proper ref also.'

Barcelona captain Carles Puyol was presented with the trophy by UEFA president Lennart Johansson. The attention after the match centred on the decision to send off Arsenal's goalie. Mark Lawrenson said, 'The game changed when Arsenal goalkeeper Jens Lehmann was sent off,' and Wenger commented, 'When Jens Lehmann got sent off, that left us with 70 minutes to play with ten against eleven, against a team that retains the ball very well.'

Van Bronckhorst said, 'It's special to win the final, and even more special to do it against your old team.'

It was Larsson's last game for the Catalan giants. 'I want to play football,' he said. 'I feel I haven't played as much as I would love to because of the great players we have at Barcelona.' He rejoined his former club Helsingborg.

Larsson was not the only one leaving his club after the match. There was much speculation that Henry would be leaving Highbury for Barcelona at the end of the season. On 19 May, Henry signed a four-year contract with Arsenal – although it was a deal that he would not see out.

Another who would sign a deal he would not see out was Reyes. After the 2005 FA Cup Final (see page 167), there was conjecture that the talented young Spaniard would leave for Real Madrid. However, in July he signed a new six-year contract and said that he was 'looking forward to having many more successful years at the club'.

In August 2006, he asked Wenger not to select him for the Champions League qualifying match against Dinamo Zagreb as he would be cup-tied for the competition. Wenger left him out of the team. Before the transfer window closed, Reyes went off on a season-long loan to Real Madrid and Júlio 'The Beast' Baptista arrived at Arsenal from the Spanish club in return.

Speaking to a Norwegian newspaper, referee Terje Hauge said that he was pleased with his overall performance – but, regarding the Lehmann red card, 'I would have liked to have taken a few more seconds before I made a decision. If I'd done that, I could have given a goal and given a yellow card as well.

'Under other circumstances I would perhaps have done something different with Lehmann, but this mostly rested on the positioning in relation to the situation.

'Everything happens quickly on the pitch and for me it looked as if there was physical contact.

'As well as that it happened in the linesman's working area and I had no reason to doubt him in this instance.

'It was obviously a big game for Arsenal, and to lose is a huge disappointment so I understand their frustration. But we'll have to give it a few days so we can discuss this more sensibly.'

FIFA president Sepp Blatter told Radio Five Live: 'My opinion is that, when in certain actions – and not only in front of the goalmouth, but everywhere – he should let the advantage, finish the action and then he can come back and whistle.

'He was too fast.'

Liverpool 3 Arsenal 6

Football League Cup fifth round. Tuesday 9 January 2007, kick-off 7.45pm
Venue: Anfield, Liverpool, L4 0TH
Liverpool: All red
Arsenal: Yellow shirts, black shorts and stockings
Referee: Martin Atkinson (Bradford)
Attendance: 42,614

Liverpool	Arsenal
1 Jerzy Dudek	24 Manuel Almunia
4 Sami Hyypiä	20 Johan Djourou
29 Gabriel Paletta	31 Justin Hoyte
12 Fábio Aurélio	15 Denílson
37 Lee Peltier	5 Kolo Touré (captain)
28 Stephen Warnock (Alonso, 58 minutes)	45 Armand Traoré (Connolly, 88 minutes)
8 Steven Gerrard (captain)	4 Cesc Fàbregas
11 Mark González (García, 11 minutes) (Carragher, 75 minutes)	17 Alex Song
	9 Júlio Baptista
9 Robbie Fowler	32 Theo Walcott (Diaby, 74 minutes)
17 Craig Bellamy	30 Jérémie Aliadière
35 Danny Guthrie	
Substitutes	*Substitutes*
25 Pepe Reina	21 Mart Poom
23 Jamie Carragher	40 Henri Lansbury
14 Xabi Alonso	43 Mark Randall
10 Luis García	2 Abou Diaby
15 Peter Crouch	33 Matthew Connolly
Manager: Rafael Benítez	*Manager:* Arsène Wenger
Scorers: Fowler 33 minutes; Gerrard 68 minutes; Hyypiä 80 minutes	*Scorers:* Aliadière 27 minutes; Baptista 40 minutes, 45 minutes, 60 minutes, 84 minutes; Song 44 minutes
	Booking: Song

ARSÈNE Wenger would be the first to admit that he does not take the League Cup especially seriously. This is apparent by the teams he fields for the competition – he bloods kids, but most of them never progress to the first team.

In the 2006/07 League Cup, Arsenal were drawn away in the third and fourth rounds, to West Bromwich Albion and Everton, and won 2–0 and 1–0 respectively.

For the fifth round on 19 December 2006, Arsenal were selected to return to Merseyside to face the red half of the region.

Then Martin Atkinson, the referee, postponed the match due to heavy fog, a decision that angered both managers. Rafa Benítez said, 'There were a lot of people looking forward to the game and it's really difficult to explain.'

A slot was found three weeks later, and the two teams finally ran out. Both managers fielded weakened sides.

Three days earlier, the two teams had met in the FA Cup at Anfield, with Arsenal running out 3–1 winners. Wenger made wholesale changes from that side. In came Cesc Fàbregas, Júlio Baptista, Denílson, Alex Song, Johan Djourou, Jérémie Aliadière, Justin Hoyte, Armand Traoré and Theo Walcott. Manuel Almunia kept his place in goal, while Touré took on the captain's duties for the first time in the absence of Thierry Henry and Gilberto. For Liverpool, only Stevie Gerrard and Jerzy Dudek survived from the cup-losing team. Lee Peltier and Gabriel Paletta were particularly vulnerable in defence, and it showed.

Arsenal started as they meant to go on, and a Kolo Touré pass set up Jérémie Aliadière to score goal number one on 27 minutes. He took two attempts to get it past Dudek, but showed determination to succeed.

Robbie Fowler pulled one back for Liverpool after Luis García had crossed the ball in the six-yard box from Fábio Aurélio's free kick, but Arsenal were in no mood to surrender, and Baptista hit two and Song one to make the score 4–1 to the Gunners at half-time. Firstly, Baptista curled home a free kick from 25 yards for only his second Arsenal goal and first in domestic football. Song sank the third after getting a ricochet off Hyypiä, before Mr Atkinson decided that Aliadière was onside when he pulled back for Baptista, who slid the ball into an empty net to make it four.

Into the second half, and in the 56th minute Dudek saved a Baptista penalty after Sami Hyypiä had clearly brought down Aliadière; but the Beast still scored two more.

Consolation goals came from Gerrard and that man Hyypiä. Liverpool's woes were consolidated by the loss of Mark González after 11 minutes, replaced by Luis García. On four minutes, González slid into what appeared to be an innocuous tackle and screamed in agony. The trainer used the magic sponge on him for six minutes before he was taken to hospital with a suspected broken tibia, which turned out only to be a six-inch gash and serious bruising. García, too, was stretchered off and replaced by Jamie Carragher after 75 minutes.

Wenger withdrew Walcott and sent on Abou Diaby after he had spent eight months on the sidelines with a fractured and dislocated ankle. Although he seemed to come through the match without incident, Diaby's career would be plagued by injury and he was released by Arsenal on 10 June 2015.

In his match report for *The Guardian*, Daniel Taylor praised Arsenal's youngsters, 'The difference between the two teams was immense. Arsenal played with flair and purpose; Liverpool were dishevelled and short of leadership.'

It was the first time in nearly 80 years that Liverpool had conceded six goals at home (the last time was in the First Division on 19 April 1930, when they lost 6–0 to Sunderland) and Arsenal's first League Cup win at Anfield.

Baptista became the first visiting player to score four goals at Anfield since Dennis Westcott of Wolverhampton Wanderers on 7 December 1946, when Wolves won 5–1 in a First Division meeting.

The match set up a semi-final clash with Tottenham Hotspur. Arsenal beat their deadly rivals and went through to the final against Chelsea. As was and is his wont, Wenger played youngsters and threw away the possibility of taking the only domestic trophy he has yet to win.

Arsenal 2 Barcelona 1

European Champions League group of 16, first leg. Wednesday 16 February 2011, kick-off 7.45pm
Venue: Ashburton Grove, Hornsey Road, London N7 7AJ
Arsenal: Red shirts with white sleeves and red trim, white shorts and stockings
Barcelona: Pale green shirts, black shorts, pale green stockings with black stripe at top
Referee: Nicola Rizzoli (Mirandola, Italy)
Attendance: 59,927

Arsenal	Barcelona
53 Wojciech Szczęsny	1 Víctor Valdés
27 Emmanuel Eboué	2 Dani Alves
22 Gaël Clichy	19 Maxwell
17 Alex Song (Arshavin, 68 minutes)	6 Xavi Hernández (captain)
6 Laurent Koscielny	3 Gerard Piqué
20 Johan Djourou	22 Éric Abidal
19 Jack Wilshere	16 Sergio Busquets
14 Theo Walcott (Bendtner, 77 minutes)	17 Pedro Rodríguez
10 Robin van Persie	10 Lionel Messi
4 Cesc Fàbregas (captain)	7 David Villa (Keita, 68 minutes)
8 Samir Nasri	8 Andrés Iniesta (Adriano, 89 minutes)
Substitutes	*Substitutes*
1 Manuel Almunia	13 José Manuel Pinto
18 Sébastien Squillaci	18 Gabriel Milito
28 Kieran Gibbs	21 Adriano Correia
7 Tomáš Rosický	14 Javier Mascherano
15 Denílson	15 Seydou Keita
23 Andrei Arshavin	20 Ibrahim Afellay
52 Nicklas Bendtner	9 Bojan
Manager: Arsène Wenger	*Head coach:* Pep Guardiola
Scorers: Van Persie 78 minutes; Arshavin 83 minutes	*Scorer:* Villa 26 minutes
Bookings: Nasri, Song, Arshavin, van Persie	*Bookings:* Iniesta, Piqué

REGARDED by many as the pinnacle of achievements at the Emirates – until an Arsenal captain parades the Premier League or Champions League trophy around the ground, that is, Arsène Wenger said, 'It was unusual for us to go into a home game as the underdogs, but it took a bit of the pressure off. But we had a huge desire to win and viewed it as a good opportunity to show we were a different team to the previous year.'

As the fans entered the ground, they found small red and white flags had been placed on their seats, prompting one wag to say, 'It's all very Last Night of the Proms.'

David Villa and Lionel Messi kicked off for Barcelona and began to pass the ball around. Then Robin van Persie got the ball from a poor pass between Dani Alves and Gerard Piqué, but as he began to head towards the Barcelona goal, referee Nicola Rizzoli blew his whistle to award Arsenal a free kick rather than playing the advantage. Samir

Nasri took the free kick, which was missed by the Barcelona defence, but no Arsenal attacker could get on the end of it and it bounced easily into the arms of Víctor Valdés.

On six minutes, Valdés was called upon to make an excellent stop from van Persie. The goalie parried the ball and his defence cleared their lines and created an attack, which was brought to an end by Alex Song with a cynical tackle that resulted in him receiving a yellow card.

The attacks seemed to have given Arsenal an impetus, and they gained confidence. But then, on the quarter-hour mark, Messi missed a sitter. With an elegant feint he put Wojciech Szczęsny on the ground, but he then chipped the ball inches wide from five yards.

Barcelona quickly gained the upper hand and kept the ball away from Arsenal, and it was only a matter of time before the Catalans gained the upper hand. In the 26th minute, Johan Djourou and Laurent Koscielny pushed out to catch Villa offside but forgot to tell Gaël Clichy their plan, and he played the Barcelonan onside to roll it under Szczęsny. Nasri was unhappy with the situation and went into the referee's notebook for his troubles.

A minute later, Barcelona and that man Villa almost doubled their lead, but Szczęsny saved at the feet of the forward. Again, the Spaniards kept possession, taunting the Gunners. Then, after Szczęsny saved from Pedro Rodríguez, Messi nodded into the net. Fortunately, the linesman saw that the Argentinian was offside and the goal was ruled out.

When Arsenal got possession, they mostly found themselves surrounded by pale green shirts. Signor Rizzoli blew for half-time with the Spaniards leading by a solitary goal.

Arsène Wenger recalled, 'At half-time I told them it was important to keep their belief and push more on certain players because we gave them a bit too much room in the first half. I felt we could change the game, we had to remember the previous season when we came back in the last 20 minutes.'

As the second half began, Arsenal made a strong start, but Jack Wilshere's shot from 20 yards did not trouble Valdés. On 52 minutes, Song bravely dived in to tackle Messi. One miscalculation and the Arsenal man would have seen red. Six minutes later, Piqué went into Signor Rizzoli's book after bringing down Fàbregas and was banned for the second leg. Messi went close to making it two. Andrés Iniesta slipped the ball through to Messi and the Argentinian put the ball under the approaching Szczęsny but into the side netting.

On the 68th minute, Wenger and Pep Guardiola both made substitutions: the holding midfielder, Song, went off, and the creative Andrei Arshavin came on. For the Catalans, Villa went off and Seydou Keita on. Four minutes later and Messi accidentally kicked Koscielny in the face; the Arsenal fans screamed for the referee to produce a card. Wenger made another substitution, replacing the at times ineffectual Theo Walcott with Nicklas Bendtner, a striker with a very high opinion of his own abilities.

Arsenal's Dutch forward, van Persie, had also not had a great game, but then he scored. Clichy set him off and then, almost from the byline, when it looked as though he would cross, van Persie shot and the ball slipped inside Valdés's near post and into the net.

Five minutes later, Cesc Fàbregas passed through to Nasri on the right, who approached the Barcelona goal. With the goal facing him, Nasri passed across the box to Arshavin, who banged a fine shot into the net from 18 yards.

The Catalans tried to find a way back in but without success, and Arsenal recorded their first victory over Barcelona.

Cesc Fàbregas said, 'It was one of those games that don't come round very often, so when they do you just want to go for it. We knew we had to play with no fear even though we were facing the best team in the world, maybe even the best team in history.

'First of all [this time] we don't have five or six injured players. Second, we are all one year older, we have closed the gap on them. We are 23, 24, 25, 26 years old – mature enough to play big games. We showed it here but if we don't show it in the Camp Nou it's nothing to us. It's just one game – it's a nice compliment to us, that's all.

'They are the best side in football's history, in my opinion, [but] the tie is 90 minutes and we've only played 45 [minutes]. It gives confidence to the team.'

Jack Wilshere opined, 'Before the Wolves game [four days ago] all the boys had been saying, "Don't think about Wednesday," but it was hard at times. We knew we had to get in their faces, be a bit nasty and stop them playing.'

Wenger said of the second leg, 'We are not favourites. We believe we have a chance. Barcelona are still favourites and we know tonight that we can beat them – which we did not know last year.'

Arsenal had drawn at home and been walloped 4–1 in the second leg of the previous season's Champions League quarter-final, which finished 6–3 to Barcelona on aggregate.

'We were not only strong on the physical side but on the mental side; we kept resilient,' Wenger said. 'We took advantage of one special piece of skill from van Persie [for the equaliser] and that goal and the second was after some good build-up play.

'Tonight's result gives us a chance to go to Barcelona with belief. It is a special lift for my team. Our players have shown exceptional strength tonight, and togetherness. This will enforce that. I am proud for Arsenal Football Club. Everyone urged us to play differently to our nature so it is good. I believe this can strengthen the belief in our philosophy. We know it will be a very difficult game [in Spain] but we will prepare well. We will be highly focused and we go to win our game. We will go for it.

'We suffered for some periods in the game but we never gave up and stayed mentally strong. You're always on the border of collapsing against them; if you give just a bit mentally you will be punished. The team wanted to go as long as they could.

'I am highly delighted because it was a special night. The game promised a lot and absolutely fulfilled the promises between two exceptional football teams who always try to play.'

Guardiola said, 'We created more chances than last year. It's a pity, but we knew they're a very, very good team. On the counter-attack they're dangerous. But we have the second leg. They are a tough, tough team, but we dominated and more or less took control of the game. It was more or less the same as last season.'

Van Persie said Barcelona had lost because the Gunners took the contest to them. 'In my opinion, and in our opinion, if you drop back too much they are so good they will in the end beat you by far. We had to beat them in their own style. We got a bit lucky but it was a fantastic win.'

Xavi said, 'The team made significant errors, but played good football. All we lacked was the finishing touch. We didn't convert our endless opportunities. The match was up for the taking, but we failed to win.'

His team-mate Villa said, 'We played a good game and created a lot of chances. But we were up against a great team in Arsenal who caught us on two counter-attacks and hurt us.'

Unfortunately, Arsenal were not able to withstand the pressure of the Camp Nou and lost 3–1. Barcelona went on to win the final (played at Wembley), beating Manchester United by the same score.

Reading 5 Arsenal 7 (aet)

Football League Cup Fourth Round. Tuesday 30 October 2012, kick-off 7.45pm
Venue: Madejski Stadium, Junction 11, M4, Reading, Berkshire RG2 0FL
Reading: White shirts, two blue hoops, blue sleeves, blue shorts, white stockings with two blue hoops
Arsenal: Red shirts, white sleeves with red and blue stripe on bicep, white shorts, red stockings with white hoop
Referee: Kevin Friend (Leicester)
Attendance: 23,980

Reading	Arsenal
1 Adam Federici	36 Emi Martínez
2 Chris Gunter	25 Carl Jenkinson
3 Nicky Shorey	20 Johan Djourou (captain)
15 Sean Morrison	23 Andrei Arshavin
17 Kaspars Gorkšs (captain)	54 Ignasi Miquel (Meade, 105 minutes)
12 Garath McCleary (McAnuff, 73 minutes)	6 Laurent Koscielny
8 Mikele Leigertwood	26 Emmanuel Frimpong (Giroud, 62 minutes)
16 Jay Tabb	22 Francis Coquelin
19 Hal Robson-Kanu	14 Theo Walcott
33 Jason Roberts (Church, 90 minutes)	29 Marouane Chamakh
10 Noel Hunt (Pogrebnyak, 73 minutes)	47 Serge Gnabry (Eisfeld, 62 minutes)
Substitutes	*Substitutes*
41 Stuart Taylor	60 James Shea
5 Alex Pearce	18 Sébastien Squillaci
11 Jobi McAnuff	53 Jernade Meade
9 Adam Le Fondre	40 Héctor Bellerín
23 Ian Harte	64 Nico Yennaris
18 Simon Church	46 Thomas Eisfeld
7 Pavel Pogrebnyak	12 Olivier Giroud
Manager: Brian McDermott	*Manager:* Arsène Wenger
Scorers: Roberts 12 minutes; Koscielny 18 minutes (o.g.); Leigertwood 20 minutes; Hunt 37 minutes; Pogrebnyak 116 minutes	*Scorers:* Walcott 45+2 minutes, 90+6 minutes, 120+1 minutes; Giroud 64 minutes; Koscielny 89 minutes; Chamakh 103 minutes, 120+3 minutes
Bookings: Leigertwood, Morrison	*Bookings:* Miguel, Chamakh, Giroud, Koscielny, Martínez, Eisfeld

I
T would be fair to say that, like many Premier League managers, Arsène Wenger does not take the League Cup too seriously. He bloods kids among a few senior professionals, and, although he professes to want to win every game, he never seems too disappointed when Arsenal's run in the League Cup comes to an end, as it inevitably does.

The one season (2010/11) that Wenger did seem to want to win the competition and played a strong team ended in disaster at Wembley on 27 February 2011. By the time the final came around, Wenger was under pressure, with the club not having won a trophy since beating Manchester United in the FA Cup in 2005 (see page 167). It seemed that all Arsenal had to do to beat Birmingham City was turn up. As is often the case, the footballing gods had other ideas, and a mix-up between goalkeeper Wojciech Szczęsny and centre-back Laurent

Koscielny in the 89th minute sent the trophy to the Midlands. The League Cup remains the one domestic trophy Wenger has yet to win.

Having comprehensively walloped Coventry City 6–1 in the third round, Wenger put out a weakened team against Reading, managed by ex-Gunner Brian McDermott and with former Arsenal goalie Stuart Taylor on the subs' bench. Arsenal had narrowly beaten Queens Park Rangers 1–0 the previous Saturday in the league, and Wenger made 11 changes from that side. Arsenal and Reading had met nine times previously in all competitions, and the Gunners had never lost. Would this match be different?

The game started at a pace, with six corners in the first 11 minutes, and third-choice goalie Emi Martínez kept busy defending his area. But the pressure from Reading had to tell, and on the 12th minute Jason Roberts opened the Royals' account. After Andrei Arshavin gave away the ball to Noel Hunt, he played it to Hal Robson-Kanu on the left, who crossed to 33-year-old Roberts. He shook off Koscielny and gave the yellow-shirted Martínez no chance from inside the six-yard box.

Arsenal started slowly and worsened, as they seemed to be a team with no fizz and little idea. It was not surprising that Reading began to further assert their superiority. In the 18th minute, Chris Gunter crossed from the byline and Koscielny put the ball past Martínez to make it 2–0 to the home side.

Just two minutes later, Reading increased their count when Mikele Leigertwood shot from just inside the area and Martínez was unable to keep the ball out of his own net. At the Arsenal Annual General Meeting the previous week, Wenger had made it clear that the League Cup was fifth on his list of priorities. From what they had seen so far in the match, the travelling fans had no reason to disbelieve Wenger's assurance.

As the half-hour mark appeared, Arsenal finally began to move the ball around, but Reading's defence held firm. With eight minutes to go to half-time, Hunt headed home to make it 4–0 to Reading. Marouane Chamakh, who was making his first start for Arsenal since January, had been bundled off the ball and appealed for a foul that referee Kevin Friend did not give, as Reading broke.

On the 43rd minute, Chamakh managed a shot on target but Adam Federici was more than equal to the task of stopping it. The fourth official signalled two minutes of stoppage time, and just as Mr Friend was about to call a halt to the first half, Arshavin passed to Theo Walcott, who chipped the ball over the advancing Federici to make it 4–1.

As the second period began, there was almost another own goal disaster for Arsenal. Martínez pushed away Hunt's header before Ignasi Miquel nearly headed it into his own net. Chamakh brought down Hunt in the box, but Mr Friend waved away calls for a penalty. On the 49th minute, the ball was again in Arsenal's goal but Sean Morrison was adjudged to have fouled Martínez.

Seven minutes after the restart, Roberts hit the ball over the bar from 15 yards, and at the other end Walcott hit Federici's upright. Two minutes later, Gunter handled in the box but Mr Friend did not give the penalty, though he did show a yellow card to Chamakh, who protested a little too long and a little too loudly at the linesman for the referee's liking.

After 62 minutes, Wenger made a double substitution, bringing on Olivier Giroud for Emmanuel Frimpong and giving Thomas Eisfeld his first-team debut in place of fellow German Serge Gnabry. It also turned out to be Eisfeld's only appearance that season.

After being on the pitch for just three minutes, Giroud did what he would become known for four or five years later and scored after coming off the bench. The Frenchman headed Walcott's corner past Federici to make it 4–2. Reading were beginning to show why they sat in the Premier League relegation zone without any wins. On the 70th minute, Leigertwood went into Mr Friend's notebook after a sliding tackle on Eisfeld. From the free kick, Walcott shot over the bar. Two minutes later, Giroud nearly had his second as he forced the Reading goalie to palm away his 20-yard shot.

Arsenal continued to push, and Federici had to be at his best to stop a Giroud diving header before the Arsenal man was shown a yellow card for a late challenge. With just minutes to go, Arsenal played four up front, which left their defence vulnerable, and Koscielny was booked for a cynical tackle on Roberts.

Koscielny was all over the match – a first-half own goal, then a trip into the referee's notebook, and with one minute of normal time left, he scored Arsenal's third from a corner from six yards out.

Four minutes into stoppage time, Brian McDermott pulled off Roberts and sent on Simon Church in a bid to run down the final few seconds. It was not enough, as two minutes later Walcott scored his second and Arsenal's equaliser. The players went mad, with Giroud throwing his shirt into the crowd before realising he still needed it.

In the first five minutes of extra time, Arsenal had two great chances, but their execution was poor – Eisfeld made a hash of a slickly executed move before Arshavin hit the ball into the crowd. Chamakh then gave Arsenal the lead for the first time in the match, hitting the ball through Gorkšs's legs and into the bottom corner.

With the second period of extra time underway, Walcott almost scored his fourth, but Federici was equal to the task. Unbelievably, Martínez tried a little time-wasting. Three minutes into the period, Johan Djourou brought down substitute Church to give the Royals a free kick. Nicky Shorey took the kick, and Morrison was on the other end to force a save by Martínez, although it turned out that Morrison was offside. Two minutes after that excitement, Morrison went into the referee's book for a bad foul on Jernade Meade. Nine minutes into the second period and the Arsenal goalie again tried some time-wasting, this time receiving a yellow card for his troubles.

In the 115th minute of the match, Pavel Pogrebnyak headed the tenth goal of the game to make it level at 5–5 and seemingly set up a penalty shoot-out. The Arsenal defenders appealed for offside, but Mr Friend was having none of it and the goal stood.

Eisfeld became the sixth Arsenal player to be booked, before Giroud sent the ball wide. The fourth official signalled two minutes of additional time. In the first, Arshavin went on a run down the left before crossing it, and, after a goalmouth scramble, Walcott put it in the back of the net from three yards. In the following minute, Gunter missed a simple header and put Chamakh through with only goalkeeper Federici to beat, which he did easily with a cool lob.

McDermott said, 'It was kamikaze football. It was extraordinary. It's the worst defeat of my career. It is embarrassing but we have to take it on the chin and move on. It's hard to take positives but we have to.'

The Reading manager was unhappy with the decision to add extra time to the extra time. 'Obviously it doesn't help that the referee added two minutes on to the four minutes of injury time to make it six,' he said. 'You can't tell the time as wrong as that, but he did.'

He added: 'I wasn't comfortable at 4–1. I don't know why, I just wasn't. We had to go in at 4–0. That gave them impetus they didn't need. It was suicide what went on in that second half and extra time.

'At full time nothing needed to be said to the players. Sometimes the less said the better. We know what happened.'

In a burst of optimism, Walcott said, 'That wasn't the real Arsenal in the first half, but we showed our character. Hopefully we can take that into the Premier League now.'

The brace of goals did not help Chamakh. He went on loan to West Ham United on 4 January 2013 until the end of that season. He said, 'I didn't have opportunities to play recently, but I did well before and I know I am a very good striker. We played only one striker at Arsenal, so I didn't play a lot, so I hope to do so more with West Ham.' He played just three games for the Hammers and never made the score sheet. On 10 August, Chamakh left the Emirates for Crystal Palace.

McDermott could not halt Reading's slide and was sacked on 19 March 2013. The club was relegated after just one season in the top tier. McDermott returned to the Madejski Stadium for a second managerial stint on 17 December 2015 but was sacked again on 27 May 2016.

Arsenal 5 Tottenham Hotspur 2

FA Premier League. Saturday 17 November 2012, kick-off 12.45pm
Venue: Emirates Stadium, Hornsey Road, London N7 7AJ
Arsenal: Red shirts, white sleeves with red and blue stripe on bicep, white shorts, white stockings with red and blue hoop mid-calf
Tottenham Hotspur: Black and grey halved shirts, black shorts, black stockings with yellow stripe at top
Referee: Howard Webb (West Riding of Yorkshire)
Attendance: 60,111

Arsenal	Tottenham Hotspur
1 Wojciech Szczęsny	25 Hugo Lloris
6 Laurent Koscielny	28 Kyle Walker (Dawson, 46 minutes)
3 Bacary Sagna	16 Kyle Naughton (Dempsey, 46 minutes)
8 Mikel Arteta	11 Gareth Bale
5 Thomas Vermaelen (captain)	13 William Gallas (captain)
4 Per Mertesacker	6 Tom Huddlestone (Carroll, 72 minutes)
19 Santi Cazorla	5 Jan Vertonghen
12 Olivier Giroud (Oxlade-Chamberlain, 86 minutes)	7 Aaron Lennon
9 Lukas Podolski (Santos, 80 minutes)	30 Sandro
14 Theo Walcott	10 Emmanuel Adebayor
10 Jack Wilshere (Ramsey, 72 minutes)	18 Jermain Defoe
Substitutes	*Substitutes*
24 Vito Mannone	24 Brad Friedel
11 André Santos	20 Michael Dawson
25 Carl Jenkinson	29 Jake Livermore
22 Francis Coquelin	46 Tom Carroll
15 Alex Oxlade-Chamberlain	22 Gylfi Sigurðsson
16 Aaron Ramsey	31 Andros Townsend
23 Andrei Arshavin	2 Clint Dempsey
Manager: Arsène Wenger	*Head coach:* André Villas-Boas
Scorers: Mertesacker 24 minutes; Podolski 42 minutes; Giroud 45+1 minutes; Cazorla 60 minutes; Walcott 90+1 minutes	*Scorers:* Adebayor 10 minutes; Bale 71 minutes
	Bookings: Lennon, Sandro
Booking: Podolski	*Sending-off:* Adebayor

I T seemed that 2012 was the year when Arsenal enjoyed putting five past their closest rivals. In the Premier League on 26 February, Arsenal beat Spurs 5–2. What made that first match all the more satisfying was that at one stage Spurs were two goals to the good and looked to be on course for the first back-to-back league wins at the home of their arch-rivals for 86 years – they came from 2–0 down to win 3–2 in 2011 despite having Scott Parker sent off late on. A goal from Louis Saha and Emmanuel Adebayor's penalty put Spurs in the driving seat. Then, in a span of 27 minutes, Arsenal hit five goals.

With a 4–0 thrashing by AC Milan in Italy and an FA Cup exit at the hands of Sunderland, Arsenal had their pride to play for. Bacary Sagna's header and a world-class shot from Robin van Persie put Arsenal on equal terms before half-time. Tomáš Rosický gave Arsenal the lead just after the resumption, and a brace from Theo Walcott completed the rout.

The result still left Arsenal in fourth, seven points behind Spurs in third and trailing leaders Manchester City by 17 points. The season ended with Arsenal pipping Spurs to third place by one point and Spurs manager Harry Redknapp being sacked.

Fast forward nine months to the Emirates and the two teams prepared to do battle again. Spurs had appointed the youthful Portuguese sacked by Chelsea, André Villas-Boas, to manage the club. In the week leading up to the fixture, Spurs chairman Daniel Levy had constantly impressed upon Villas-Boas how vital, how important it was to beat Arsenal at the Emirates.

Villas-Boas picked Jermain Defoe and former Arsenal player Emmanuel Adebayor as a two-pronged strike force. Spurs' crocked players included Mousa Dembélé (hip injury), Scott Parker (Achilles), Benoit Assou-Ekotto and Younes Kaboul (both knee).

For Arsenal, Wenger was without Gervinho (ankle), Kieran Gibbs (thigh), midfielder Abou Diaby (thigh) and Rosický (hamstring). A number of players – Olivier Giroud (hamstring/calf), Walcott (buttock muscle), Mikel Arteta (hip), Sagna (leg) and Wojciech Szczęsny – all passed last-minute fitness tests. Jack Wilshere was available again after completing his suspension.

After nine minutes, referee Howard Webb awarded a free kick on the right-hand side to Spurs. Gareth Bale took it, but the ball did not seem to have much power behind it. Giroud headed it directly at Tom Huddlestone, who shot, and the ball deflected to William Gallas, who put the ball past Szczęsny – back after a two-month injury layoff – but the defender was offside.

A minute later, and Arsenal left a huge gap in defence. Jan Vertonghen was allowed to stride forward and found Defoe, left alone by Per Mertesacker and Bacary Sagna. Szczęsny was able to save Defoe's shot, but not the follow-up from Adebayor who opened Spurs' account. Breaking (again) the convention that you do not celebrate goals against former clubs, the Togolese striker jumped over the advertising hoardings and performed an odd dance, much to the annoyance of the Emirates faithful.

Spurs sensed blood, and Aaron Lennon shot just wide from a Bale pass. The Arsenal defence looked shaky in the face of attacks by the men in the horrible black and grey shirts.

Then it all changed. Adebayor went in for a lunge on Santi Cazorla studs up, both feet off the ground, and caught the Spaniard's ankle about a foot in the air. Mr Webb flourished a red card, and Adebayor was ready for his early bath as both sets of players rounded on each other.

Six minutes later, Mertesacker made up for his earlier error by getting on the end of a Walcott cross and putting the ball beyond the reach of Hugo Lloris. Three minutes before half-time, Lukas Podolski gave Arsenal the lead when his shot ricocheted off Gallas, leaving Lloris in no man's land. Just before half-time, Giroud added to Tottenham's woes when he met a cross from Cazorla and slid it past Lloris.

At half-time, Villas-Boas, in charge of his first north London derby, sent on Clint Dempsey and Michael Dawson for full-backs Kyle Walker and Kyle Naughton.

On the hour mark, Giroud headed a pass to Walcott, who sent it wide to Podolski on the left, who crossed low; and Cazorla tapped it past Lloris to make it 4–1.

Eleven minutes later, Bale nutmegged Laurent Koscielny to pull one back for the visitors, but it was too little too late. In the 91st minute, Walcott wrapped up the afternoon's proceedings to make it exactly the same scoreline as in February. And the season ended with Arsenal one place and one point ahead of Spurs.

AT LAST ... THE DROUGHT ENDS

46

Arsenal 3 Hull City 2 (aet)

FA Cup Final. Saturday 17 May 2014, kick-off 5pm
Venue: Wembley Stadium, Middlesex, HA9 0WS
Arsenal: Red shirts, white sleeves with red and blue stripe on bicep, white shorts, white stockings with red and blue hoop
Hull City: Black and amber striped shirts with amber sleeves with black band, black shorts with amber trim, black stockings with three amber hoops at top
Referee: Lee Probert (Wiltshire)
Attendance: 89,345

Arsenal	Hull City
21 Łukasz Fabiański	1 Allan McGregor
3 Bacary Sagna	27 Ahmed Elmohamady
28 Kieran Gibbs	2 Liam Rosenior (Boyd, 102 minutes)
8 Mikel Arteta (captain)	14 Jake Livermore
4 Per Mertesacker	6 Curtis Davies (captain)
6 Laurent Koscielny	5 James Chester
9 Lukas Podolski (Sanogo, 61 minutes)	4 Alex Bruce (McShane, 67 minutes)
16 Aaron Ramsey	8 Tom Huddlestone
12 Olivier Giroud	12 Matty Fryatt
11 Mesut Özil (Wilshere, 106 minutes)	29 Stephen Quinn (Aluko, 75 minutes)
19 Santi Cazorla (Rosický, 106 minutes)	7 David Meyler
Substitutes	*Substitutes*
1 Wojciech Szczęsny	22 Steve Harper
17 Nacho Monreal	15 Paul McShane
5 Thomas Vermaelen	24 Sone Aluko
22 Yaya Sanogo	17 George Boyd
10 Jack Wilshere	3 Maynor Figueroa
20 Mathieu Flamini	10 Robert Koren
7 Tomáš Rosický	20 Yannick Sagbo
Manager: Arsène Wenger	*Manager:* Steve Bruce
Scorers: Cazorla 17 minutes; Koscielny 71 minutes; Ramsey 109 minutes	*Scorers:* Chester 4 minutes; Davies 8 minutes
Booking: Giroud	*Bookings:* Huddlestone, Meyler, Davies

I T was the match that Arsène Wenger had to win – or he would surely lose his job. Arsenal had not won a trophy since triumphing in the FA Cup in 2005, and the Gunners boss was under extreme pressure.

The competition began for the Gunners, who were top of the Premier League at the time, in the third round with a home tie against deadly north London rivals Tottenham Hotspur on Saturday 4 January 2014. The Reds scored either side of half-time, with Santi Cazorla and Tomáš Rosický doing the honours as Arsenal ran out 2–0 winners.

Towards the end of the match, Theo Walcott was injured after appearing to catch his studs in the turf as he raced back to make a defensive tackle. He had to be carried off on a stretcher. As he left the pitch, he infuriated Spurs fans by signalling the score from his recumbent position with a huge smile on his face. The gesture may have been Walcott's revenge after Spurs fans threw coins at him. The injury – a ruptured anterior cruciate ligament of the left knee – turned out to be long-term, and Walcott missed that summer's World Cup.

Wenger said, 'The game was played at a good pace and I think we controlled quite well both sides of it, the defensive and the offensive.'

In the fourth round, Arsenal were drawn at home against Coventry City from League One, 54 places below the Premier League leaders, and playing in an unfamiliar yellow and blue kit. The match was an easy 4–0 win for Arsenal, although there was excitement 42 minutes into the first half when some of the floodlights at the Emirates went out. Making his Arsenal debut was 16-year-old Gedion Zelalem, who was born on 26 January 1997, which meant that he was the first Arsenal player born after Wenger took over as manager in September 1996. The goals came from Lukas Podolski (two), Olivier Giroud and Cazorla.

In the fifth round, on Sunday, 16 February, Arsenal had another home tie to look forward to – Premier League opponents again in the shape of Liverpool. The Scousers had walloped Arsenal 5–1 in the league the previous week, so the Gunners were looking for revenge. The match was end-to-end stuff, and the result was the same as the 1971 FA Cup Final, although no extra time was needed for Arsenal to win. Alex Oxlade-Chamberlain opened the scoring before Podolski got his third goal in two cup games. Steven Gerrard scored a penalty in the 59th minute to pull one back for Liverpool, and the Reds thought they should have had another penalty when Luis Suárez – the subject of a failed £40,000,001 bid from Arsenal in the summer – was sent tumbling inside the Arsenal area by Oxlade-Chamberlain. Referee Howard Webb decided that the tackle was clumsy but fair. Arsenal held on, and their name went into the hat for the sixth round.

In the quarter-finals on 8 March, Arsenal faced the other major side from Merseyside, and again at home. The Toffeemen from Goodison Park were underdogs and not expected to provide much difficulty – but they proved the doubters wrong and were in competition for much of the match. The scoreline did not really do justice to Everton's efforts.

Mesut Özil gave Arsenal an early lead, but Romelu Lukaku tapped in from almost on the goal line to equalise for Everton before half-time. The match remained deadlocked until Gareth Barry brought down Oxlade-Chamberlain on 66 minutes and referee Mark Clattenburg pointed to the spot. Mikel Arteta converted to give Arsenal the lead. Two goals in two minutes from substitute Giroud ensured Arsenal's victory.

Sitting on the bench as the substitute goalie against Spurs, Coventry, Liverpool and Everton was Emiliano Viviano, who had come to London on 2 September 2013 on a one-year loan deal from Palermo. There was an option to make the move permanent at the end of the season.

However, when the season finished, he returned to Palermo without having played a competitive game for Arsenal.

In the semi-final at Wembley, Arsenal were drawn against cup holders Wigan Athletic. In the previous year, the Latics had been managed by Roberto Martínez – now the Everton manager – who had been hoping to create history by becoming the first manager to retain the FA Cup after moving to a different club.

Arsenal's big German defender Per Mertesacker gave away a clumsy penalty, bringing down Jordi Gómez to give Wigan the lead. With the match looking increasingly like a win for the holders, the German redeemed himself with a late equaliser eight minutes from time that took the match to penalties.

Łukasz Fabiański saved Wigan's first two spot-kicks, from Gary Caldwell and Jack Collison. Arteta, Kim Kallstrom and Giroud all found the target for Arsenal, while James McArthur and Jean Beausejour scored for Wigan. Cazorla took the fourth penalty for Arsenal and found the back of the net, sending Arsenal to their 18th final – and the second they reached without leaving London (the 1950 tournament was the previous time: see page 52).

Arsenal equalled Manchester United's record of FA Cup final appearances, while Hull City made their first appearance in an FA Cup final. In their entire 110-year history, Hull had won just the Third Division North in 1933 and 1949, the Third Division in 1966 and the Championship Play-Off trophy in 2008.

Both sides faced selection difficulties. Arsenal were without Theo Walcott and Serge Gnabry, while club captain Thomas Vermaelen and Alex Oxlade-Chamberlain faced late fitness tests. Vermaelen was passed fit, although only as a substitute, while the Ox was ruled out.

'Every defeat is a scar on your heart that remains for life,' said Wenger. 'You have to sacrifice your life for this job.'

Hull attackers Shane Long and Nikica Jelavić were cup-tied; James Chester, Paul McShane, Sone Aluko and Robbie Brady faced fitness tests and all passed except Brady. Allan McGregor was back between the sticks after recovering from a kidney injury.

Hull manager Steve Bruce said, 'We'd obviously had a week to prepare. The big thing was: it's a red-hot day, you've got to be 100 per cent fit to play against Arsenal, and I couldn't risk too many.'

After the teams were introduced to the Aston Villa-supporting HRH the Prince William, 'Abide with Me' and the national anthem were performed by *X Factor* winner Leona Lewis, accompanied by the Band of the Welsh Guards.

As with the League Cup Final against Birmingham City three years earlier, Arsenal were clear favourites, and it looked like Wenger would get his hands on his first piece of silverware for nine years or 3,283 days.

Hull, however, had other ideas as they kicked off the 133rd FA Cup Final. The East Yorkshire side went two ahead in the opening ten minutes, with goals from Chester and Curtis Davies. It looked as though disaster loomed for the Londoners as Hull continued to dominate possession.

The opener came from a corner that went to the edge of the penalty arc, ready for Tom Huddlestone to smash it goalbound from 25 yards. He miscued his shot, however, and Chester back-heeled the ball past Fabiański from close in.

Four minutes later, Stephen Quinn crossed the ball and Alex Bruce headed at goal, bringing about a brilliant save by Fabiański – but the Pole could do nothing to stop Davies hitting the ball into the far bottom corner of the Arsenal net.

Wenger was furious because, prior to the second Hull goal, the Tigers were permitted to take a free kick eight yards further forward from where the foul had been committed.

On 13 minutes, Hull almost got a third but for Kieran Gibbs clearing a header from Bruce off the line. Everything seemed to be going Hull's way, but Arsenal had a glimmer of hope. In 1966, Everton came from two goals down to beat Sheffield Wednesday and win the cup final 3–2.

Then it all changed. Arsenal won a free kick on the edge of the Hull penalty area. Cazorla hit the ball over the Hull wall and into the top left-hand corner of McGregor's goal. Arsenal had a few chances, but Özil mis-hit two opportunities. The rest of the first half was played out with both sides fluffing chances.

The second half began in much the same way, with a blistering run down the left-hand side from Özil, but Aaron Ramsey could not get a boot on the ball from the German's cross.

Meanwhile in Spain, Barcelona were playing Atletico Madrid, and, on 33 minutes, the Catalans opened the scoring through the good offices of a chap called Alexis Sánchez.

Arsenal had claims for a penalty in the 58th minute, when Huddlestone put his arm across Giroud's shoulder, and four minutes later Wenger withdrew Podolski for youngster Yaya Sanogo. Another penalty claim came in the 68th minute, when Davies brought down Cazorla but referee Lee Probert waved play on.

The pressure finally told in the 71st minute, when Cazorla sent over a corner that Bacary Sagna headed against Giroud before it dropped for centre-half Laurent Koscielny on the edge of the six-yard box, who swivelled and put the ball past McGregor, injuring himself in the process.

With 11 minutes to go, Kieran Gibbs could have sealed the game for Arsenal, but skied the ball over McGregor's goal with just the Hull keeper to beat. A minute later, Santi Cazorla was bundled over again in the box, this time by David Meyler, but again Mr Probert wanted nothing to do with it.

Arsenal continued to pound Hull, who had all 11 men in their own half when the fourth official signalled five minutes of stoppage time. Both teams had chances to win the match, but neither could, and Mr Probert blew for full time and 30 minutes of extra time.

Olivier Giroud hit the crossbar after five minutes, and Ramsey hit low shots at goal, forcing the Hull keeper into a number of saves. Hull scrapped and fought to score, while Arsenal tried to put together a more masterful way to get a goal.

Wenger made two substitutions in the 106th minute of play, bringing on Wilshere and Rosický for Özil and Cazorla. Could their fresh legs make the difference?

In the 109th minute, Arsenal attacked again and the ball went to Giroud in the penalty area. He executed a smart back-heel to Aaron Ramsey, who put the ball just inside McGregor's left-hand upright to give Arsenal the lead with his 18th goal of the season.

With six minutes to go, Yaya Sanogo could have wrapped it up for the Arsenal – but no, he dragged the ball across the goal, to the frustration of the fans who nicknamed him Sa-no-goals.

Łukasz Fabiański, in his last match for Arsenal, performed heroics to save from Aluko, and 60 seconds later Mr Probert blew for full time, giving Arsenal their first trophy in nine years.

With the trophy safely gathered in, Wenger said, 'We wanted to make history and win the game. We made history both ways: how not to start a cup final, and how to come back. This is a turning point in the life of this team. I have praised many times the spirit of this team. Congratulations to Hull, they played fantastic for the whole game.'

Kieran Gibbs commented, 'We got over the line, and that's what matters. It's a positive season, and we're going to celebrate now. This is why we're here, why we're in the business. We can use this to push on for next season.'

'It's been a long nine years,' said Jack Wilshere. 'We've felt it as well, but this is for the fans. This is for them. We never do it easy, do we? Sitting on the bench, I felt sick.'

The trophy Arsenal collected was a new version of the FA Cup. It stands 24.2in high and weighs 13lb 14oz. Made of 925 sterling silver, it replaced the previous trophy, which was first presented to Liverpool in 1992. The base of the old trophy, containing the winners' names, was kept.

On 30 May 2014, Arsenal announced that Wenger had signed a new three-year contract.

Manchester United 1 Arsenal 2

FA Cup sixth round. Monday 9 March 2015, kick-off 7.45pm
Venue: Old Trafford, Sir Matt Busby Way, Stretford, Manchester M16 0RA
Manchester United: Red shirts, white shorts, black stockings with red stripe at top
Arsenal: Royal blue shirts with pale blue diagonal panels, royal blue shorts, pale blue stockings
Referee: Michael Oliver (Northumberland)
Attendance: 74,285

Manchester United	Arsenal
1 David de Gea	1 Wojciech Szczęsny
25 Antonio Valencia	39 Héctor Bellerín (Chambers, 66 minutes)
12 Chris Smalling	18 Nacho Monreal
5 Marcos Rojo (Januzaj, 73 minutes)	34 Francis Coquelin
3 Luke Shaw (Jones, 45 minutes)	4 Per Mertesacker (captain)
17 Daley Blind	6 Laurent Koscielny
21 Ander Herrera (Carrick, 45 minutes)	19 Santi Cazorla
7 Ángel Di María	15 Alex Oxlade-Chamberlain (Ramsey, 51 minutes)
10 Wayne Rooney (captain)	17 Alexis Sánchez
31 Marouane Fellaini	23 Danny Welbeck (Giroud, 74 minutes)
18 Ashley Young	11 Mesut Özil
Substitutes	*Substitutes*
32 Víctor Valdés	26 Emi Martínez
2 Rafael Da Silva	21 Calum Chambers
4 Phil Jones	3 Kieran Gibbs
16 Michael Carrick	16 Aaron Ramsey
11 Adnan Januzaj	38 Chuba Akpom
8 Juan Mata	12 Olivier Giroud
9 Radamel Falcao	14 Theo Walcott
Manager: Louis van Gaal	*Manager:* Arsène Wenger
Scorer: Rooney 29 minutes	*Scorers:* Monreal 25 minutes; Welbeck 61 minutes
Bookings: Herrera, Fellaini, Young, Rojo, Di María, Januzaj	*Bookings:* Bellerín, Ramsey
Sending-off: Di María	

THE match that was decided by the player no one seemed to want. Manchester United manager Louis van Gaal had decided at the start of the 2014/15 season that striker Danny Welbeck was surplus to his requirements at Old Trafford, after signing Radamel Falcao on loan from Monaco. Arsène Wenger was said to be interested in Welbeck, but only as a loanee, not a permanent move. In his first season at United, van Gaal was adamant – sale or no deal – so Welbeck signed for Arsenal for £16 million on 1 September 2014 and made his debut in a 2–2 draw against Manchester City 12 days later. This was his first return to Old Trafford, and so he had a point to prove.

Arsenal had begun their defence of the trophy on 4 January at home to Hull City, the losing side in the 2014 final. Unlike at Wembley, Arsenal did not mess around, and beat the Tigers 2–0 with goals from Per Mertesacker and Alexis Sánchez. Hull manager Steve Bruce said,

211

'If we're going to be honest Arsenal deserved to win. We just needed to stay in there but unfortunately, at the top end of the pitch, we were unable to create anything. The disappointing thing for me is that the first goal is the first we've conceded from a corner this season. Mertesacker is huge – we should be doing better than that. We battled on valiantly but we weren't quite good enough.'

In the fourth round, Arsenal travelled to the south coast and the Falmer Stadium to play Brighton & Hove Albion. Arsenal triumphed 3–2, with Theo Walcott, Mesut Özil and Tomáš Rosický getting on the scoresheet. Middlesbrough were the opponents in the fifth round, and they visited the Emirates. Olivier Giroud scored twice in two minutes to dismiss Boro in the game that saw Gabriel Paulista make his debut.

Wenger said of the Middlesbrough tie, 'We started well, with a good pace and we controlled the game with our movement and technical quality. We had good team focus overall, we maybe lost our cohesion a little bit at 2–0 but I am happy. Overall we were serious and focused over the whole game. Olivier Giroud was very sharp. He has improved a lot compared to the player he was when he arrived here. He is mobile, technically good, and he works with great focus in training. He has become a top player. Gabriel Paulista made a great recovery tackle in the box. He wants to defend, he has good urgency levels and a good physique and technical qualities. He is short language-wise but the intelligent players compensate with vision. They look at what their partners are doing, and he did that well.'

The sixth round clash with Manchester United was the second time the two teams had met that season; United had beaten Arsenal by two goals to one the previous November at the Emirates, thanks to an own goal by Kieran Gibbs and a Wayne Rooney strike.

Although Arsenal were the cup holders, the Red Devils were favourites to go through to the semi-final, as Arsenal had failed to score in each of their last four FA Cup matches against United. The Red Devils had won 11 of the past 15 meetings between the sides in all competitions, and none of the 18 players in the Gunners squad had previously won a game at the Theatre of Dreams while playing for Arsenal.[18] Van Gaal was determined to get to Wembley. 'What's the plan? That we beat Arsenal! That's the most important thing in a cup tie. Arsenal are one of the best teams in the Premier League but I

---

18 Danny Welbeck had been on the winning side, of course, while playing for United; and so had Theo Walcott for England and Mesut Özil for Real Madrid.

have noticed that they have played more defensively lately with a lot of success. I have been to Wembley as a spectator but not as a coach and that is more interesting.'

The match was a closely fought game – some might say dirty. The first attack, after two minutes, came from Arsenal, before Nacho Monreal ran out of ground on the left. A minute later, Sánchez took on Antonio Valencia and a shot from the Chilean ended safely in the arms of David de Gea – but it showed that Arsenal were not afraid to attack.

After just four minutes, Héctor Bellerín became the first player to go into referee Michael Oliver's notebook, for a rash tackle on Ashley Young. By the end of the match, Mr Oliver would have shown eight yellow cards and one red.

A corner from United almost resulted in the first goal, as Rooney met the ball on the volley but it ran across the face of the Arsenal goalmouth. A few minutes later, the curly haired Marouane Fellaini went close but Wojciech Szczęsny and Per Mertesacker managed to clear their lines. After Bellerín and Santi Cazorla missed chances for Arsenal, Young also messed up at the other end.

And then, after 25 minutes, it all changed. Özil found Alex Oxlade-Chamberlain on the right; he cut inside and went past Luke Shaw, Chris Smalling and Valencia before finding left-back Monreal inside the area. He had one touch, and beat de Gea at his near post. It was the Spaniard's second goal for the club since signing from Málaga on 31 January 2013 as a replacement for Gibbs.

Four minutes later and United were level, thanks to a flying Rooney header, from Ángel Di María's cross, that gave Szczęsny no chance. A minute later, Arsenal demanded a penalty as Marcos Rojo manhandled Welbeck, but the referee was not interested. Then Szczęsny made a mess of collecting a cross and was fortunate the ball did not end up at the feet of Wayne Rooney for a tap-in.

As half-time approached, both sides had chances to take the lead, but the goalies were equal to all the challenges. When Mr Oliver blew his whistle, Manchester United had had six attempts on goal, Arsenal five.

As the teams emerged for the second half, United had made a double change: Phil Jones replaced Shaw, and Michael Carrick came on for Ander Herrera. Three minutes in and Oxlade-Chamberlain stretched for the ball and looked to have torn his hamstring. He managed another three minutes before being forced to call it a day, to be replaced by Aaron Ramsey.

The quick tempo of the first half slowed in the second, but the mistakes by both teams continued to come, and Fellaini went into Mr Oliver's notebook for two awkward hacks in a matter of seconds. On the hour mark, Young joined his team-mate in the book for a foul on Welbeck.

A minute later and United made a total hash of defending their goal. Valencia's back pass was weak, and Welbeck charged in and beat de Gea to slide home the loose ball. To say that Welbeck was pleased would be a gross understatement. He had scored 29 goals in 142 appearances, and now he had got the goal that would knock his old club out of the FA Cup and ensure that van Gaal's first season in charge ended trophyless.

Wenger pulled off Bellerín, who had committed a couple more fouls, before Mr Oliver sent him off, and Calum Chambers took up a berth at right-back. Then Arsenal replaced Welbeck, who was booed by some and cheered by others, with Olivier Giroud.

On 75 minutes, Ángel Di María had a moment of madness and was booked for diving. Then, apparently annoyed at the decision, he pulled Mr Oliver's shirt. The referee immediately reached into his pocket and showed the Argentinian a red card. Incredibly, the United fans applauded the winger as he trudged off.

With five minutes of regular time to play, Adnan Januzaj went down inside the area as he went past Monreal – but rather than award a penalty, as many referees might have done, Mr Oliver booked the substitute for a dive.

The fourth official signalled five minutes of stoppage time and Arsenal hearts went into their mouths. Could they hang on? Wenger turned away in disgust after seeing that five on the board and then shook his head.

With a minute to go, de Gea made a brilliant save from Sánchez after Özil had put him through. Then, at last, it was all over and Arsenal were through to the semi-final. The match was Arsenal's first win at Old Trafford since 17 September 2006, when Emmanuel Adebayor scored the only goal of the game with four minutes to play.

Roy Keane, a former United hard man and no fan of Arsenal, said, 'The shocking defending meant Arsenal made the most of it. You couldn't begrudge Arsenal that win, they thoroughly deserved it.'

Wenger said, 'Last year we played a tricky game at Wembley in the semi-final and we expect that again. Tonight I thought we played well and deserved to win the game. We had to start without apprehension and play at a high pace and we did that well. Danny Welbeck, I believe, is just happy to score. He worked extremely hard today and deserved his goal. We live in the real world and want to compete in every competition. This result can give us good morale for the Premier League and the [Champions League] game in Monaco.'

Van Gaal made no excuses for Di María's sending-off. He said, 'In Spain he knows that he doesn't touch the referee, but that is also in his emotion. I've already spoken with him, he knows my opinion but also I have to see on the video. I think he's touched the referee and that's forbidden in every country, so he has no excuses.'

Of the match as a whole, the United manager added, 'I've said in the dressing room we gave [the game] away by ourselves and that is the biggest disappointment. In the second half, we had the first chance also then we gave it away again. We don't lose from the opponent, we lost from ourselves and it was very disappointing. You play this match to win; to beat the opponent, we wanted to be in the semi-final.'

Arsenal captain Mertesacker commented, 'In the second half there was a feeling we could get something out of it. The crowd got nervous, we were rewarded with the second goal and then we defended from the top in a special way. Danny Welbeck was a great player here at United, he's a bit quiet in the dressing room at the moment. I think it hurts him a bit as well as he was here for a long time. We tried to get him going and to tell him he can enjoy special moments with Arsenal.'

RECORD BREAKERS

Arsenal 4 Aston Villa 0

FA Cup Final. Saturday 30 May 2015, kick-off 5.30pm
Venue: Wembley Stadium, Middlesex, HA9 0WS
Arsenal: Yellow shirts with blue sleeves, blue shorts, yellow and blue hooped stockings
Aston Villa: Claret shirts with sky blue pinstripes and blue sleeves, white shorts, sky blue stockings with four thin claret hoops
Referee: Jon Moss (West Yorkshire)
Attendance: 89,283

Arsenal	Aston Villa
1 Wojciech Szczęsny	31 Shay Given
39 Héctor Bellerín	21 Alan Hutton
18 Nacho Monreal	18 Kieran Richardson (Bacuna, 68 minutes)
19 Santi Cazorla	15 Ashley Westwood (Sánchez, 71 minutes)
4 Per Mertesacker (captain)	5 Jores Okore
6 Laurent Koscielny	4 Ron Vlaar
34 Francis Coquelin	8 Tom Cleverley
11 Mesut Özil (Wilshere, 77 minutes)	28 Charles N'Zogbia (Agbonlahor, 53 minutes)
17 Alexis Sánchez (Oxlade-Chamberlain, 90 minutes)	20 Christian Benteke
14 Theo Walcott (Giroud, 77 minutes)	16 Fabian Delph
16 Aaron Ramsey	40 Jack Grealish
Substitutes	*Substitutes*
13 David Ospina	1 Brad Guzan
3 Kieran Gibbs	2 Nathan Baker
5 Gabriel Paulista	7 Leandro Bacuna
10 Jack Wilshere	9 Scott Sinclair
12 Olivier Giroud	11 Gabriel Agbonlahor
15 Alex Oxlade-Chamberlain	12 Joe Cole
20 Mathieu Flamini	24 Carlos Sánchez
Manager: Arsène Wenger	*Manager:* Tim Sherwood
Scorers: Walcott 40 minutes; Sánchez 50 minutes; Mertesacker 62 minutes; Giroud 90+3 minutes	*Bookings:* Hutton, Cleverley, Delph, Westwood, Agbonlahor

BACK in the FA Cup Final – for the record-breaking 19th time. Arsenal and Aston Villa had met twice in the league by the time the final came around, and Arsenal had scored eight goals (three at Villa Park and five at the Emirates without reply). In days of old, the television schedules were cleared for cup final-themed programmes, and in 2015 the BBC revived the practice.

Since 2008, when the FA has apparently needed the money, the semi-final has been played at Wembley rather than at one of the big club grounds such as Villa Park, Hillsborough, Old Trafford or Stamford Bridge as they should be, and Arsenal travelled there to play against Championship side Reading.

As with the League Cup (see page 205), the Royals took Arsenal to extra time, but two goals from Sánchez were sufficient for Arsenal to reach the FA Cup Final for the second consecutive year. Their opponents, Aston Villa, had seen off Liverpool in the other semi-final.

It was expected to be a keenly fought final, but how wrong the experts were. Arsenal came out motoring and never took their foot off the accelerator – winning free kicks with only two minutes on the clock. After nine minutes, Koscielny got on the end of a Cazorla corner but was unable to put it in the Villa net.

After 14 minutes, Tom Cleverley became the first player to be booked. A minute later, Koscielny got on the end of a Sánchez cross, but was again unable to put it in the Villa net. On 17 minutes, Ramsey went close but missed, and he missed again three minutes later.

All the pressure was coming from Arsenal, and it had to be only a matter of time before the deadlock was broken. On 33 minutes, Alan Hutton joined his team-mate Cleverley in the referee's book, and four minutes after that Fabian Delph was the third Villa player to see a yellow card.

Then, with 40 minutes gone, Monreal overlapped on the left and sent a deep cross into the area, where Sánchez beat Ron Vlaar and headed to Walcott, who placed his left-footed shot from the centre of the box into the bottom left-hand corner to open Arsenal's account. It had been coming.

Five minutes after the restart, Sánchez made it two to the Gunners. Ashley Westwood, in the 52nd minute, became the fourth Villan to be booked.

With 62 minutes gone, Arsenal won a corner, which was taken by Cazorla. Mertesacker rose above everyone else to give the Reds their third. In the 77th minute, Wenger sent on Giroud for Walcott and Wilshere for Özil. Six minutes later, Gabriel Agbonlahor of Aston Villa was shown the yellow card – number five.

In the last minute of normal time, Oxlade-Chamberlain replaced Sánchez. Three minutes later, the Ox passed to Giroud – who had got his hair specially highlighted for this match – who slotted it into the bottom right-hand corner of the net to make it four. Villa keeper Shay Given, playing in his first FA Cup final in 17 years, belied his 39 years but was unable to stop Arsenal.

Arteta collected the trophy from Aston Villa supporter HRH the Duke of Cambridge, and, with Per Mertesacker taking one handle, the two men lifted the cup to a chorus of Curtis Mayfield's 'Move on Up' and an explosion of ticker tape.

Villa manager Tim Sherwood said, 'We gave the fans nothing to cheer about today but I promise them it will get better. We've stayed in the division but we have a losing mentality. We don't want to be scrapping relegation next season.'

Wenger said, 'Of course I think we can push on. Why not? We have won the league in the past when we have had potential to do it and that's what we want to do again.

'That's what we want to show next season but you also don't know how good the other teams will be.

'It is about consistency at the top level and in the past we have won leagues when we have been consistent.'

Midfielder Aaron Ramsey, convinced that Arsenal would go on to win the 2015/16 title, said, 'It's a great feeling. We really wanted this one. Winning back-to-back FA Cups is not an easy thing to do and we have done it.

Now we can look forward to next season and kick on and give it a real go in the Premier League.'

'If we keep this squad, with one or two more players, we will have a good chance to challenge for the title,' said Olivier Giroud. 'The Premier League title is the target. Hopefully we will be there.'

49

Arsenal 2 Bayern Munich 0

European Champions League Group F. Tuesday 20 October 2015, kick-off 7.45pm
Venue: Ashburton Grove, Hornsey Road, London N7 7AJ
Arsenal: Red shirts with white sleeves, white shorts and stockings
Bayern Munich: Black shirts, shorts and stockings with pink trim
Referee: Cüneyt Çakir (Istanbul, Turkey)
Attendance: 49,824

Arsenal	Bayern Munich
33 Petr Čech	1 Manuel Neuer
24 Héctor Bellerín	21 Philipp Lahm (captain)
18 Nacho Monreal	18 Juan Bernat
19 Santi Cazorla	14 Xabi Alonso (Kimmich, 70 minutes)
4 Per Mertesacker (captain)	17 Jérôme Boateng
6 Laurent Koscielny	27 David Alaba
34 Francis Coquelin	23 Arturo Vidal (Rafinha, 71 minutes)
16 Aaron Ramsey (Oxlade-Chamberlain, 57 minutes)	11 Douglas Costa
14 Theo Walcott (Giroud, 74 minutes)	9 Robert Lewandowski
11 Mesut Özil	6 Thiago Alcántara
17 Alexis Sánchez (Gibbs, 82 minutes)	25 Thomas Müller
Substitutes	*Substitutes*
49 Matt Macey	26 Sven Ulreich
2 Mathieu Debuchy	8 Javi Martínez
21 Calum Chambers	13 Rafinha
3 Kieran Gibbs	15 Jan Kirchhoff
8 Mikel Arteta	16 Gianluca Gaudino
15 Alex Oxlade-Chamberlain	29 Kingsley Coman
12 Olivier Giroud	32 Joshua Kimmich
Manager: Arsène Wenger	*Head coach:* Pep Guardiola

Scorers: Giroud 77 minutes; Özil 90+4 minutes
Booking: Giroud

PEP Guardiola's Bayern Munich arrived at Ashburton Grove (UEFA rules ban clubs from using sponsorship names in the Champions League) full of confidence – brought about by their unbeaten 12-match run stretching back two months. Before the match, they had not conceded more than one goal per match in their season's previous 13 games, in which they had won a dozen and drawn one. They topped Group F with maximum points, scoring eight goals and conceding none. Arsenal went into the match with no points and two European defeats under their belt – in Croatia against Dinamo Zagreb and at home to Olympiakos.

Arsenal had to contend with having been knocked out of the group of 16 by the Germans in the two previous seasons. Arsène Wenger said, 'We don't look at the history. We look at the potential performance on the day, that is what we try to do. After that, the history doesn't play the game.

'What will decide the game is the performance we produce, and that comes from if we believe that we can do it. In Europe it is true we have been poor in our first two games, so that is what we want to correct.

'I must say we have our backs to the wall and we play against a top team, so I can understand the scepticism of people, but we have to prove them wrong.'

Of Bayern's Polish centre-forward Robert Lewandowski, the Arsenal manager opined: 'First, the best way to combat him is for us to have the ball, and after that you have to be shrewd with him.

'Inside the box he is outstanding, because his technique, his finishing, his movement inside the box, that is where we need the experience of [Per] Mertesacker and [Laurent] Koscielny to deal with that because that will be one of the important things on the night.'

The Germans recovered from a minor incident before the game, when their coach driver had driven into a parked car as they left their hotel. Witnesses at the scene alleged that the coach reversed into the black Mercedes as they prepared to make their way to the Grove.

In his pre-match interview, Wenger said, 'I believe the urgency will be different. They have the best striker in Europe at the moment.

'I believe that they are the favourites but I know we can beat them if we play at a high pace and turn up against them in a compact way. If you want to grow as a team we can win these kinds of games.

'You never know how open it will be. That will depend on the team that scores first but it can be a very interesting game because on both sides are top level players.'

Petr Čech returned between the sticks for Arsenal, as regular cup keeper David Ospina was injured. The match nearly started with a Bayern goal, as Lewandowski got the ball and made a run for the Arsenal box and almost managed to get a shot in. After five minutes, the Pole won a corner for the Germans, but Arsenal cleared their lines.

A couple of minutes later and the Bayern Munich fans made their way into the stadium, having staged a protest outside at what they saw as the exorbitant £64 ticket prices at Ashburton Grove. Arsenal's fans, also unhappy at the cost, applauded their German counterparts. For the first five minutes, much of the Bayern end was almost empty, occupied only by a few fans and large banners bearing the legend '£64 a ticket but without fans, football is not worth a penny'. A BBC survey showed that Arsenal was the most expensive team in the country to follow, with the highest single ticket price costing £97. A spokesman for Bayern Munich fans said, 'This kind of a price structure makes a stadium visit impossible for younger and socially disadvantaged fans.'

With 12 minutes gone, the Germans almost broke the deadlock as Thomas Müller shot but unfortunately straight at Arsenal goalie Čech. Two minutes later and David Alaba took a shot from 25 yards out and got a corner. Douglas Costa quickly took it in a bid to outfox the Arsenal defence, but Aaron Ramsey was equal to the task and cleared the ball. The statisticians pointed out that in the first 15 minutes of play, Bayern Munich had put together 110 passes while Arsenal had managed a paltry 34.

Having cleared the danger from a corner, Arsenal counter-attacked, but it all came to naught as Santi Cazorla gave the ball away instead of passing to Theo Walcott. Wave upon wave of German attacks pounded the Arsenal box, and the Čech resistance helped keep the scores level. Douglas Costa was too quick for Bayern down the left-hand side, leaving the hapless Héctor Bellerín for dust. By this stage of the match, the Germans excelled in every department, and on the rare occasions they lost the ball, they chased back. Arturo Vidal went close on the half-hour mark, but Čech denied him.

Arsenal finally began to make some moves, and after 34 minutes Manuel Neuer made a brilliant save to stop Walcott's header from hitting the back of the net. The Englishman came close in the next few minutes but was unable to finish, causing one reporter to remark, 'Walcott is so frustratingly close to being really good at football. Maybe one day.'

His play, though, became an inspiration for his team-mates, and Cazorla and Alexis Sánchez looked dangerous. However, once again, having got himself brilliantly into position, Walcott was let down by his finishing.

The second half started the same way the first had ended, with Bayern Munich moving the ball around and leaving the Arsenal players for dead. Lewandowski forced Čech into a great save, and then the Czech goalie gathered the resulting corner without too much trouble.

Arsenal had their woes added to when Ramsey was forced off with a hamstring problem and was replaced by Alex Oxlade-Chamberlain. By the time the hour mark passed, Bayern had had 71 per cent of the possession and had completed 441 passes compared with Arsenal's 117.

With about 16 minutes left to play and neither side able to break the deadlock, Wenger sent on Olivier Giroud for Walcott. Three minutes later, Arsenal were awarded a free kick 35 yards out and Santi Cazorla chipped it into the box. Neuer came off his line but failed to gather it, jumping over the ball, and somehow it hit Giroud on the head and rolled into the back of the Bayern net.

Bayern stepped up the pace, but Arsenal found themselves equal. Having been outpaced in the first half, Bellerín got the better of Costa with a sliding tackle. With eight minutes to go, Wenger made a defensive substitution, replacing Sánchez with second-choice left-back Kieran Gibbs. A couple of minutes later, Giroud stopped Neuer from clearing the ball and found his name in Turkish referee Cüneyt Çakir's book. More pressure from the Germans, and Nacho Monreal came to his side's rescue, heading out for a corner.

Four minutes into stoppage time at the Grove, confusion reigned. Bellerín made a blistering run into the Bayern box and crossed the ball to Özil, who had an open goal. He could not miss and did not – but then Neuer appeared from nowhere and grabbed the ball off the line. The Arsenal players began to celebrate as the crowd was confused. The Turkish referee signalled a goal after his colleague behind the goal notified him that the ball had crossed the line, and the match ended 2–0 to the Arsenal. No team had ever managed more shots on target against a Pep Guardiola side in the Champions League than the eight Arsenal did in this match. In the final tally, Bayern completed 765 passes to Arsenal's 278.

The Gunners remained bottom of the table, but were level on three points with Dinamo Zagreb and three behind both Olympiakos and Bayern Munich.

Fifteen days later, Bayern took their revenge at Football Arena Munich, beating Arsenal 5–1. Arsenal managed to win their final two games by the same 3–0 margin to progress to the knockout group of 16 stage. Unfortunately, they drew Barcelona and lost 5–1 on aggregate – losing 2–0 at home, in a match also refereed by Cüneyt Çakir, and 3–1 at Camp Nou.

Arsenal 2 Chelsea 1

FA Cup Final. Saturday 27 May 2017, kick-off 5.30pm
Venue: Wembley Stadium, Middlesex, HA9 0WS
Arsenal: Red shirts with white sleeves, white shorts, red stockings with white tops
Chelsea: Blue shirts and shorts, white stockings with blue hoop at top
Referee: Anthony Taylor (Wythenshawe)
Attendance: 89,472

Arsenal	Chelsea
13 David Ospina	13 Thibaut Courtois
16 Rob Holding	28 César Azpilicueta
18 Nacho Monreal	24 Gary Cahill (captain)
24 Héctor Bellerín	15 Victor Moses
4 Per Mertesacker (captain)	30 David Luiz
29 Granit Xhaka	7 N'Golo Kanté
15 Alex Oxlade-Chamberlain (Coquelin, 82 minutes)	21 Nemanja Matić (Fàbregas, 61 minutes)
7 Alexis Sánchez (Elneny, 93 minutes)	3 Marcos Alonso
23 Danny Welbeck (Giroud, 78 minutes)	11 Pedro (Willian, 72 minutes)
11 Mesut Özil	19 Diego Costa (Batshuayi, 88 minutes)
8 Aaron Ramsey	10 Eden Hazard
Substitutes	*Substitutes*
33 Petr Čech	1 Asmir Begović
34 Francis Coquelin	5 Kurt Zouma
35 Mohamed Elneny	6 Nathan Aké
9 Lucas Pérez	26 John Terry
14 Theo Walcott	4 Cesc Fàbregas
12 Olivier Giroud	22 Willian
17 Alex Iwobi	23 Michy Batshuayi
Manager: Arsène Wenger	*Head coach:* Antonio Conte
Scorers: Sánchez 4 minutes; Ramsey 79 minutes	*Scorer:* Costa 76 minutes
Bookings: Ramsey, Holding, Xhaka, Coquelin	*Bookings:* Moses, Kanté
	Sending-off: Moses

IT was the match that Chelsea had only to turn up to win and complete the Double for the second time in their history. It was the match that would signal the end of Arsène Wenger's 20-plus year reign at Arsenal and probably the last games for Alexis Sánchez and Mesut Özil, both in the final year of their contracts at the Emirates.

The Gunners had finished the season in fifth place and failed to qualify for the Champions League for the first time since Wenger had been manager. Defeat was assured in the FA Cup Final – Arsenal's 20th appearance in the last game of the tournament. Except the Arsenal players had not read the script and, like Aston Villa two years before, Chelsea failed to turn up for much of the match.

The route to the final had been a mixed one – they were drawn against one Championship side and two non-league teams on the road to Wembley. On 7 January 2017, Arsenal saw off the challenge of Preston North End away at Deepdale, 2–1. Aaron Ramsey and Olivier

Giroud got the all-important goals in the first minute after half-time and the last minute of normal time as the Lilywhites led for all of the first half and looked as if they would at least force a visit to north London.

The fourth round, three weeks later, was another away tie – this time to St Mary's Stadium to face Southampton. Arsenal ran riot, winning 5–0 – Danny Welbeck got a brace and ex-Saint Theo Walcott scored a hat-trick. It was revenge for the Saints knocking Arsenal out of the League Cup in the fifth round tie at the Emirates on 30 November 2016. As was his wont, Wenger had chosen a mix of youth and experience for the competition, and as usual the gamble had not paid off.

On 20 February, Arsenal faced non-league Sutton United at Gander Green Lane in the fifth round. It was a match that Arsenal could not afford to lose, coming five days after a 5–1 drubbing in the Champions League round of 16 by Bayern Munich in Germany's third largest city.

Wenger made seven changes from that side, and it was enough to see off a team 105 places below the Gunners in the league system. Sutton's management complained that each Arsenal player had been assigned a bodyguard for the trip. Lucas Pérez's cross-shot gave Arsenal the lead after 26 minutes, and Walcott doubled the advantage from close range ten minutes after the break with his 100th goal for the club. He thus became the 18th player to score 100 goals in all competitions for Arsenal.

Sutton play on a plastic pitch, which caused the ball to bounce more than is usual. It may have been the bounce or skill, but Sutton had their moments. A poor clearance from goalkeeper David Ospina in the first half gave Adam May a chance, but he wasted it. In the second half, Roarie Deacon smacked a 25-yard shot against the crossbar, but Arsenal hung on. Wenger said, 'We did the job. It is very different on this kind of pitch. It was not an easy game at all. We have to give them credit because every error we made they took advantage of. They played very well. It is basically division five and when I arrived here 20 years ago, in division five they were not as fit physically as they were today. They were organised and had a huge desire. If we were not mentally prepared we would not have gone through.'

In the quarter-final, played on 11 March, Arsenal faced their second non-league side of the competition: Lincoln City of the National League. It was the first time the two teams had met for almost exactly 102 years – the previous encounter had been on 6 March 1915 in the Second Division, when Lincoln ran out 1–0 winners.

The 21st-century result would be different. It was another nail-biting first half, as Arsenal could not make their Premier League advantage tell. Cup goalie Ospina was injured, so regular first choice Petr Čech was entrusted with the gloves.

Arsenal wore their usual red and white, while Lincoln played in green shirts and stockings and black shorts, with their goalie Paul Farman clad in a fetching all-pink kit. Lincoln battled through eight games to get to the quarter-final, beating Premier League Burnley and Championship high-flyers Brighton & Hove Albion along the way to become the first non-league side to reach the quarter-finals of the competition in 103 years.

Arsenal, on the other hand, had reached the semi-finals 28 times previously.

Lincoln started the game 88 places below Arsenal in the league system, but kept the Gunners at bay until the first minute of stoppage time, when Walcott's deflected strike opened the Arsenal account. Giroud put the hosts in control with a clinical strike eight minutes after the break. Kieran Gibbs, getting a rare start, crossed the ball five minutes later, and Luke Waterfall scored an own goal to make it three. Sánchez, with his usual brilliance, made it four before assisting Aaron Ramsey to complete the rout.

Outside the ground, around 200 supporters had staged a protest demanding that Wenger not be offered a new contract. They carried banners bearing the legends, 'Arsène 4th place is not a trophy. Arsenal FC not Arsène FC' and 'Wexit'.

Speaking after the game, the Frenchman said, 'There was always a level of anxiety because these boys are unpredictable. They knocked out Burnley, Ipswich and Brighton, so we have to respect them.

'It was all us in the second half but you have to congratulate Lincoln for what they have achieved in the FA Cup.

'We have been short of confidence after some disappointing results recently. When the confidence was there in the second half the quality came back.'

Lincoln's manager, Danny Cowley, had nothing but praise for his opponents. 'Arsenal were frightening in the second half and for us it was a pleasure to see world-class players first hand,' he said.

'It felt like Arsène Wenger had brought 15 players on. If we can learn from this experience today and throughout this FA Cup journey, we will be better players and better people.'

This tie was Arsenal's 300th competitive fixture at the Emirates and the match in which they registered their 200th win in competitive games at home. (They had drawn 61 and lost the other 39 games.)

The semi-finals were an all-Premier League affair, with three teams from London and one from Manchester, both games to be played at Wembley again. There were dreams of a north London semi-final – or better still, final – but the hopes were dashed when Arsenal drew Manchester City, with Chelsea facing Tottenham Hotspur. The all-London clash took place on the Saturday, while Arsenal met Manchester City on St George's Day: Sunday, 23 April.

Arsenal were the underdogs as City manager Pep Guardiola attempted to win silverware in his first season at the Etihad. Wenger chose to play three at the back, with Paulista, Koscielny and Holding in defence, and Monreal and Alex Oxlade-Chamberlain as wing-backs.

It was a system that worked: as Henry Winter wrote in *The Times*, Oxlade-Chamberlain 'truly shone, the Englishman proving he can seize the big occasions … his jet-heeled belief stirring his team-mates and delighting the huge Arsenal following, whose support for their team here at Wembley was unconditional and loud.

'When Oxlade-Chamberlain performs with this intensity and threat, not in highlights but sustained application, he looks one of the best players in the country.'

In a match full of fouls, City took the lead in the 40th minute – or thought they did. A cross from Leroy Sané on the left sailed over Čech's left hand and was met by Sergio Agüero, who hit the ball at Čech, standing behind the line, before Raheem Sterling buried the loose ball into the roof of the net.

By that time, however, linesman Steve Child had waved his flag to signal that the ball had gone out from Sané's cross, and referee Craig Pawson disallowed the goal.

On the stroke of half-time, Sánchez appealed for a penalty, going down at the far post. However, he was already on his way to ground when Jesús Navas laid a hand on his shoulder.

The atmosphere was strained in the stands and on the pitch, so both sets of players were relieved when Mr Pawson blew the whistle to signal the end of the first half. Arsenal had just had one shot in that half, but it was on target and forced Claudio Bravo to make a save.

Arsenal came out showing more passion in the second half. On the 62nd minute, however, Agüero broke the deadlock for City. From an

Arsenal attack, Ramsey lost the ball, and Yaya Touré punted it upfield to the Argentine, who was chased by Monreal.

The Arsenal man could not reach the City player and was fearful of making a tackle lest he commit a foul and, in that goalscoring position, receive a red card from Mr Pawson.

Čech came off his line, but the result was never in doubt and the Czech was unable to stop Agüero lifting the ball over him to score his 30th goal of the season.

Arsenal legend Martin Keown said, 'Agüero there produces such a clever finish. The ball to him from Yaya Touré was excellent, and he's too quick for Monreal.

'He waits for the keeper to come out and makes it look so easy. Petr Čech didn't know whether to come out or not, and that made it so easy for Agüero to make up his mind.'

With City looking to arrange their second visit to Wembley in a matter of weeks, it was Arsenal's unorthodox wing-backs who combined to equalise.

On the 71st minute, Oxlade-Chamberlain received the ball on the right and headed along the line. He crossed, but the ball was too much for Giroud – but not for Monreal, who arrived in the six-yard box, and with his right foot volleyed the ball past Bravo in the City goal.

Keown again: 'Oxlade-Chamberlain has been outstanding on the right-hand side, and Monreal, the wing-back on the other flank, comes in to finish. Monreal has just taken charge. It was his destiny to get on the end of that.'

The Spanish left-back does not score often for Arsenal, but when he does, it tends to be in the big games against clubs from Manchester.

City came close to retaking the lead, hitting the post (with a little help from the Arsenal goalie) and the crossbar.

Tired legs made mistakes, and the referee started making use of his notebook. Kevin De Bruyne's name was taken in the 89th minute.

Mr Pawson blew to signal the end of the 90 minutes and 30 more of extra time. In that period, three more City players and Granit Xhaka for Arsenal were shown the yellow card.

In the 101st minute, Arsenal were awarded a free kick and Özil placed it into the middle from the left-hand side. Substitute Welbeck, on for Giroud, missed the ball; but Sánchez, in the six-yard box, did not and put the ball past Bravo to give Arsenal the lead. The score remained that way until half-time.

In the 105th minute, Guardiola substituted a substitute (Kelechi Iheanacho replacing Sterling), making use of a new extra time FA Cup rule that allowed four substitutes to be used. It was the first time any side had used a fourth substitute.

It made no difference, and Arsenal hung on to reach their 20th FA Cup Final.

Wenger said, 'I am very proud of our performance and spirit. I felt we became stronger. In the first half maybe we were a bit cautious, accepting to be dominated, and then we became stronger and stronger. It was a very tight game but overall I think we deserved to win the game.

'I am very pleased, it was a big game today. Overall it was a great performance not only technically but mentally. We became stronger and in the end deserved to win the game.

'The team performance was there. When the players give their best and are completely focused you always stand up for them.

'We were close to scoring and on the break they are very good. We lost the ball and conceded the goal but we showed the right response.

'Alexis Sánchez was like the team. He had problems to start and became stronger and stronger. He is an animal, always ready to kill the opponent. He will never give up. He will be here next year because he has a contract and hopefully we will manage to extend it.

'At Arsenal Football Club we want the team to turn up in big games and I think we've done that today. Overall I am very pleased. People questioned us; we went through tough times. In these times you can be divided or united and today we have shown the right response.'

Alex Oxlade-Chamberlain said, 'I'm tired but delighted. We set out to reach the final. Our league form has not been good enough and this is something we could hold on to.

'We have given ourselves every opportunity to go and win it.

'It's a new and interesting position for me at wing-back. I have to focus on the defensive side of things and we have adapted really well.'

Aaron Ramsey commented, 'I love this competition. We have been quite successful in recent years and you can see the passion that the players play with. We went behind and kept on going and got a result.

'I made the mistake for the goal. I know in these situations you have to respond. I carried on trying to work my socks off and ultimately it paid off. That is the second time we played this formation, credit to the boys. We have shown the character we have in this team.

'It was important to win today, to have something to look forward to. But now we have another seven cup finals to try [to] get into the top four.

'We have let [the boss] down at times this season. We want to win it for him and ourselves.'

Guardiola said, 'In games like this, you can't expect to control all the situations but we did most of the time.

'We performed like we would want to in a final. We did absolutely everything. Congratulations to Arsenal. We'll improve next season. We competed here, we had more chances but the finishing was like it has been throughout the season.

'We played like we wanted to and that's all. We are sad but tomorrow we have to stand up to finish the games we still have to play.

'I don't have regrets about the team. We just have to compete in these games. We are here for the results. Next season we will be stronger.'

The day before the final, a rumour broke that Wenger had plumped for his cup goalie rather than the regular first choice between the sticks. Petr Čech's performance against his old team in the league on 4 February at Stamford Bridge had been dire – he had even thrown the ball to former Gunner Cesc Fàbregas for the Blues' third goal in the 85th minute, as Chelsea ran out 3–1 winners, and so it was said that he had something to prove. He was not to get the chance, though, as the rumour turned out to be true and David Ospina's name was the first on the team sheet.

With team captain Laurent Koscielny suspended after being sent off in the last league match of the season (a 3–1 victory over Everton at the Emirates), and Shkodran Mustafi and Gabriel Paulista both injured, Wenger was limited in his defensive choices. Club captain Per Mertesacker was recalled despite having played only 37 minutes all season. Wenger chose to play 3–4–3, with the inexperienced Rob Holding and regular left-back Monreal keeping the captain company in defence.

If Chelsea attacked as was expected, Wenger could be in even more trouble, as he did not name a single defender among his six outfield substitutes. In the end, he did not need to worry. Holding more than stepped up, Monreal was excellent and Mertesacker was superb, showing why he had won more than 100 caps for Germany.

Phil McNulty, the BBC's chief football writer, said of the German defender, 'He was faultless throughout, giving a masterclass in positioning, timing and making crucial interceptions time after time in a display that made a mockery of his lack of action.'

Come matchday and security was tight around Wembley Way, after the terror attack in Manchester after an Ariana Grande concert had left more than 20 adults and children dead and scores injured by a terrorist loser. Armed police were on duty. The national anthem was sung by soprano Emily Haig, although few of the players joined in on either side – Chelsea captain Gary Cahill sang out. The Duke of Cambridge, the newly elected mayor of Greater Manchester, the culture secretary and the chairman of the FA laid wreaths on the pitch before a minute's silence was observed.

Ninety seconds later, someone came along and took the wreaths off the pitch so the match proper could begin.

And what a match!

Diego Costa got things started on referee Anthony Taylor's whistle. The first attack came from Chelsea but fizzled out. Arsenal then took control and rarely let up.

They won the first corner of the match in the fourth minute, but the giant Thibaut Courtois in the Chelsea goal safely gathered Özil's cross. The pass out, however, was a poor one and quickly recaptured by Arsenal.

Then it all began. Nacho Monreal went down the left wing and crossed to Aaron Ramsey, who passed to Alexis Sánchez. As Ramsey ran forward, Sánchez tried to chip the ball in to him but David Luiz headed it back to the Chilean. The ball hit Sánchez on the knee and bobbled up towards his face. Sánchez used his hands to protect his handsome good looks, and the ball dipped forward. Ramsey was in an offside position but did not attempt to touch the ball, and with three minutes and 49 seconds on the clock, Sánchez, with the outside of his right boot, put the ball past Courtois to give the Gunners the lead – or did he?

Gary Beswick, the linesman, flagged – but was he signalling handball (Sánchez) or offside (Ramsey)?

The referee went over to consult his colleague as Chelsea's Luiz and Cahill followed him, remonstrating as they went. Mr Taylor sent them away as Granit Xhaka wandered over. It was a painfully difficult time for Arsenal fans as the two officials spoke.

Then, 41 seconds after the ball had gone into the net, Mr Taylor signalled a goal for Arsenal. The underdogs were in the lead.

Chelsea began an attack, but Holding brought down Costa. Mr Taylor was quickly on the scene to defuse matters as Holding, with gestures to his temple, soon made it clear what he thought of Costa's mental state.

Two minutes later and Ramsey's name went into the referee's book for a foul on Pedro. Courtois just about managed to clear as Welbeck approached. Chelsea made hard work of keeping possession, and Arsenal looked like a side energised, not the one that had struggled so much in the season just gone.

With a quarter of an hour gone, Diego Costa shot from the penalty spot, but Monreal blocked his effort. Straight from the save, Arsenal went upfield and Özil chipped Courtois to try to ensure a second for Arsenal, only to see Gary Cahill acrobatically back-heel it off the goal line. Two minutes later, Nacho Monreal stopped Pedro with a blocking tackle.

From a corner in the 19th minute, Danny Welbeck rose and hit the ball with his shoulder from six yards out. Courtois could only watch as the ball hit his right post before cannoning into Ramsey's chest and back on to the post. It could have been Arsenal 3 Chelsea 0 and not even 20 minutes had elapsed.

Three minutes later and Mertesacker made a brilliant tackle to stop Costa from shooting. Just before the half-hour mark, David Ospina spread himself to stop that man Costa again and took a boot to the head for his troubles.

A minute later, Welbeck found himself free on the left-hand corner of the six-yard box and crossed to Ramsey for a tap-in, but Cahill again cleared off the line. Arsenal fans wanted to know where this Gunners side had been hiding all season.

On 33 minutes, the excellent Nacho Monreal broke up an attack from Eden Hazard. Despite having little playing time under his belt, Mertesacker, along with Monreal, was immense in the Arsenal defence. The half-time whistle was blown and the north Londoners went in with a one-goal advantage over their west London neighbours.

Three minutes into the second half and the BFG was called upon to block Pedro before Ospina was called upon to save a swerving 25-yarder from Kanté.

The following minute, Mertesacker brilliantly slid in to tackle Costa and even won a goal kick by deflecting the ball off the Chelsea striker. Arsenal fans, and indeed the football world in general, had difficulty believing that before this match Mertesacker hadn't started a game for 392 days.

Moses attempted a shot, but Ospina was not troubled, before Monreal stopped an attack from Costa and won a free kick into the bargain. The Chelsea player was not impressed and thought for a second of kicking the ball into the crowd, but common sense prevailed in time.

In the 54th minute, young Rob Holding went into the referee's book for a foul on Costa. Then Bellerín made a break down the right with lots of space, but made a hash of the cross, and Courtois easily gathered. Arsenal could – should – have been five or six ahead.

Danny Welbeck cleared a corner and was pulled back by Victor Moses, who found himself with a yellow card. With just over an hour gone, Conte pulled off Matić and replaced him with Cesc Fàbregas.

With 68 minutes gone, Moses dropped a shoulder to go past Oxlade-Chamberlain in the penalty area and then took a dive. The Chelsea fans screamed for a penalty, only to have their screams die in their throats when referee Mr Taylor pulled out a yellow and then a red card to send Moses off. Moses became the fifth player to be sent off in an FA Cup Final.

Then, on the 76th minute, Costa hooked the ball towards the goal. It clipped Mertesacker, and that was enough to send it past Ospina and into the bottom left-hand corner of the goal.

It took just three minutes for Arsenal to retake the lead. Olivier Giroud, on for Danny Welbeck, caught a pass from Sánchez and crossed to Ramsey to get his head to the ball and into the net past Courtois.

Then with three minutes of normal play remaining, the upright again saved Chelsea. Özil sold Cahill a dummy, and then from eight yards hit a low shot, which hit the right-hand post, rebounded on to the Chelsea keeper and went out for a corner.

Arsenal managed to see out the four minutes of stoppage time to win their 13th FA Cup and make Arsène Wenger the most successful FA Cup manager of all time.

Aaron Ramsey said, 'It's been an up-and-down season, but to finish it with an FA Cup has to make it a successful one. I just love this competition. The boys deserve it, and I'm happy for the manager, I'm delighted. He's been fantastic for me, fantastic for these players. Fair play to him, he's changed the system and it's paid off. So hopefully he'll be here next season, because we owe him a lot.'

Le Professeur added, 'It was an outstanding performance from the first minute onwards. This team has suffered, united, and responded. I said last week this team will win the championship with one or two good buys, and keep them together. They showed strength and we played spectacular football today to win the game. I am very proud [to have won seven FA Cups] because you see the fight you need even to win one. I am proud of doing two things that have never been done: to win a championship without losing a game, and to win seven FA Cups. It is not easy, believe me.

'We have a board meeting on Tuesday, and [my future] will be clear on Wednesday or Thursday.'

ACKNOWLEDGEMENTS

I would like to thank my incredibly patient publisher, Paul Camillin, for putting up with the delays on this book – as protracted as an Arsène Wenger contract negotiation. Many thanks to Graham Hughes for copy editing and Dean Rockett for excellent proofreading who caught a number of errors – without me they could not have done it. Thanks also to Graham Hales and Duncan Olner for layout and design. Vince Wright was his usual helpful and encouraging self and delved into his Arsenal archive when mine was found wanting. Thanks also to my agent, Chelsey Fox – 20-plus years and counting; Don Wright, Nottingham Forest's archivist, supplied information unavailable elsewhere; UEFA's Media & Public Relations Department; *mille grazie* to Cristina Demarie from the Juventus press office and club historian Ermanno Vittorio; and the same to Alice Scarsi, my executive assistant.

Books

Adams, Tony with Ian Ridley, *Addicted* (London: CollinsWillow, 1998). *Sober* (London: Simon & Schuster, 2017).

Barclay, Patrick, *Football – Bloody Hell! The Biography of Alex Ferguson* (London: Yellow Jersey Press, 2010). *The Life & Times of Herbert Chapman* (London: Weidenfeld & Nicolson, 2015).

— *Sir Matt Busby: The Definitive Biography* (London: Ebury Press, 2017).

Belton, Brian, *The First Gunners: Arsenal from Plumstead to Highbury* (London: Pennant Books, 2008).

Best, George, *Hard Tackles and Dirty Baths* (London: Ebury Press, 2005).

Bolam, Mike, *The Newcastle Miscellany* (London: Vision Sports Publishing, 2007).

Brown, Deryk, *The Arsenal Story* (London: Arthur Barker, 1972).

Clark, Rob, *Manchester United Greatest Games – The Red Devils' Fifty Finest Matches* (Pitch Publishing, 2014).

Crick, Michael, *The Boss: The Many Sides of Alex Ferguson* (London: Simon & Schuster, 2002).

Cross, John, *Arsène Wenger: The Inside Story of Arsenal Under Wenger* (London: Simon & Schuster, 2015).

Donovan, Mike, *Manchester United: On This Day* (Pitch Publishing, 2012).

Fox, Norman, *Farewell to Highbury* (London: The Bluecoat Press, 2006).

Gibson, Alfred and William Pickford, *Association Football & the Men Who Made It* (London: Caxton, 1906).

Glanville, Brian, *Arsenal Stadium History* (London: Hamlyn, 2006). *The Real Arsenal* (London: JR Books, 2009).

Groves, Perry with John McShane, *We All Live in a Perry Groves World: My Story* (London: John Blake, 2007).

Harris, Jeff, *Arsenal Who's Who* (London: Independent UK Sports Publications, 1995).

Hayes, Dean, *Arsenal: The Football Facts* (London: John Blake, 2007).

Joy, Bernard, *Forward, Arsenal!* (London: The Sportsmans Book Club, 1954).

King, Jeff and Tony Willis, *George Graham: The Wonder Years* (London: Virgin, 1995).

Lawrence, Amy, *Invincible* (London: Penguin, 2015).

Leighton, James, *Duncan Edwards: The Greatest* (London: Simon & Schuster, 2012).

Macdonald, Malcolm with Colin Malam, *Supermac: My Autobiography* (Newbury: Highdown, 2003).

Maidment, Jem, *Arsenal: 100 Greatest Games* (London: Hamlyn, 2005). *The Official Arsenal Encyclopaedia* (2nd Ed) (London: Hamlyn, 2008).

Matthews, Tony, *Who's Who of Arsenal* (Edinburgh: Mainstream Publishing, 2007).

McCartney, Iain, *The Official Manchester United Players' A–Z* (London: Simon & Schuster, 2013).

McLintock, Frank with Rob Bagchi, *True Grit: The Autobiography* (London: Headline, 2005).

Mitten, Andy, *The Man Utd Miscellany* (London: Vision Sports Publishing, 2007).

Neill, Terry, *Revelations of a Football Manager* (London: Sidgwick & Jackson, 1985).

Parlour, Ray with Amy Lawrence, *The Romford Pelé* (London: Century, 2016).

Peskett, Roy (ed.), *Tom Whittaker's Arsenal* (London: The Sportsmans Book Club, 1958).

Pirès, Robert with Xavier Rivoire, *Footballeur* (London: Yellow Jersey Press, 2003).

Ponting, Ivan (credited to Joe Rose) *Arsenal: Player by Player* (London: Hamlyn, 2004). *Manchester United: Player by Player* (Studley: Know The Score Books, 2008).

Potter, David, *Newcastle United: On This Day* (Pitch Publishing, 2012).

Robertson, John, *Arsenal* (London: Hamlyn, 1985).

Soar, Phil and Martin Tyler, *Arsenal: The Official Illustrated History 1886–2008* (London: Hamlyn, 2008).

Spurling, Jon, *Highbury: The Story of Arsenal in N5* (London: Orion, 2006). *Rebels for the Cause* (Edinburgh: Mainstream Publishing, 2003). *Red Letter Days* (Pitch Publishing, 2014).

Stammers, Steve, *Arsenal: The Official Biography* (London: Hamlyn, 2008).

White, John, *The Official Manchester United Miscellany* (London: Manchester United Books, 2005).

Wilson, Bob, *Life in the Beautiful Game* (Thriplow: Icon Books, 2008).

Wright, Ian with Lloyd Bradley, *A Life in Football*: *My Autobiography* (London: Constable, 2017).

Websites

Arsenal FC – https://www.arsenal.com/

Arseweb – http://www.arseweb.com/

Association of Football Statisticians – https://www.11v11.com/

BBC – https://www.bbc.co.uk/

Historical Football Kits – http://www.historicalkits.co.uk/

History of Arsenal – http://www.blog.woolwicharsenal.co.uk/

Leicester City FC – https://www.lcfc.com/

LFC History – http://www.lfchistory.net/

Manchester United: The Official Statistics Website – http://stretfordend.co.uk

My Football Facts – http://www.myfootballfacts.com

Rec.Sport.Soccer Statistics Foundation – http://www.rsssf.com/

Reuters – http://www.reuters.com/

Roger Wright & Sally Davis – http://www.wrightanddavis.co.uk/

The Arsenal History – http://www.thearsenalhistory.com/

ToffeeWeb – https://toffeeweb.com/

toon1892 – http://toon1892.com/

YouTube – https://www.youtube.com/